W9-ACI-052

He Called Them By The Lightning

Also by Lura Beam

A Maine Hamlet
Bequest From A Life

With Robert Latou Dickinson, M.D.

A Thousand Marriages
The Single Woman

He Called Them By The Lightning

A Teacher's Odyssey in the Negro South, 1908-1919

by Lura Beam

THE BOBBS-MERRILL COMPANY, INC.
A Subsidiary of Howard W. Sams & Co., Inc.
Publishers / INDIANAPOLIS • NEW YORK • KANSAS CITY

The author acknowledges with gratitude permission to quote from the following works: W. H. Auden, "The Chimeras" in *Nones,* Copyright © 1951, Random House Inc.; B. A. Botkin, editor, *Lay My Burden Down,* Copyright © 1957, University of Chicago Press; Paul Laurence Dunbar, "Angelina" in *The Complete Poems,* Copyright © 1930, Dodd, Mead and Co.; Claude McKay, *Harlem Shadows,* Copyright © 1922, Twayne Publishers, Inc.; Ridgely Torrence, "Simon the Cyrenian" in *Plays for a Negro Theatre,* Copyright © 1917, The Macmillan Co.

First Printing, 1967

LIBRARY OF CONGRESS CATALOG CARD NUMBER 66-30501

DESIGNED BY *Helen Rostagno*

Printed in the United States of America

"I hear far voices out of Darkness"

Augustus Field Beard
H. Paul Douglass
George Edmund Haynes
Elizabeth Ross Haynes

Except in the case of the well-known, the names, appearance of people and other clues to identity have been disguised.

Contents

The Return of Memory 1

ONCE I HAD a friend named Julia. When she was gone, her daughter, "Little Julia," began to send me Christmas cards. I have never seen the daughter, but I always fancy the mother's thin intellectual face and delicate aloofness behind the continuing name.

My friend's daughter is colored and lives in the Deep South. A few years ago she wrote me a letter along with her holiday greetings.

Julia and her husband thought they could see what would happen to their fifteen-year-old son in the local high school. He was doing well in his studies, but they asked whether I thought it would be better to send him to a Northern boarding school. They did not see how they could afford boarding school when college and professional school would be so expensive, but what might be the psychological damage he would suffer if he remained? Would distance now be better for his life?

I asked whether it could mislead the boy to send him away.

There was a 1941 opinion that the bomb shelters in London spoiled people by making them feel safe, and by "keeping them from the reality of the battle, whose participants they ought to be."

"Whose participants they ought to be." To take this position about other people's children is so Spartan that I attempted to say that no matter where he lived, a high-school boy now would be in a battle. The familiar setting of his native city, school, home, and parents would support him. A remote environment might make him brood alone.

The Christmas letter stood for affectionate ties of long ago, but my Negro yesterday ended in 1919. As the pioneers of that time passed on, I had no way of knowing the young who were growing up to take their places, so this part of my life misted over and was forgotten.

Now the screaming around schoolhouses in Southern cities I used to know has brought the past back with intensity. Not at first; I assumed that Little Rock and smaller cities were exceptions. When the sound came from New Orleans, a favorite city, in one flash I remembered everything.

I began to know Negroes so long ago, that most of them still walked everywhere they went. They liked walking under the trees, or they lived too far out for a car line, or they just wanted to save a nickel. White people walked too, in those days, but the two races never walked together. These figures walking separately in a landscape were my introduction to the racial customs of the United States.

I saw them first in 1908, from the train, against the fall foliage of Virginia. I was on the way to Wilmington, North Carolina, to teach in a Negro high school. Public education for colored children then ended with the seventh grade and the school was private, under the auspices of the American Missionary Association.

The AMA was founded in 1846 by a group of come-outers on issues of the day about slavery. Its functions were antecedent to those now carried on by the American Civil Liberties Union, educational foundations, and the Peace Corps.

My father was in South America and my mother did not want me to go. I had had no missionary interests or tradition whatever; I even disliked the word "missionary." In college I had avoided causes; I had not even gone to watch the big Women's Suffrage Parade. I had never had a chance to notice Negroes. None lived in the country where I spent my childhood—only one in Machias, Maine, where I went to high school. Two I saw at the University of California were not in my classes. I had not studied American History since the eighth grade and had not traveled south of Trenton, New Jersey.

The attraction was that I would be allowed to teach the subjects mentioned in my notice from the Pratt Teachers' Agency, and I wanted to see a new part of the country. I was twenty-one and I liked the unknown.

I am here recalling my impressions of Negro life as I saw it, over half a century ago. I regret the absence of factual data, but that lack has rarely made any difference to people writing about the South.

My impressions were skewed favorably by seeing only the better side of the Negro personality. I traveled at lovely times of the year—in the fall, when money was going into pockets after the cotton-picking; in the winter, when I left snow for reddening strawberries; in the spring, when blossoming peach trees ran up every slope. I knew that the water hyacinths on little Florida rivers were a menace, but I was infatuated with the look of them, and I felt this ambivalence about many aspects of Southern life.

I knew Negroes only as pupils in the first grade through college, or I knew them as adults in connection with their work or their children. That is, I knew them at their best when they were occupied with their dearest aims and greatest responsibilities. Mothers were planning for their children, fathers for the community, teachers were living their hopes at last, ministers were reading from the Bible, children were learning, voices were singing.

I knew only emerged or emerging classes when the aim was to follow the white cultural pattern. I knew the Negro aristocracy and the changing middle class rather well. I knew a lot about the looks and life of the poor, but nothing about their thoughts. The lowest economic group—the "arms and legs" folks, who had only simple farming skills—I never knew at all.

My recollections were shaped during a time span that Negroes then called a period of Lost Hope. Almost my first impression was that now they were losing what they had thought they had. I believe that most periods appear like this to the submerged, but the basis for it here was that the South resurgent began to conquer the North in the 1890's, certainly by 1900. The region was restoring pre-Civil War attitudes by implementing new laws of segregation. The last state to ratify these new laws did so in 1908, the year I began to know the South.

Whiteness was consolidating itself with vigor. The whitest of all, the aristocracy, was being thrown by the "rednecks"—men whose necks are sun-reddened as they plow—the mill crowds, and the new middle-men with fox faces. Thrown according to rules which kept them on top socially, but diminished them practically; the new politicians bowed as they walked the greensward, but they rediscovered the machete.

On their side, Negroes had lost to death the Northern movers and shakers of the Civil War and were losing their own Black Puritans. They claimed that 1875–1900 had been a better time; the present was stagnant, they felt empty.

Migration was not yet an answer, and possibly it is true that my eleven years—1908–1919—were a static interval. Local movements in art and sociology stirred in the 1920's, but nothing lifted the colored people nationally until the New Deal of the 1930's.

I worked in the only zone where the lights grew brighter: in education. Time and distance give any story of education an illusive calm. No one can tell now how bad some of the past was.

Until I experienced the wind-swept screaming, I never had any idea of writing a book about Negroes. When I left them, they did not seem different enough from other people to write about. I kept no diary, no records—nothing.

When my memory began to recover the past, it rushed upon me in the order in which I am writing. First came the Southern rules for the Negro and his life as lived within them, then the

Northern assertion of the rights of national culture over regional culture.

The first two-thirds of the manuscript are approximately factual; that is, everything happened somewhere.

The "Cold Journey," which appears early in the sequence, functions as a prediction of doom. In this dual culture, some Negro was always approaching the high jump and every Northern white participant knew a chill from the heights and depressions of the culture. It is also reasonably factual, reminding one, through the shocks to one person's nervous system, of the massive shocks that tremble under the surface of Negro culture.

The last third of the manuscript is only an individual impression which came about slowly and falteringly. I know that I was at once arrested by the manifestations of religion and music and that I had the sense of death and of the shadows over the Negro potential of self-expression before the end of the first year. I did not hear the sound of the trumpet which stood for affirmation until some time during World War I, and the Southern landscape only spoke to me in detail after I had traveled it many times.

My return to my lost country occurs because I knew this fifteen-year-old boy's great-grandparents. They were old when I was young. The distinction of their looks, home, and lives attracted me when I was twenty-one. They were disciplined, worn, and wise; their vitality showed in the minds, character, and education of their children.

Little Julia's son, their great-grandson, must be at least the fourth generation in the United States, because I have known four. He will be the third generation in college. He should not be given so bad a time in high school.

His parents kept him at home. Whatever happens to him now, in his home town, before he finishes his education, will come out in the man of fifty-five he will be in about the year 2000.

I do not know the boy's first name. He stands for many.

A Stranger Enters 2

THE NIGHT BEFORE I left home in a New York City suburb, my mother came into my room just as I was going to sleep and sat on the foot of the bed. She said, "Papa is not going to like this North Carolina teaching when he hears. I am going to give you plenty of money. Look over the school as your father and I would. If the Teachers' Home and the faculty are not exactly as the New York office told you, you must come home by the next train." I telegraphed her, "Conventional Massachusetts atmosphere." My parents practically commuted to Boston and when I was small I thought it was right around the corner. It was the metropolis of a Maine hamlet in the woods and when the teacher wished to explain the position of ancient Athens, she always said it was "like Boston for us." After a little while, I sent back the extra money and wrote that the institution was even on Nun Street.

Wilmington, North Carolina, seemed like a piece of Boston,

but set among roses and dropped further back in history. I liked it better than Berkeley, California, before the earthquake, where the lushness of nature could not subdue the new. This city had had 200 houses before the Revolution. The 1755 records showed owners of twenty to eighty slaves in the river-trading days of timber, rice and indigo.

The old and civilized trees still come back to me in dreams. Live oaks, magnolias and chinaberry trees grew along the streets; bouquet trees of holly and palms set off the boulevards. The long leaf and the loblolly pine grew in the outskirts and the sweet gum fringed the black and glassy swamp. Out of the water grew the swamp cypress, misshapen and human.

I had been born within sight of the Machias River, and shipbuilding and the waterfront easily seemed the core of the life. The Cape Fear River had ships and tankers at anchor, and stevedores handling cotton bales swarmed the wharves. Men in bowler hats stood around Front Street, calculating deals for lumber and fertilizer.

The chief public buildings were churches. The white high school was in an old mansion; there was no public library, no museum, movie or restaurant, no public lectures, not much of a newspaper. The one drugstore was small, aromatic, dirty, and cluttered beyond belief. The owner and his colored porter had been marinated in the well of pre-war courtesy a long time and the name over the door had been known in the area since the seventeenth century.

A belt line of trolley cars racketed around the city and horses and buggies were hitched in the Square, but life was planned for the pedestrian who lived at home. Cotton royalty lived among trees, boxwood and azaleas, in houses of the Classic Revival, but even little dogtrot houses were buried among oleander, japonica, and bougainvillaea. My window looked out on a huge magnolia. The flower of this tree is so perfect a statement that the South does not need the Grand Canyon or Niagara Falls. It could be Tennyson's nineteenth-century flower:

> *. . . . if I could understand*
> *What you are root and all and all in all,*
> *I should know what God and man is.*

Recreation was walking, going to the beach or down the river, or out into the country. Hunting, fishing, and clamming were for food; vendors peddled vegetables and fruit up and down every block; housewives in long skirts and large hats were always buying for dinner.

The tempo was slow. Between the Past, the river, the swamp, and the ocean eight miles away, the little city had many boundaries of the infinite. I used to walk downtown to see the mingling of elegance and shabbiness in housing and to look at the river. The light was different here, and so was the quality of the darkness; so were the street sounds and the flower fragrance. A stranger could feel mystery at hand and to come.

As I faced the school on the first day, the dark faces swam into a whole, as evergreens unite going uphill to the forest. The mass had inaccessible form, more like nature than like people. Rock, mist or mountain, the stranger had come to the valley where the hills press downward after sunset.

I used to sit reading on a platform, keeping the study hall for 150 adolescents from grades eight to twelve. Suddenly a humming tone would fill the room. No face looked up, no lips moved, no body changed. The young might have been painted there, while above them floated this unhuman dissent of wind in the trees, or surf on the sand. The vibrations gave, in another way, the sense of fir trees crowded in the frozen North.

These fluent harpstrings brought me a defiance. It said convincingly that I did not know anything; possibly I could not learn. I tried to remember that white teenagers would also have their way of trying out the novice.

I began to understand this accusing voice when it sang the morning hymn. The month was warm October. The sun shone, bells rang, goats walked by outside, my feet felt old hollows on the unpainted stairs. A piano tinkled, and melody wound in spirals:

Christian, dost thou see them
On the holy ground,
How the powers of darkness
Rage thy steps around?

The minor cadence loved its own despair. Then the piano crashed, and the caged flung out a shriek of triumph:

Christian, up and smite them,
Counting gain but loss,
In the strength that cometh
By the Holy Cross.

This hymn, where protest melted away into faith, was in a world removed from the brisk and cheerful hymns I had sung in a New England high school. We had not known menace or darkness; we hardly knew pain. We were agreeably alive, and musically monotonous; these people had music in them and they knew about an abyss. The singing told me more than I grasped with my mind for a long time.

On Sundays at sunset I played the piano for the Congregational church song service. When a singer raised a song, I picked up an accompaniment, listening the while to the orchestration of the congregation. They inclined to minor keys and they could make daring variations. They had a way of letting go in acceptance:

Oh, reign, Oh, reign,
Oh, reign, my Saviour,
Reign, Master Jesus, reign,
Oh, reign, salvation, in my poor soul,
Reign, Master Jesus, reign.

In our quartet, the soprano had a voice like a bird, the town barber had a good tenor, the bass gave certainty. The contralto washed clothes for a living on weekdays; on Sundays she prayed for mankind with "Look unto Me and be ye saved."

When the old burst into prayer at the Wednesday evening prayer meeting, the Hebraic-Christian tradition soared with the elation of Negro imagery. The sea of Isaiah and Jeremiah swept over us, drew back, repeated, receded. I began to see that I could understand the schoolroom better in the church.

On Sunday mornings I traveled to St. James's, Westminster, Wesleyan, Shiloh, Ebenezer, Rose of Sharon, Church of the Pentecost and Pillar of Fire, until I had taken every step from the Protestant Reformation through the history of American sectarianism. After I left the paved streets and walked in the sand beyond the jungles of sweet bay trees, the preacher putting on the rousements was every kind of figure. I saw the actors in *The Emperor Jones, Green Pastures, Porgy* and *Hallelujah* long before they reached the Broadway stage.

Church ushers took a teacher from "Old Gregory," as Gregory Normal Institute was called, to the front pew with a flourish, because the AMA school was the local Harvard. Pupils walked an average of two miles a day to get there. The dreary gray frame buildings had stood on the lot since soon after the War. The pioneers and the years had earned them merit and at least they were not crowded. The public schools were gray and dreary too, and stuffed to the doors with children.

The long low study hall was sunny, with every window full of plants, seedlings, and experiments in agriculture and gardening. Chalky stretches of blackboard and cases of library books broke the green walls. The favorite corner was the reading table, stacked with Webster's *Dictionary*, the *National Geographic, The Outlook*, and *The Independent*. In winter, children liked to sit near the tall sheet-iron stove.

No one minded that this school was a place of books only; no athletics, no clubs, no entertainment, except one concert a term and perhaps a poetry reading. Parents agreed solidly that books were the thing; "one punishment at school, two at home," they would say to a pupil kept after school for not paying attention. Girls pleaded for business courses although there was hardly a Negro business in town, and the great desire unsatisfied was always Latin. The parents thought Latin was the mark of an educated man, and their children were being kept back. The major subject of study was mathematics and no child was willing to study another lesson until he had first done his utmost in a fine and orderly notebook for algebra and geometry.

I taught English. A child in pink gingham would lean over my desk, earrings and pigtails projecting like double antennae, and say, "Please, Ma'am, Mama say she been try but this all the money she gots for my book; she send the ten cent Monday."

A lanky country boy, hearing about Mary Stuart, rolled his eyes and said, "That Queen sure favor the other world; she bound for the Judgment." Life poured into me every day from the delightful and bewildering talk of the children.

As soon as I knew their names, the children began to be James, Herbert, Harry, Dorothea and Asphodel; the beautiful brown eyes and faces took on their own looks. As the full figure emerged, an exotic litheness belied the drawling voice and sliding walk; it had every grace of motion and gesture.

I used to walk in the city to observe the appearance and manner of colored strangers about whom I knew nothing. They were much less regimented than now. The easy variation of body and posture from a tree to a panther had convincing design. The body's curves could appear liquid and undulating as a forest vine; at home in daily life, its motions were conditioned by work; in ceremony, it magnified stateliness.

The soot-black face, the thin-lipped brown face, the tiger lily face under a brush of red hair presented new statements to the imagination. The skulls roused the sense of volume; they were sculpture felt in the round. The narrow feet and hands when not moving took on something unfootlike and unhandlike. Just so at high noon in the sun, a great green leaf hides its paler underside from the light.

The blur of faces turned lighter in color as I got used to them. Individuals stood out like petunias in the pansy bed—the bitter, the lazy, the lovesick one with her five-pound boxes of candy, the little spoiled one. I discovered accidentally the one who carried a knife. When I held my hand out to Fred one day he put a white mouse in it. Pairs of fourteen-year-old girls could not look at each other without giggling, and gangling boys hoped someone would trip over their feet in the aisle. The notes, gum, tardiness, spitballs, and crushes that I remembered from my own schooldays were just as always. I became used to things. When a mother said to me about her daughter, "I told her never to lie except to white people," I understood that she was paying me a compliment; I was colored too.

Mischief freed children a little from books. They handled books with feeling, and volunteers always wanted to help with the library for the sake of touching books and talking about them. Their respect for property was extreme; school desks did not have Whittier's "jackknife's carved initial," although boys carried jackknives, and no one ever wrote anything on white and gray-painted walls.

I was never able to please parents about discipline; they said I was too easy. Ellie was old enough to be memorizing "The quality of mercy is not strained," but if she felt obstinate and said "I won't" about anything and I sent her home as punishment, she was back in an hour, led by an old man who held his hat between worn and wrinkled hands and reproved me.

"Why didn't you strop her, Ma'am? I'm her grandfather and I put her into your hands. If she don't learn, please Ma'am, use your strap."

Handwriting in pencil on flimsy ruled paper was always entreating me "Please, Ma'am, whip Isaiah. I pays for him to learn." One dominating old mother whipped her daughter after she had been graduated from high school because, she said, "You come along with this new riffraff. I got to learn you." Colored teachers were defeated by this faith in corporal punishment. They said old people were hopeless; whipping would go on in the homes until slavery's generation was gone.

I began to feel stabilized in work as soon as I made the first perfectly natural contact. It was with the homes and the mothers. School opened at eight o'clock in the morning and ended at one because so many pupils had afternoon jobs. I made a spot map of the homes and I spent every afternoon calling, sometimes about matters of discipline, beginning over again when I had gotten around once.

Walking down shady streets until the sidewalks ended, I came to deep sand where horsedrawn wagons creaked and swayed. Students here lived in little unpainted houses behind picket fences. Violets fringed the brick walk, and bottles, stuck upside down, marked off round flower beds of marigolds. In the back yard, a big iron kettle boiled clothes over a low fire.

The mother, folding her hands over her apron and asking about Blanchie May, was lovely and unmistakable. My sense of her motherhood was stronger than any sense of race, and I felt at home. She inquired about my mother, asked what my father did, admired my hat, said that I "favored" a teacher she remembered from the olden times. Her house had no clock, but

"Blanchie, she listen for the school bell"; no lamp, but "She have plenty time to study befo' sundown."

It was the first time I had known about people who had so little and the first time I thought about family heroism. "My old man been sick a right smart, but my Hetty she go right thu. She teachin' now, over in Haypatch, she bring me somethin' ever' Friday night. . . . I scrubbed my first boy, my Isaac, into high school and he been taken from me with the typhoid. But the Lord raise me right up my second son."

I came from where women had other interests than their primary function. Life had fixed it so that these women had nothing else. The mother helped support the family, cherished men, children, and the old, went to church—that was all.

She could look as if she had just arrived from West Africa, be widowed or deserted, live in a house that had no more furnishings than a tent, be unable to read, have no skill except washing and ironing by hand, but she had dragged two children into high school. I often met her—incoherent to whites except about her children.

At first I never thought of Negroes as poor. I was impressed instead with their speech, manners, goodness to the old, and their ambition. The women were so rich in the significant values of women that I felt a depth in them as I did in my mother and grandmother. I left many homes feeling that, proportionately, my life would never turn out half as well.

In pregnancy, colored women looked even more slow, stately, and enriched than white women. They raised many children because they would take on nieces, nephews, grandchildren, and orphans. The largest brood I knew was twenty-nine; the last seven were grandchildren who had lost one parent. The young, when they were old enough to realize, ought to have known that their mothers had been almost superhuman.

I rarely met fathers, unless they were professional men or community leaders. They often worked on trains or on night shifts. A few were said to have poor jobs or no jobs, nothing but their roving feet.

Every house had its drama. One hostess bringing out a plate of fruit cake had been brought up on her white father's plantation, playing with her white half-sisters. After sixteen, they never spoke to her again. An old man of wise gravity had stood on the auction block. Men opened his mouth to look at his teeth and he was once sold for $1,200. A photograph shown to me was "our eldest, when she was with the Jubilee Singers and sang before Queen Victoria." One family of nine all had malaria, out where the city edge ran into the marshes. They ate quinine as steadily as they ate cornbread. Another family dropped from seven to one with tuberculosis; the survivor was listening for the saw-whet owl, and waiting, for "Before a death, the owl hoots at night."

Mothers mourned audibly for the long past of their school days. The first principal had prayed and caned boys equally well. He was consecrated, "His name is written in God's Book." At the same time, there was an algebra teacher who marked every mistake in red ink: "When she was here, this school could hold up its head."

As the life drew me into its web, I began to say, "My children." A few were splendidly gifted, and even the average was intelligent. Their trouble was that books were not part of their lives. They worked at home chores and sometimes for pay; boys were porters and messengers, girls had to practice their piano lessons.

Textbooks were duller than they are today, and if grammar was not dramatically presented, eyes looked wistfully out the window. They were afraid to talk lest they not give back what the book said; afraid to write lest they spoil the fine white paper.

I got around the perils of writing by dividing it into two stages; the first was an outpouring, written as fast as possible. We criticized it only for the thought and laid it aside. Later, we returned to it for grammar and composition only. I memorized Leona's paper on her hates because I liked her definiteness. It is the first stage of a paper written when she was thirteen:

MY HATE

I going to rite about the thing I hates.
I has a lot of hate but the thing I hates the
most is little childern, dogs and turkys. The

*childern is my Mother childern and she go out
and leav them on me all day. I has to keep them dry
and I has to iron they close. The dog is my
Father dog. They is houn dog and they has to be
kep home and they is five narsty dog. The turky
is my Grandmother turky and they is the hatfullest
of all. If they gets wet they dies. Seem like it
all the time rain and turky don't wants to live.
What I wants I wants to get reddy to teach school
and then I will not have to do none of this Hatfull stuff.*

In spite of the Christmas roses, winters could turn sharply cold. Houses were not built for winter, clothes were not warm enough, the walk to school was long. Children who had not eaten enough breakfast had to wait until a three-o'clock dinner in order to eat.

Poor scholars gave in at once. They wanted to pull their coats over their heads and sleep. Better scholars sat up straighter than ever. At home, they had heard this giving in referred to as "nigger behavior."

It struck me that whole families acted this way before tuberculosis. It was the pattern of a psychic strike before something they could not master; it showed when confronted with books they could not read, talk above their reach, and sickness they regarded as hopeless.

At the foundation of every trouble was the apprehension about destiny. The immediate difficulty was that all learning had to pass through the special sieve of being black. Every hour had its contradictions.

My children said that they hated the mass of white people, but they were proud of learned people, the local cotton king, his home, his family, and his horses. They had the white names of contempt for Jews, Chinese, and Italians—the "foreigners" in town. Our first talk about the word "Nigger" came about because their lips were so careless with "Sheeney," "Chink," and "Dago."

They lived by the Old Testament but looked down on the Egyptians as heathen; they disliked even to know about mummies and the pyramids and what they called "worship of cats and beetles." They looked far down on Africans—"Savages and cannibals!" They admired Greece and Rome and went around town looking fiercely for the Doric and Ionic in architecture. Their cruel Latinless school was denying them their birthright and when they went "off" to school, they would learn to read both Greek and Latin. The classes in cookery, sewing, gardening, and carpentry were sending them back toward slavery.

When I told them the story of the Four Hundred at Thermopylae, it fell cold. The boys said a last stand did no good and a pert fair girl who had already lived half her life said, "Those Spartans just died for obstinacy and left everything on the women. There's a lot of men like that."

They liked the heroic to be presented in a single person. When they began high school, they brought only Washington and Lincoln and some Old Testament characters, especially Moses and Daniel. They began at once to be interested in the showy. They were possessed with Alexander the Great; they called Louis XIV "The Sheik," and for everything I could say against warlords, they gloated over Napoleon; "That's a man."

The Revolutionary War was not real to them since the Civil War had swallowed everything else. What they did get out of the Revolution was not Paul Revere and Lexington and Concord. The big news was that Crispus Attucks, a runaway slave, was one of the first to die in the Boston Massacre of 1770. He was a martyr and he had a monument, the Attucks Monument in Boston. They repeated softly the poem about him:

His feet were the first in perilous place
to pull the King's flag down.

I could not at first fathom why they were so interested in my grandmother's Civil War stories: the cost of food, her brother in Andersonville, her three nephews who died, her brother-in-law who, as a veteran, proved a claim in Montana, so that she never saw her sister again, and the year she could only buy oranges for the children's Christmas. When they heard that she had stopped the family dancing at the news of Lee's surrender, saying, "Think of the South tonight," a girl said, "What did she look like? What was her name?"

They had never thought of the North as suffering from the

War, and my grandmother had suffered in terms they could understand. So had my father; his father had come into a room, turned to his mother and said, "Lincoln's been assassinated." They said no more; both sat down and both began to cry. Their six-year-old son was terribly frightened; he had never known that grown people could cry. My class sat in silence after hearing this story and a boy asked, "Did you ever go into that room?"

They worshipped Lincoln, wanted to stamp their feet to "Marching Through Georgia," and never were willing to hear "Dixie." I knew better than to ask Jim why he did not sing "America," but someone else did and he said, "I'm going to be a man can't vote; when I can vote I'll sing, 'My country, 'tis of thee.' "

I said, "Jim, I can't vote either," and before he thought he blurted, "But that's different, you're a woman."

Every girl in class began to taunt him, "Explain to us, Mr. Woman-Hater, just how it's different. You go to New York where she lives and you can vote and she can't."

Shakespeare became the fashion. They wanted to stage a play and said, "Will we ever have a Negro Shakespeare?" Next to Shakespeare, they quoted Milton. To their high school vocabulary they added his phrases: "iron tears . . . moon-struck madness . . . Death . . . on his pale horse . . . Hence, loathed Melancholy . . . Whoever knew Truth put to the worse." The girls shuddered at "He for God only, she for God in him."

Cooper seemed too wild to them and the talk of Dickens' characters too inaccessible. It put them off Scott to learn that he had been the favorite novelist of the Old South, but Scott's "The Lady of the Lake," where Frederick Douglass found his surname, won them over. They were taken with Bacon's "Revenge is a kind of wild justice," until they read of his bankruptcy. No failure could write for them any rules for success.

Romanticism on the classical level was entirely new and they believed or disbelieved according to their ideas about character. They loved Keats, but refused Shelley; the Shelley of Harriet and Mary, "God drowned him." Coleridge and De Quincy affronted them because of drug habits. A boy whose father drank hard jerked in his seat and said, "Woe unto you, ye scribes and Pharisees, hypocrites!" The seventeen-year-old who always carried his

Omar Khayyam talked in happy intolerance, "I shan't read any more little poets now and I don't ever want to hear any more Dunbar. I'm surprised they can try after this fellow has said it all."

Shakespeare and Milton and Keats had no color. My children took them as theirs at once, but unless literature was powerful, they had nothing to pin white names to, so they remembered Negro names better. Any child would boast about Toussaint L'Ouverture, Frederick Douglass, and Paul Laurence Dunbar. They knew that Henry O. Tanner was "our" painter, though they had seen only small black and white reproductions, and Coleridge-Taylor was "our" musician, although they had heard only "Listen to the Lambs."

They resented loudly the white stereotypes about Uncle Tom, Topsy and Aunt Jemima, Negro preachers and guitar players. They laughed at slapstick from Williams and Walker and if I said that these jokes held the race up to ridicule, they laughed more and said that the race deserved it. I realized that they might say this, but I might not. This was true about so many things.

At fifteen, the better students already felt that they were intellectuals, separate from the masses. Already they had only a fringe connection with the Main Street in the Sauk Center where they lived.

When the hero was not in a book, just a man at hand, they did not recognize him as a hero. One day when their teacher of carpentry bent over to pick up some wood, one of the boys kicked him. For a weary while, no one would tell. When the sinner owned up, he said, "I don't see how I came to do it, except I think Hampton Institute men are so meeching. I wondered how much he would take."

My children were too young to care about the history of their city, but they were proud of the historic sites and monuments, the Cape Fear River, the cotton production, the trees and formal gardens, and all the views no man can own. I never got used to their being proud of the Old Testament in a similar way; some part of them lived there.

The mores and the student's plan about his own life somehow delayed interest in the other sex. Evening parties were not customary; walking out by twos was not permitted. All were rabid about class spirit, but they ran in crowds and pairing off did not happen. Boys patronized girls a little and girls had to show that they could not care less.

I never heard any ambitions about money. The attitude and aims were those of young adults. The ideal life would be to go to college and "do something to advance the race." This thought was so dominant that even a child who appeared of small potential had it and anything less was regarded as a disgrace.

Educational Beginnings 3

THE BEGINNING WHICH formed the background for my children's talk about Milton's "iron tears" and the need for a Negro Shakespeare began in West Africa in 1838. In the days when my grandparents were children, there came a rapid sequence of events: Negroes kidnapped, the ship *Amistad*, ex-President John Quincy Adams speaking about slavery, Massachusetts granite coming out of the ground in new founders and organizations—the American Missionary Association, other Protestant missions.

A *Secretarial Paper* of the AMA tried about 1914 to explain how the strength of national issues made missionary work possible:

For forty-five years following 1841, a club-footed preacher dragged his apostolic course, beginning with the wilderness roads of the new Black Hawk Purchase, until he had founded twenty-five churches in Iowa and Illinois. . . . Because the Lord started him as only half a man physically, He made him two men in spiritual vigor and strangely gave him always a roving ministry. . . . "Nearly every sermon I have preached," he writes, "has been at a time and place where the people would have had no preacher at all but for my presence. To preach to the destitute I have felt to be my vocation."

In 1843, he renounced the commission of the National Home Missionary Society on account of what he esteemed its complicity in sin by reason of aid given to churches fellowshiping slave holders. For the next two years, he lived almost at the point of starvation, his sole support being people as poor as himself. In 1846, he accepted the commission of the organization . . . which was about to become the American Missionary Association. This connection he continued until slavery was dead.

I have chosen Father Oliver Emerson for my text at this hour because he almost perfectly incarnated the genius of this Association in its origin. He was before the Association was. The Association became because he was and others like him. . . . .

I have pictures of the founders who decided to begin the AMA at a two-day meeting in Albany, New York, in 1846, but photographs are not necessary; their looks can be visualized from what they did.

Some years previous to this meeting, the nation had been aroused by the famous *Amistad* case in which a boatload of slaves, illegally captured in Africa, had landed at Montauk Light and been jailed at New Haven under charges of murder and piracy. Before the case came to trial, Josiah Willard Gibbs, Professor of Theology and Sacred Literature at Yale, talked with the prisoners. He learned the sound of some of their words and betook himself to the New York City waterfront, looking for an African sailor; when he found him, he took the sailor to New Haven and, between the interpreter and what he could put together, heard the story. During transshipment from Havana to another Cuban port the Africans had somehow been given to understand they were to be killed and eaten. Since the trip was a short one, they were not in irons; the Africans resolved to die trying to escape their fate and in the ensuing melee several men died, including the *Amistad*'s captain. The captive slaveowners were ordered to steer the ship back to Africa; instead they anchored at Montauk after 63 days and the charges of piracy and murder followed.

A District Court decision directing the Africans' return to Africa as free men was appealed to the United States Supreme Court by the Cuban planters who claimed them as slaves. In 1840, the Court heard the appeal. Ex-President John Quincy Adams, then seventy-three years old, pleaded for the Africans: "Is there a law of Habeas Corpus in the land? . . . . Has the Fourth of July of '76 become a day of ignominy and reproach?" He won the case.

The two chief movers of the *Amistad* Committee then became chief movers of the new AMA. Arthur Tappan, a native of Northampton who had been in the silk business in New York since 1817, became chairman of the Executive Committee, and his brother, Lewis, became its treasurer.

The AMA began writing again in the South the seventeenth-century words upon the Harvard gates— "to advance learning and perpetuate it to posterity." Out in the brush with a frame building and a clutter of pupils who could not read, they started primary schools meant to grow into colleges and adjacent churches to be aided until they came to self-support. The larger Protestant denominations—Methodist, Baptist, Presbyterian—started with similar aims and methods and smaller denominations and new Negro groups proceeded in the same pattern.

The goals and policies of all show well enough in the one organization I know from experience. I visited the colleges and schools of other denominations and knew their educators; AMA policies, practices, and financial backing were duplicated a dozen times and all the organizations were striving for the religious and educational aims of the time.

They were a bulwark in the national life. If Southern poverty and reluctance and the Negro's weak status had been left untouched, Negro education would not have been more than industrial for a long period.

George W. Cable said at the University of Alabama in 1884 that Northern gifts to schools had reached $20,000,000 and had supplied most of the colored teachers for public schools. By 1919, I noticed that I never knew well any Negro who was not educated by Northern personality on Northern money; this includes all my close friends and many connected with colleges and organizations, who were to be leaders of the third generation.

When I worked for the American Missionary Association, it was still an independent organization supporting within the national borders schools, colleges, churches, hospitals, clinics and social service centers for "the unassimilated peoples for whom the Americanizing energy of the nation has hitherto failed." These peoples were Indians, Negroes, the Spanish-speaking in Puerto Rico, New Mexico and Florida, white people isolated in the Western and Southern mountains, Orientals in California, and Eskimos in Alaska.

The Congregational church made annual gifts, but such gifts never equalled the income from endowments designated for Negro education, some going far back: The Slater Fund dated from 1882; the Daniel Hand Fund gave $1,000,000 in 1888, later $500,000. The AMA did not come under Congregational church control until after the beginning of World War I. As long as I knew the budget, its chief support was from endowments.

The receipts from 1888 to 1908 totaled $10,230,569.87, distributed chiefly among twelve Southern states. The budget covered four theological schools, four colleges, twenty-nine secondary schools; "seventy-three schools of all grades" which had 15,000 pupils and 560 teachers.

In the year of Emancipation, the organization already supported 353 teachers and had spent $377,000. By 1908 Berea College (1855) and Hampton Institute (1863) were independent, Fisk University (1865) and Howard University (1867) needed support for only selected departments and Talladega College (1869) was moving toward independence with its own board of trustees.

The churches were less fluid; a total of 194 received aid, likely to be only part of the pastor's salary. When I went to North Carolina, they were all around—Concord, High Point, Raleigh, Beaufort, Lawndale, Wilmington—but I question if the founders ever expected the faith of Plymouth Rock to spread among the orange blossoms. It functioned remarkably in the early days, offering a certain nourishment to the mind instead of the extreme excitability of the more popular religious groups.

The money canalized into the South would be a respectable sum even now. The financial records were meticulous, school by school, church by church, person by person, down to the number of reindeer in the Alaskan reindeer herd.

I think highly of the Association's rigor in publishing annual financial and educational records. The school at Wilmington has been gone for forty years or so, but in yellowing books there could still be found its cost, its personnel, and the entry of a person of my name.

Cold Journey 4

WHEN I PICKED magnolia blossoms from my balcony in the first North Carolina spring, I had already learned that the magnolia's social climate is cold. It rises out of human permafrost; beyond the first foot down lies the Arctic ice.

The stranger's journey over permafrost is so slow and so cold that he finally gives up. The South can hardly be understood by an outsider, whatever his attempts at redirection.

My family had tried to prepare me for this. In offering me the teaching position, the Executive Secretary of the AMA told me that if I accepted it, I would not afterward be able to live or work among whites below the Mason and Dixon line, and that while teaching in a colored school I would be ostracized.

My mother had spent winters in Florida. When I went home with my news about a job, she said that taking on this work showed my ignorance. Philanthropic organizations would never get anywhere with ignorant girls who did not know what they were getting into. The South was in a condition of fallen elegance and the level I was going to reach would be really down at the heel. She did not mind my teaching Negroes—she resented the lack of any child's public high school education—but she was unwilling for me to go nowhere, a nowhere with no social life.

My uncle, who had been in business in Charleston during the bombardment of Fort Sumter, remained an unreconstructed rebel; he thought Tilden should have been President. The family heard his pure and unvarnished opinion. My parents' dear old friends in Delaware, who entertained me on my way South, cautioned me not to tell anyone at their parties what I was going to do. I never stopped at their house again while I was involved in any form of work with Negroes.

My Barnard College friends were dismayed. As seniors we had visited all the New York City institutions for the afflicted: the deaf, dumb, blind, and the mentally defective. They thought Negroes were in the same afflicted category and that I was throwing away my chance of professional advancement, going backward and downward with Topsy and Uncle Tom.

The Northern form of brainwashing did not impress me; it was exaggerated. But as soon as the Southern school year began, I heard of little but race relations. Each race is a staple of conversation for the other. The Old South had only two forms of art. The historical school was that of interpretation and preservation of Southern white life as it existed before the war. The college sorority could not afford to buy a house with ante bellum pillars, but the sisters saved money and put them on. The Negro was the subject of the contemporary school and both races were always involved in its study. White people among themselves talked an incredible lot about colored people. The colored, in turn, spread the word about whites all over town.

Among the first discoveries that I made was that my older associates, teachers for a lifetime, were dropping me into a pit. I was the youngest, and after dinner, as we visited together before settling down to the evening's work, the experienced marked me as their own special innocent.

I supposed that the warnings were the prejudice of the older generation, for I could already see that here lies were a form of good manners.

"They steal now," I was told. I must never leave my rings on the bureau or my watch on the desk. . . . I must keep an eye on the monitors and see that the hymnals were collected after chapel. . . . I must keep the bookcases locked. "They lie." I must get ready for children to look me straight in the eye and lie.

The children's grandparents had been wonderful pupils. They had walked ten miles to learn their ABC's. The fathers and mothers had studied by firelight, humble and grateful to have a chance. The older brothers and sisters had worked and saved and earned their way through college. Look at this generation now! Spoiled children, petted at home, never had to work, they actually said college would be too hard. They did not really love their books, would put them down on the sidewalk, the children of parents who had never let a book out of their hand. It would be a mercy if they ever graduated.

When talk turned to the white teacher's position in the community, I listened intently. I was told that I must understand that we were still fighting the Civil War. We lived over a tinder box, hands with matches always ready. The best whites tolerated our outrages against Southern custom, but the worst believed in torches. We were pointed out as "trespassers . . . carpet baggers . . . nigger-lovers." After dark I was not to step outside the door without a male escort. I had to cultivate distance and reserve, be inconspicuous, never become involved with either race, better not even look at people directly.

The white teacher from Massachusetts who warned me most severely on policy was over sixty years old and a vigorous and rational woman. She had lived through Wilmington's race riot of ten years earlier in 1898. She knew where twenty-three murders had taken place; she told me the very street corners where blood had run. The fires had started along streets where I walked every week. She remembered which of our school families had to run for their lives.

An editorial in the Negro newspaper, which went "too far" for the whites, had started the riot which ran on for four days and nights. This was a long time in so small a city in 1898. The white mob drove the newspaper editor out of town and smashed his press.

I had already sensed the smell of fear, as I had heard the story in the children's homes. This family had slept in the marshes, that one had buried the silver and never found it again. A brother had been shot; a son had gone North, swearing that he would never come back. The mother of one of my children said, "It come so that we in this town is afraid of a white face."

I could see the running figures and the pursuers in the torchlight, the crowd, the black swamp where men pretended they were cypress trees. I could hear the threats, the baying bloodhounds, the guns and the rumors.

The riot stories gave me my first understanding of how danger might come to others from something I could say or do. Danger gave me a brightening of perception; I meant to stop a long way before risk.

The atmosphere induced me to beware of whites. More, and worse, I was told to beware of Negroes. I must not expect parents or pupils to speak to me on the street. They could not be seen doing so. They would cross the street or cut me to protect us both.

For that matter, I must expect to be looked down upon by everyone. The father of our girls was used to Southern standards for women—his image was the lily-of-the-field; he knew I was doing something no "Southern lady" would do. He supposed that Northerners were mercenaries, teaching for big money, or because they could not get a job at home. I must do nothing in the way of manual labor, it was the sure sign of poor white trash. The dry leaves must lie on my balcony until the matron noticed and sent a maid to sweep them up. I must not dust my school desk—the janitor would notice. I must not wash my white gloves—the laundress would gossip about my morals.

I must hurry by every ghetto corner store and never go in even to ask directions—it might be a gambler's hideout. Everything could be something else and the ordinary concealed the disreputable.

I was told to get used to the fact that a Negro does nothing with me unless he is waiting on me. He walks behind me. He stands while I sit. He knows better than to eat in my presence. Keep well in mind that if the Negro drank, the Southerner smashed the glass.

Yet, my ears rang with the sound of the breaking glass of

tradition and my eyes saw the pieces in both Negro and white family homes. I could note the peculiarities of the sexual mores. I heard nothing about sexuality, nothing my grandmother might not have heard, but observed extravagant evidence about its consequences.

I was teaching pupils fairer than I, blue-eyed boys with pale Anglo-Saxon faces and fair hair, girls with the pink and white skin that goes with auburn curls. Violation of the Northern sexual taboos was all around me.

The white father of one of our families came to the school once a month to pay the tuition and sign the report cards. He waited uneasily until the principal came, for he wanted to talk with a man about his children's prospects for college. A white man of the area who died had two funerals: one in his downtown mansion behind the elaborate iron gates and one in the Negro quarter, among his colored family.

Women used to say easily that this preacher or that lawyer in their circles was "living in sin." Living near these dramas was like living in a Greek theater, and all the plays seemed of long ago. I had heard that Sojourner Truth bore five children to a man "given" to her by her master. Slaves made some prize understatements: "Papa went off when Freedom come. Mama didn't care. He was give to her." Adult mysteries had little to do with my young pupils. They were trying to find out about being themselves.

Eating mixed me up more than anything else. I had eaten candy with the children and taken the Communion wine from the silver cup at the mission church before I heard about the eating taboo. It ranked next in importance to the sexual taboo. There was no question of who was to be offended. No matter what you did, you offended everybody. I could not eat with Negroes privately, "because they will not respect you. News gets around and you will not be able to control the children."

An individual had no freedom to eat, an organization might have. Our Teachers' Home entertained for lunch or dinner any speaker who spoke at the school and, once in a while, the Congregational minister and the manual training teacher, a bachelor who lived in the city.

Talking so much about eating put a fence around these routine civilities. When I sat across the table from the first mild and harmless young guest, a poet, I tasted history on the plate. His slender hands closed their pale palms around his knife and fork while he talked to me about the Ben Franklin Library in Philadelphia. I cut my steak as if I, not he, were the outcast.

I felt outcast because I saw that this taboo had local sanction. The mothers who brought me cake and homemade wine or lemonade when I called never brought food or drink for themselves. At first I had believed them when they said they had "a little upset," or that they had just finished dinner.

An irrational wish not to make any more calls arose in me. Was I to go around claiming little upsets? If quicksand was everywhere, why should I think I could pick my way? And yet I had learned most of what I knew in the homes and there was no mistaking a woman's wish to talk about her children.

At this distance, it seems as if even a beginner could have distinguished between major and minor rules and would have known which were balderdash. I could not, because there was so much balderdash. Mothers telling me about some interracial triangle would explain that "of course" the white sheriff's dead body had to be taken to his wife after the heart attack, although he had not lived with her for twenty years. Everyone knew that he lived with his colored mistress in another part of town. Few would consciously differentiate between fact and fiction when speaking of the other race.

Those who instructed me were more than forty years old and I meant to conform exactly, lest I discredit the tradition or bring reprisal on the school. I would have liked to have received perspective from the public library, but there was none, and I grasped the feeling that outside of college centers, the bookish slant would be Southern. The local newspaper sneered about Negroes very often. The school library of 300 books or so was made up chiefly of literary classics; possibly by intention it had no books on race. I noticed that Charles W. Chesnutt, author of the first short stories about Negroes, had to make his narrator in *The Conjure Woman* a white man before the tales could get underway. This was the policy in 1899, and he could not protest his publisher's practice of beginning Negro with a small letter.

Ceremonies told me more than books could ever tell. The

first funeral was a revelation. I had been to only two funerals before, one the Congregational brevity of thirty minutes, the other the Roman Catholic ritual.

The funeral was for a girl of fourteen who had been enrolled in my freshman English class. When I arrived at the announced time, two o'clock, hardly anyone was in the church. The auditorium must have held 500 when the minister finally appeared in the pulpit. He intoned:

I wish to announce that the coffin
is now in the churchyard and
The pallbearers stand ready,
This church is $200 behind on the pastor's salary and
A collection for this debt will now be taken.
When the sum is received,
The coffin will be brought into the church.
Freely ye have received,
Freely give.

The crowd began to stream up the aisles to the table, where two deacons waited, changing their bills and clinking their silver. After an interval a deacon called out:

We thank you for $100
Half-way . . . half-way.
Just another hundred . . .
"Rock of Ages, cleft for me,
Let me hide myself in Thee."

The donors marched up and down again three times, responding to song and announcements.

"When I draw this fleeting breath"
Fifty dollars now . . .
Just fifty . . . just fifty . . .
"When mine eyelids close in death,
When I rise to worlds unknown"
Ten dollars more . . .
"And behold Thee on Thy throne"
Who will give the last dollar?
"Rock of Ages, cleft for me"
Bless God . . .

I sat shaking with anger, counting the strikes against the girl out in the hearse. Her older brother had died of the same disease in the same house the year before. The brief life had had only plain food, plain dark clothes. Nothing about her was pretty except her round girlish handwriting.

She had come to school within six weeks of her death from tuberculosis and I had noticed nothing. I had blackmailed her about her grammar as her church was blackmailing her now. The mother was a passive countrywoman, "Mus' be God punish me."

She looked young, lying in the open coffin, but no one's eyes dazzled. The neighborhood was used to losing children. Few had known her; she was hardly there at all. The mass had come together for the drama of death. This was what colored friends meant when they laughed in a pained way and said, "My people like funerals." The peaks of life they had were not many; they wanted something intense.

This was the first ritual I saw as distinctly the Negro's own. It had to contain clues to his arts, beliefs and behavior. It went beyond the boundaries of taste to some other depth. I was unable to realize that church ceremonies I had not questioned at home might have had a similar origin.

I looked at the minister. He was a man in business and he knew that people jinxed into masochism gave more when they were played upon. The rhythm and volume of his voice varied according to the need for $100 or ten dollars or one dollar. As the audience became more incoherent, he became more coherent. The reproachful and callous aspects of this death seemed a kind of cannibalism.

Gradually I began to withdraw. Instead of calling at homes, I went on long walks to look at the swamp life, comforting myself with frogs and dragonflies. Near the swamp I saw the foliage of the mandrake. The mandrake root suggests the human form, and superstition said it screamed when pulled out of the ground. The sound of the scream carried death or madness, so the mandrake's power must never be roused by human hands. Men hitched animals to the root and drove them to tear it out of the ground. The race business was full of malevolent hitchings, like this poison in a flower. I felt alone and became silent, remembering my mother's remark about "ignorant girls."

But it was not possible to stay frozen toward people who were so put upon. Every able member of a family who wanted to get off the treadmill had at least ten pairs of hands pulling him back. The father's hernia made him give up his job as piano mover. The son became the wage earner, carrying also the demands of his mother's malaria, his grandmother's medicines, and the little brother's shoes. After getting hold of his earnings, these crows in family life gradually picked his brains.

An awfully thin skin showed in those who got away from the cave of family obligations. A seventeen-year-old girl admitted to a Northern university in 1905, when such admissions were few, went to a little party for freshman girls, given by senior girls. It was only a get-together at five o'clock, with flowers, tea, sandwiches, and a girl playing the piano for dancing. She stood around eating and talking but when the president of the Undergraduate Association asked her to dance, she was shaken up. She danced, but she left at once. Crossing the campus she was already in tears. "I'll do something to myself. I won't stand it."

The next day she went to the Dean's office to say that she was leaving college. The young man who attempted to understand the trouble could make out nothing and turned her over to a woman advisor. The freshman was no match for the advisor's experience. She said she was going away because she had been patronized at the dance. A freshman was too insignificant to get an invitation from such a glamorous senior; it was an insult to her race.

The Dean's assistant explained to her that at these little tea parties, it was the policy that seniors dance with every freshman and never with each other. She had only happened to get the president.

Posted around everywhere at beaches, waiting rooms, drinking fountains, on streetcars and trains, the word *Colored* made my own liberty a reproach. To feel its barriers in full, I stayed away from areas and amusements closed to my children. I did not go to see Sarah Bernhardt play "Phèdre" at a matinee. After I could only read, walk, take pictures and study flowers for recreation, I lived behind Du Bois' "Veil."

I had small reminders of status. Two sisters who called at the Teachers' Home once a year explained heavily that to call on the ostracized was their Christian duty. They were white, but a little alien; Lutherans in the Methodist-Baptist sea.

Except for the pious sisters, I never spoke to a white person except on business during the eleven years I was connected with Negro education. Arguing began the moment I stepped off the first train. The hack driver said, "Lady, that's a nigger school, you don't want to go there."

The ostracized probationer is timid. He is in what prisons call "solitary," yet in this solitary, eyes look at him, criticism rolls above his head. Men are fairly tough about being in solitary. They do have business contacts, perhaps they have better sense. Women advertise that they have neither; some of them never go downtown. After a time, another mood succeeds. The ostracized becomes the invisible one. He pulls down a visor of unconcern as he walks along. He feels an evil exaggeration of what used to be a love poem:

If she be not fair to me
What care I how fair she be?

He no longer looks at people, he lets them swim indistinctly on the edge of vision. I imagine that a mental patient becoming disassociated from life chooses this willful blur.

John Howard Griffin in *Black Like Me** writes about how a Texas white man made up as a Negro felt traveling in the South. He could not eat or sleep properly, seemed never to be where he could find a public toilet, was afraid of being shaken up by both policemen and stray white men. His mind emptied out all thoughts except those of food and safety. Sometimes he had to give in suddenly, wash the stain off and turn white. His face in the mirror took on the long melancholy lines of certain Negro faces. This disconsolate look may begin in fatigue, but it becomes set from the gnawing of whatever gnaws the person, fixed

* *Houghton-Mifflin Co.: New York,* 1961.

to the look of those behind bars. I can recall a few white women who in the hostile environment became less erect in posture, more hesitant and uncertain in motion and in decisions. These are the women who must not stay; I never knew a man so affected.

The white taboo against Negroes creates special conditions—the emotional and divisive behavior, the substitutes for family relationships, the interracial attachments, the typhoons of lust for or against the other race. In defying the taboo, the forbidden, the adventurous rebel expands to a size able to overcome it.

Tracking down the music and words of spirituals found me the first friend of my own age. She was a thin olive-skinned girl, a college graduate then teaching music, a delicate cynic who hated ragtime and dancing because people thought Negroes could do nothing else.

Ours was the world of music and conversation. I never ate with her or walked with her. I asked her to explain Negroes and we lent each other books.

In her early twenties, she already accepted humiliation as she accepted nature. Although she practiced Bach every day, she was not allowed to touch the keys of a newly delivered piano. The salesman instructed "Kate," as he called her, in "Chopsticks."

In New York she felt wonderfully free, did a year's shopping, went to the theater and concerts, but was vaguely homesick on Fifth Avenue—"Never a sight of a colored face."

Her haunting soprano was for Schubert and Schumann and nothing but music gave any answer to her life. She often said she did not belong to either race. She lived long enough to sing and to love and to wear an engagement ring, but not to marry.

Death must have opened the exit sooner because she loved a man who was one of the accursed. He was whiter than the average white man, handsome and volatile. He had had two years of college, did not want to teach, was not musical and not religious in any professional way. Without capital and dangerously gentle, he was never able to find a job that would permit their marriage. Local employers would hand him no more than a broom.

After her death, he lived on only a year. My first sight of romance in the world to which I had come was these two babes in the woods, so early covered by leaves.

Very many Southern experiences ended abruptly and definitely like this. There was so often a foretaste, like the one the novelist uses when he puts a suicide in the first chapter; the reader need not expect the happy ending.

Because of my friend's long disembodied spirit, I have sometimes understood elements that have gone into music since World War I. Because of her, too, I began to expect the knife among the roses. It was not only that she died; I had to assimilate the fact that there were those who would have preferred that colored people die in some violent interracial fiesta.

One initial effect of the new region was to throw me back toward childhood. Books were inaccessible. My learning depended surprisingly on the five senses. My eyes taught me most, but my ears heard more than they would have in a big city; the taste of two hundred years of Southern living went into my mouth every day.

After two years in Wilmington I told the New York office of the AMA that I found it too hard to be neither black nor white. The executive secretary said that a transfer to Memphis would be easier, for it was already a generation ahead in education. He meant that scholarhip was on a more stable footing. Possibly he knew that some recent racial trouble there had temporarily suspended calling in the homes and attending the churches.

Memphis on these slight terms was like teaching anywhere. Le Moyne Normal Institute (now Le Moyne College) had a good library and the students were more mature. In a sense, I forgot the racial limitations. The city itself took the place of contacts with the colored community. I heard no one's troubles; there were concerts and lectures to go to. I used to walk by the Mississippi River and memorize the looks of the gorgeous clutter of Negro business of Beale Street.

I paid no attention to the egg thrown at me as I sat reading in the living room on a Sunday afternoon. It broke against the window pane. An egg was nothing. In 1866, a chapel, the first built by the AMA for Negro worship, was burned in a furor which destroyed all the city's colored churches.

After a year in Memphis I was planning to leave teaching for postgraduate work, but when I said so, the AMA offered me its new position of assistant superintendent of education. I took it eagerly because of the chance to see all the Southern schools and to acquire a new perspective.

Whenever I was not caught in the issues, the dual culture dazzled me. It roused in me all the heat of the search. In college I had not been searching for anything beyond the assignments. I turned *Horace* into English verse, wrote short stories in French "in the style of Zola," crammed the decisions about the Standard Oil Company and the Chicago and Alton Railroad. I was aware that I was only learning methods.

The race question drew me into concentration. It drove me. I did not believe I could do anything about it except as a teacher, but I wanted to know the educational possibilities. While I was traveling in the South, I visited public schools, colleges of other denominations and other landmarks of Negro life from 1911 to 1919.

Life on the Edge 5

WHAT I KNOW about Negro life began in talks with mothers in their homes about their children and their plants and flowers. Once in a while we agreed that she should not try to push Mary so hard, but usually we were involved in happy conversation. Then she began to tell me that the old cactus came from a leaf enclosed in a letter and I told her about the heliotrope that grew thirty feet high in California.

She questioned me cannily about my parents and home, and what year I had left college. My reputation was enhanced when she learned that I had owned a horse as well as a bicycle. She apparently thought I had the right possessions for my age, but perhaps she wanted to give me something out of her more ample life, for she said, "You inexperience." She often told me about the hard times of her life, the children's illnesses, how she and her husband saved money, and when they began to buy the house.

The homes I knew were clean and tidy. They were crowded,

since families often ran to six because of the old grandmother or a relative's child. The more comfortable had a living room and a dining room; others had to use every room as a bedroom. The big white bed with the ruffled pillowshams edged toward the door. The bureau and mantelpiece were jammed with boxes, shells, medicine bottles, and vases marked "Souvenir." Enlarged photographs—"my Mother, my Father, my Husban' "—pressed down from the walls. Rooms had the smell of clean clothes, piles of them were airing by the fireplace, baskets of them waited to balance on the head for the evening walk to the owner.

I admired the way colored women made good homes. Everything they did had savor. When the family sat down to three-o'clock dinner, the food was as well-cooked and palatable as it was in the big house where the mother had once cooked or might still be cooking. She liked to feed people and she had a generous hand. Her own table had plenty of fish, cheaper parts of the pig, turnips and collards instead of fruit, syrup instead of dessert. At the lowest dip of the income curve, fat back, corn pone, greens, and pot liquor were staples. My children shivered when chitterlings, pig's tail and pig's feet were mentioned; they said old people ate disgusting meat.

Relative extravagance in eating was a balance against daily worry and aggravation. Families who lived a hand-to-mouth existence bought meat steadily and kept fruit cake and other rich and tasty sweets in the cupboard.

Stimulants were not customary. Fathers smoked pipes, but our boys did not smoke and the only liquor I knew about was homemade wine. Coffee was not usual, but when health was so often uneasy and courage low, the body took solid comfort in replenishment by meat and sugar.

The poor never had enough warm clothes for rain or cold and old women tied the head up in a bandanna and perched a rusty black sailor on top of it, but in general, use of clothing was the practice nearest to the American norm. School girls wore cotton frocks which were made at home and laundered to perfection. A shack on the edge of nowhere would send to Sunday church two well-dressed children and a teenager with daisies on her hat and that indefinable look of being sixteen.

The color combinations were exciting. Negroes put red and

pink and orange together before Matisse did. Children wore pale blue, a color of innocence. Their mothers rejected the navy blue so often chosen for durability by women of small income. No color is more unlike them than navy blue. Women who could wear only gray and blue in slavery came out in yellow, orange, cerise, green, scarlet, magenta and purple. Matrons in their best clothes displayed an opulent color sense, topped by hats that were extravaganzas. They had a characteristic style, a genuine prediction of what was to come in Negro arts. Dress afforded another prediction. They were often in mourning and they wore it a long time. I remember girls of fifteen dressed in black for two years at a time.

The racial separation into upper, middle, and lower class was taught me casually by high-school students. It was no different from what I knew about whites, except that I never heard about it as an adolescent, and would not have used it as a classification in ordinary speech.

Class and caste defined the broad patterns of aim, order, warning, and reward. Their hair-splitting about these matters was worse than that of whites, because they added more categories.

The two uppermost, moving toward white middle-class life were the pace-setters. They were schoolmates and friendly, but pocketed separately in housing, church, education, and occupation. Neither knew much about the lower class. They were deathly afraid of getting dragged back to what their grandfathers had left behind.

"The talented tenth" was, at birth, farther along than the others. It was lighter in color and had inherited land or education or money from white or free ancestors. It had the first higher education and produced most of the early professional men.

In middle life, this group supplied the community leaders. Schools, churches, social clubs, charities, alumni organizations, the literary and music clubs, and the beginning of the library depended on their initiative. Leaders owned a frame house, with electricity, bath, and refrigeration. Money was spent for Northern travel in the summer, for medical and dental care, for books, magazines and a piano. Children might have afternoon jobs, but all were brought up hoping to go to college. The ordinary standards of the day were there, and some extra jewel, like a peach tree or a wisteria, or a child with musical gifts.

They told me that their particular problem was being colored at all. Being too white themselves, they could not assimilate the lower class. They were the prestige pattern, but too high on the hill—a traget for snipers. They suffered in conscience about trouble that could hardly be expressed. Those who came North were sometimes fair enough to pass, but "passing" was then regarded as treason to the race. I never knew anyone who did not think so.

Secretly, they held on to certain whites as models of conduct; public and historical figures predominated, of course, but locally, they venerated the first principal of their missionary school, and they measured a man by President Cravath of Fisk University or President Ware of Atlanta University.

The middle-class channel was narrower, provincial in outlook. The women especially had not been far from home. Wives continued to work in white homes, unless they took in washing; husbands were carpenters, cooks, butlers, gardeners, hostlers, post office sorters, Pullman waiters, and porters. This seemed the most selfless group: for themselves they wanted only the Methodist or Baptist church, visiting relatives, small comforts, fishing, crabbing, hunting. Their children were the first of their line to get through high school and become teachers in the country. They supported grandchildren; their bungalows had shrubs and flowers and big back yards, but only kerosene lamps and unpaved streets, and usually fireplaces for heat and cooking.

The lower class lived in more ramshackle houses in poorer neighborhoods; the peach tree and the wisteria were gone. Rent was about $3.50 a month; a woman who did laundry at home at fifty cents to $1.00 a wash, worked three or four days to earn the rent money. The now-and-then roomer, the unattached day laborer, working in anything heavy and dirty, crowded in with these families.

I could never understand how the lowest group made out financially. They could not scrape together the month's tuition of $1.10 all at once and used to send it in two payments. I knew from experience that the doctor was not called until the illness reached the frightening stage. The children's shoes were scuffed, the winter coats sleazy, the dress only one fading calico.

They were the very dark people, sometimes the last lot into the city from the open country. Their skills were the crudest, their religion the wildest; they sang and shouted half the night at the Church of the Morning Star.

I do not think the lower class was as stagnant as it appeared. It was anonymous, had little tenure anywhere. Men passed from job to job, women from wash to wash. Without a steady job, there could not be the white protector to refer to in time of trouble. The gossip was that men carried razors and women carried icepicks. A grandmother of one such ghetto once said to me, "I have never had a child arrested and I am proud of it." Menfolk were said to get into prison two and a half times as often as the white man. I always imagined the connection within the race was weak because the upper classes were afraid to mingle.

In the cotton-picking area, the sharecropper could show the unwilling walk, the sullen look, the whining voice or the teeming silence. Asked the way to John Smith's house, a cluster of field hands would shake their heads and say "I doan' know, I ain't never seen him . . . Nosuh . . . Nosuh." If, however, the stranger let them know that he was not a bill collector but looking for a song, they said, "Oh! You means *John Smith.* I ain' understan' what you say. He right down in yonder field."

The median Negro home of about three rooms without conveniences may have been no worse than the first homes of famous men of our early days, and European immigrants to big cities found worse in the nineteenth century, but the Negro never seemed able to get away as the others had done. In World War I, he was worse off in housing than rural whites in his state had been when Frederick Law Olmsted had observed the whites in the 1850's.

All in the region shared threats from nature and from the economic shifts that go on above the average head, but color drew additional blows. A good crop year, a bad year, an election, a new state policy, each swayed life according to the white life at the center.

The 1900 Negro employment in the South was close to the peasant tradition:

AGRICULTURE, FISHING, MINING	57 per cent
DOMESTIC AND PERSONAL SERVICE	31 per cent
MANUFACTURING, MECHANICAL INDUSTRIES	6 per cent
TRADE AND TRANSPORTATION	5 per cent
PROFESSIONAL SERVICE	1 per cent

Unless he was a farm hand, the man in agriculture was a tenant. The landowner provided the land, house, tools, mule, seeds, fertilizer, and a charge account for food, clothing, and incidentals at the commissary.

When the owner and the tenant settled up—once a year after cotton picking—the owner must have owed money sometimes, but the records seem to be about those who did not. The tenant might hear a rumor that he "broke even" or that he had cleared $25 on his year's work. Because he could neither read nor write, he was likely to be told by the accountant that he owed, not was owed, $25. The tenant had only remembered charging such necessities as corn meal, bacon, blue jeans and tobacco.

White tenants in Kentucky had the same trouble growing tobacco. They fell so far into debt that they could not get out, and became peons attached to the land.

Before World War I, peonage was big news as a shifty trick that restored slavery. Young university men did research in what rated as a dangerous occupation. Newspapers told of mysterious disappearances:

When I was in peonage in Mississippi
And they watched us with guns,
I saw a man kill more than one and
just throw them in the river.

The bulk of personal service was still carried out in private homes. Barbers, valets, and waiters were included, but not women's beauty salons. A white family had to have a servant or lose face. She might be a ten-year-old to wheel the baby, sweep the yard, and run errands.

A girl who studied beyond high school could teach in the elementary grades, but her parents opposed nurse training, saying that there would not be enough hospital jobs and that white men would make private nursing impossible. She might do dressmaking or give music lessons, but she yearned to do stenography and typing, perhaps because they were out of reach. There were not enough positions in colored offices and those few were filled by women relatives of the owner.

Yet, compared to men, women had the favorable work situation. School teachers worked among their own race and had steady employment and high social status. Those who did housework for others were at least using feminine skills in which they had served an apprenticeship. They had a craftsman's pleasure in work, in proportion to their own initiative, and in good furnishings.

The man had little luck. The buffets of the world canceled his ego, made him stick with the monotonous and accept the fact that the color line would freeze him at a low point. The white employer did not want him to have a job that would adequately use him and let him grow as a worker—and as a man. The Negro man could not be sure that he could support his family and he had to wear a terrible meekness: "Yes, sir . . . Yessuh . . . Yassuh." Let one dark Monday morning betray him into over-assertion and he would get his walking papers as "an uppity nigger."

It was said that when the Kentucky Derby began, the jockeys were mostly Negroes, but when the salary got to $12,000, white folks were riding. The colored men were stable attendants, caring for horses and throwing dice:

Our Fadder which are in Heben
White man owe me leben, pay me seben.

A few boys were going into law, the ministry and dentistry. Their parents groaned. The race took no care of its teeth. The courts pushed colored lawyers around. It was no use to study for the ministry. Baptists could be ministers if they just felt the call.

The profession which all were willing to sacrifice for was medicine. The physician was the top man in the top caste. Parents would pinch fearfully to put a boy there. They wanted their sons to be of service to the race and they dreamed of getting back at white doctors who had been rude in their houses.

The modest jobs in clerical work, selling and industry were closed to the colored male. He had to leap over the middle-range occupations straight to the professions. Professions that required long preparations and Northern study were beyond his financial reach. As well, these professions were those which provided services beyond the reach of the poverty-stricken Negro. Teaching and the ministry were full of men who were there because there was so little else to do.

The unmuscular literate males whose looks suggested that they might make trouble were automatically labeled unemployable. Some took their revenge by turning into a liability. They cut up as clowns, drank, or rolled dice, or they had a wandering foot.

In some little entryway with a counter, anywhere and anytime, a submerged cluster of young males loafed and lived out their doctrine. "A nigger is a nigger . . . he lives in the basement . . . no use to run upstairs." Just as some men appear to have a natural goodness, these set out to make a career of natural badness. Gay, sly, and vicious, seeing no top to life, they planned to reach the bottom. The older women of his race characterized this type as they tested a hot iron with a wet finger—"He eats, sleeps, drinks, gambles, jokes, womanizes, sings, spits, mimics, sharpens his razor."

Yawning on the edge of the drop, fighting, playing the buffoon, there were only three ways of graduating from the apprenticeship in entryways: into prison by way of a cutting scrape, with tuberculosis, or by migration to a place big enough to sustain sports and shady characters.

Outside the three economic classes, the nucleus of a sporting group floated; the man who made the dice shake, the liquor flow, and the dance go round. Only two or three might be in evidence, peeling bills off big rolls, going to the fights, and wearing the ring with the large stone. Their wives had lace curtains and pianolas, but not every cleaning woman was willing to clean for them. She told the wife that her back was bad, but by the time she was telling her neighbors, she was saying, "I thinks too much of myself. I don't has to clean up after niggers." Gambling was disapproved of by those who did not gamble and church members spoke of it as a threat.

I missed in all male occupations an element I had heard about from childhood. Sea captains and lumber men used to say that a man could never reach his full development until for once he had been able to go greatly beyond himself. Their stories of men's big moments made me realize how little chance colored men had for daring. Another reason the man was trapped in his cabin was that health and strength were the family's chief capital and some of his household so often had poor health.

The sunset colors the women wore to Sunday church were chosen by people who were going to live such a brief time. When I lived in Maine death seemed to come only after eighty; in California, the population was so young and almost no one was ever sick. Now I saw illness and death, from infancy to thirty-five, around me everywhere. The death rate was then about double that of white. Deaths from tuberculosis were at the rate of three colored to one white.

A few ex-slaves were always around, but by Clement Eaton's figures in *The Growth of Southern Civilization*,* only 1.2 per cent of the slaves lived to be over seventy. They were subject to fevers, dysentery, pneumonia, hernia, cholera, lockjaw, malaria, and venereal diseases. Every ailment but lockjaw seemed to continually run its course among the populace.

The buzzards circled slowly over the urban slums. The city's outskirts were always in danger of typhoid and even in the center, water trickled through cisterns and could be contaminated by old leaking sewage mains. In out-of-the-way places I ate and drank only according to the rules, but in 1914, I caught typhoid fever in a little Alabama college town. This fever, once started, sweeps through whole families; they cannot provide the nursing care for so long and so contagious a disease.

At the time, Negroes were so illiterate they could hardly have been taught even on an emergency basis. By the United States

* *Harper and Row: New York,* 1961.

Census of 1900, about one-third of the population of the South was Negro and half of them were illiterate. Illiteracy had a dreadful integration, because eleven per cent of the whites were illiterate too. In the best state of the South for literacy, thirteen out of every one hundred could not write their own names; in the worst, thirty-eight could not.

The five border states and Texas then enrolled nearly two-thirds of all the pupils in Negro high schools; the other eight states enrolled only 1,100 among them.

Northern parents, hearing today that the annual cost of their child's public education might run to $1,000, can hardly believe that even fifty years ago, some Southern states were spending only $5 per pupil. A state might allot around $7 per capita, $4.42 on every white child, $2.21 on every Negro. Truancy helped the taxpayer and no one troubled that a third of the white children and half of the colored did not go to school at all.

Money scarcity made for short school years, sometimes only half as long as the Northern school year. A Negro elementary school could be held in a colored church or lodge hall for five months. Costs included the teacher's salary—about $35 a month—and practically nothing else. Overcrowding was commonplace. Not every child had books. Of one hundred children registered in the first grade only about twenty-five held on to "graduation" from the sixth or seventh.

The basic deficiencies went unnoticed by Southerners who did not get interested until it was time for "vocational education." The whites preferred book learning for Negro children when it was accompanied with the plowing of fields. Old people said that the craftsman's work deteriorated as soon as the overseer with the spyglass was gone. Politicians used to tell audiences how healthful it would be to have overgrown lots near the school cleared, plowed and planted.

These vocational ideas received nation-wide approval. When General Armstrong at Hampton Institute had to educate grown young men and women who had worked for years but could not read well, he devised a program of education using the classroom, vocational shop, practice sessions and projects—a plan considered desirable for many children. Virginia subsidized Hampton Institute, Alabama subsidized Tuskegee Institute, and every state improved its agricultural and mechanical college. AMA schools in Southern cities got subsidies from their towns for household arts, woodworking and ironworking and printing shops, although requests for the addition of a fourth year to the high school or for a science department were refused.

The founders of this educational program had mature pupils, a controlled environment and fabulous equipment. No wonder it took hold. I once heard Dr. George Drayton Strayer of Columbia University's Teachers College say that to have full educational expression in this country, a child had to be deaf and dumb, blind, mentally defective, Indian or Negro. After the founders departed, a lot of money was lost because teachers with proper skills were hard to find and the layman could not understand how various, expensive, and seemingly unreasonable the equipment had to be.

The Southerner's devotion to lumbering and plowing came out of his dream to live again in his agricultural past. The commercial traveler often assumed that his Southern territory was almost wholly agricultural. Riding the red plush seats of the Southern Railroad, drowsy after a meal of fried chicken, spoon bread, and pecan pie at the station restaurant, he might take a nap. When he awoke the type of landscape he had passed two hours ago was still before his eyes. Cotton fields and cabins seemed endless, and he liked the change when the locomotive rushed through pine forests or swamps. King cotton, lumber, turpentine, oxcarts, mules, goats seemed to float by as they had before the War.

This impression was a false one. Iowa around 1910 had farm values equal to those of all the south central states. Rice, indigo, and Sea Island cotton were already gone and cotton's day was soon to pass. Industry was promoting the growth of new cities, some on Northern capital.

Textile mills were drawing whites down from the mountains. The father of a family was getting his job and his company house with an agreement to put his whole family to work in the mill during the busy season. The poor white came from an area that had its own interpretation of the Dred Scott Decision and he hardly knew that the South had lost the War. He had grown up hearing boasts that no Negro could stay overnight in his county.

The Northerner who came as superintendent or manager of the textile plant was credulous and co-operative. He discovered in himself a hobby of visiting battlefields and he hung out the Stars and Bars on Confederate Memorial Day.

These white migrants from two new backgrounds tightened the color line as Thomas Dixon had tightened it with *The Leopard's Spots* in 1902 and *The Clansman* in 1905. No one then talked about letting the Negro laborer leave. Northern agents recruiting him in Jacksonville, Florda, were charged $1,000 for a license fee. Only two per cent of Chicago's population was Negro; Harlem had fine roomy old houses and apartments for the early migrants.

Life on the edge had its own unique and wonderful signs. Church was the one great steeple that pointed upward for all. After the starvation of slavery, there were no unbelievers. A church rose for every degree of education, every location and purse. Families talked easily about conversion:

My boy found the Lord
in the trenches,
in France.
I bless His name.

The few eccentrics who were not really religious would never have been outspoken about it. They might not feel they had the Spirit, but they went to church anyway; it was where they met everybody and heard everything.

The Congregational, Presbyterian and Protestant Episcopal churches were regarded by the masses as stuck up and impossible. Northern Congregationalists thought that part of their function was to liberalize the more popular denominations, while waiting for educational evolution.

Language revealed social orgins as plainly as church membership and residence areas. The small upper class met the standards of good American speech with the expected regional flavor. Not only professional people, but craftsmen spoke well and brought up their children in the local standard. They called everything else "dialect" and the professional heard it as the clank of chains.

The large middle range—surely more than half the people—spoke with the variations in tense and number, the unmatched subject and predicate, and the elisions often quoted in this book. Local mannerisms in the white upper class and grammatical faults in the lower class whites were copied by many Negroes. The singing tune and the slurs over words had to be learned by the outsider, but the speech of three generations was moving in the direction of the models of the area—the orators, lawyers, and aristocracy.

The speech had the attraction of a foreign tongue. I thought that I must not speak it and that I must teach children how to get away from some of it, but it had novel adjectives, adverbs and figures of speech, and wonderful racy sayings. I would hardly call the variation I heard "dialect," but rather a fluctuating intermediate stage which might even be generally approved some day.

Three speech levels could be found in one home. An old grandmother spoke the Gullah dialect of the coastal region around Charleston, or something explained to me as "back country." Tune, inflection, and vocabulary were strange. I could not understand her. The mother spoke with a fluent and gorgeous incorrectness, somehow graphic and pleasing as soon as one became used to the idiom. A daughter in high school, explaining in class something learned from a book, spoke the prose of the book. The whole town thought I ought to beat her if she ever spoke differently. Her family wanted her to get a teaching job and as they put it, "She gots to talk good." Yet the excitement of telling a story or writing one always made her want to speak as her mother did.

The United States Census of 1910 pictured the Negro as an illiterate rural Southerner with a short life span, working chiefly in agriculture and personal service. Usually poor, he was segregated, lynchable, and masochistic.

Yet, the Negro defied generalization. He was a pioneer, testing to see how anyone always near the danger line could make his way into the mainstream of American life. He could hardly get away from tragedy, passing rapidly from his father's and mother's to his own and his child's. In requiring his acceptance of tragedy, the gods made him a present of some important secret weapons.

An unbeatable quality surged up in a certain kind of Negro laughter. Almost anybody could laugh at himself and some acquired a technique that made both races laugh. The unbeatable laugh expressed a secret meaning: "I can get out of every box you put me in, except the last."

Long ago, they had acquired deep within a heightened sensitivity to fear. Country people had a naked physical fear as if some slavering beast might cross the creek and carry them away. City folk, lost in urban mazes, were less afraid of white neighbors and had instead economic anxieties and hauntings about status.

The unwritten law was that Negroes should form a solid unit against the white man. It would not be polite for any Negro to disagree with this directive but some also needed to be destructive, so they were in conflict with their own race.

It would have been too tame, too conformist, to patronize the early colored doctors, lawyers, dentists, storekeepers and insurance agents. As soon as these young men began to operate, their middle and lower class brethren leaped to pull them down. They were not well-educated enough, not light enough, not experienced enough, not from an important enough family. Parents said curtly that their children must be taught by white teachers. A black Negro was not desirable to employ professionally, to buy from, to entertain, to marry, to be buried beside.

At the same moment all these beliefs were being expressed, it could be seen that the misdeeds of parents could be forgotten in the good deeds of children and that these restrictions would pass. The race did not seem to have what sociologists call the under-class—the folk permanently in the lowest plane. It had fluidity.

I saw this shifting at its best by way of an occasional child. She would be a very dark child, hair in tight pigtails, faded pink gingham, old red sweater, at fourteen like something just out of the egg. Her favorite question was "Do it has to be that way?" The idea that what she was saying was a sentence with a subject and a predicate was one of the funniest she ever heard. She laughed and laughed and said, "I'm so tickled. Please Ma'am, tell me again. Why do it has to be?"

She had plenty of intelligence and the word "retarded" maligns her. She was an innocent trying out in a new culture.

The mother of a child like this might say to me, "She eatin' her white bread now and don't know it." This saying did not have to be true. Character, industry, and children who did well might raise the whole family to the middle class. I have seen families of five pulled up the ladder by a single girl of this type. In the end, she provided white bread for two younger children and her parents.

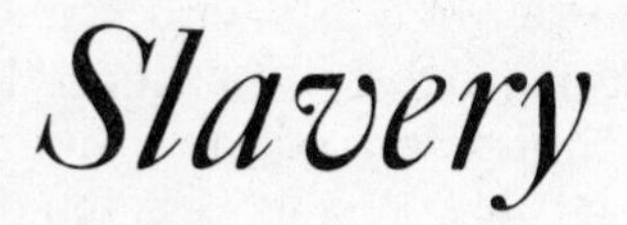

Slavery 6

My Lord calls me, He calls me by the lightning.
The trumpet sounds within-a my soul . . .

EVERY NEW YEAR I used to go to the Big Meetings, celebrations of Emancipation Day. I began attending only forty-five years after January 1, 1863, and I knew many who had been slaves. Their annual memorial service gave an immediate impression of slavery.

Freedmen attracted me as living documents. My five great-aunts and uncles, in their eighties when I was eight, telling me of frontier settlement and perilous ocean voyages, had made me understand that there was the Past.

William James and Edward L. Thorndike, psychologists of two generations, brought me further understanding of human behavior during college. I had the feeling of another world when considering ex-slaves. James had made me study men who were twice-born. If new birth could come from religion, from political creed, from love, from sickness, from nature, it could come with freedom from slavery. The rebirth did not come at the confusing moment of liberation, but at some later time it lit the new man in a burst of glory. When I knew them, Negroes experienced these transfigurations in church as a group.

When I was a teacher in Wilmington and Memphis, I saw ex-slaves every day; later I asked to meet them as I traveled. I still remember about fifty different individuals—all important to me because they let me glimpse fragments of their lives' psychological direction. I knew seven well, in intimate moments of revelation, the same way I came to know my elderly relatives.

I could look around my schoolroom and see slave ancestry in the craving for iron discipline and in the softness which atoned for being hard. I felt supported by their good manners, standards of conduct, and liking for fine things. They adapted the great moral tradition of the Old Testament to their needs as soon as they were out of "the Wilderness." They thought that they, too, were a chosen people for whom the waters of the sea had opened.

The older ex-slaves, who had been called by lightning, showed that life itself is the greatest art. They were tough as pine knots, free as flowing water. I heard the stories of slavery in their homes. These individuals provided the real source material. If they had been as old as thirty at Emancipation, they had been formed in slavery. Now in the seventies, they had a wonder about the world they would soon leave.

The more I saw of the Negro community, the more I was able to trace everything back to slavery and Emancipation. These aging half-anonymous figures, reborn naked to the world's ways during my parents' childhood, had rolled up mountains of character. They revealed to me a conquering of self that the white has no knowledge of and cannot equal. I recognized that they had received a sign and I looked up to them. They had virtue.

They were in the habit of praying about the Day of Judgment, but on earth Emancipation Day was their Great Day.

Wilmington's old church—African Methodist Episcopal Zion

—was crowded with ex-slaves and their families for the long afternoon service. They were the simpler folk, plainer, darker, and poorer by far than the Easter congregation. The young, the fair, the well-to-do and the highly educated were getting to the point where they could not bear to be reminded of the Great Day; they shrugged and stayed away.

The January weather was cold, the light came from a wan sky. Dress was sombre: brown, gray or black. Primitive types and faces from an earlier time returned. Old men were gnarled by manual labor, gaunt women had put on their look of being unfulfilled. The congregation appeared watchful, keyed up, bound together in tension; saying that they were joyful, they seemed vulnerable to fear. They were shaken because they remembered their parents, their friends already gone and their own youth. The ghosts of slave multitudes walked in the church in their immortality. The phantoms of slavery plunged the congregation back into it again.

Men called on God in agitation: "Father, we thank Thee that Thou didst lead the Israelites out of the house of bondage." They gave thanks for Lincoln and for every hand that struck off the chains. They wrestled on their knees, crying out that they be enabled to forgive those who had beaten them. A penetrating and metallic soprano began to sing:

Jordan's waters, chilly and cold,
Chill the body but not the soul.

They fled into identification with every Biblical character who had ever been in trouble and they made them real. Job and Daniel might have been in the front pews.

Memories loosened in these services. I used to walk away seeing apparitions, wondering what these men and women would dream that night, what stories they would tell their children as soon as they closed the door and built up the fire.

I never felt at liberty to ask too much about slavery. I asked about religious experience, Christmas, music, folk sayings, the development of skills, courting customs. I always asked the few who remembered Africa to tell me about their life there, but I only mentioned slavery if they spoke of it first. They had come to dignity, and I feared to remind them of the time when they had not had it. I liked to listen and watch the old Rembrandt faces—serenity and wisdom turned into flesh.

The ex-slave's graceful and remote courtesy had been inflicted by the iron rod, but became part of him because, instead of breaking, he had managed to bend with an air of acceptance. When he paid deference to those he cared about, he endowed it with beauty in proportion to his care. It shook me then—and still does—to see goodness emerging from such severe restraint; it did not come until the Negro himself had made a translation from a language of cruelty to one of love.

My children talked as if their ancestors had lived on big plantations, the domain built up out of seventeen smaller plantations and 2,500 slaves, where a horseman took two days to cover the ground. Yet, Booker T. Washington's owner had seven slaves. Clement Eaton says that in 1860 eleven masters held over 500 slaves, 3,000 held 100, and the remaining 43,000 owners held up to twenty. My pupils had heard stories of historic plantations, especially of the Pierce Butler Plantations on Butler Island and St. Simon Island, Georgia, because these provided the last great auction sales. At the Savannah race course in 1859, the last of Butler's seven hundred slaves—429—were put up for his debts. The highest price for a single man was $1,700 and for a woman with her five children, $6,180. Old couples went for $250 apiece. The proceeds of the sale were $300,000. As he walked around saying goodbye, Mr. Butler gave each slave a dollar in four bright new quarters.

A big plantation was a remote and self-contained stronghold, cut out of wild nature. Animals moved around the landscape; in season, wild ducks skimmed overhead. The air carried sounds now forgotten: cattle lowing, pigs grunting, guineas gabbling, and hens complaining; bird song and human song, calls and hollers from field to field, the sound of running water, saws and axes, horses at the gallop, the scrunch of leather, wheels turning on hard ground, bell peals, the thud of feet on the run. The master buried his money for safety and the house servants knew where it was.

The slow tempo came from weather, water, the sun, the force

of gravity, and the human body. The shirt-tail boy, playing in the cleared space between the cabin rows, was already as wild as a quail. When he was a month old, his mother went back to chopping cotton. He ate johnnycake outdoors at the call of the old woman in charge and he dipped into a long wooden trough of milk—"like the pig's trough"—along with other children. In the larger trough of a small dark cabin, he slept with his brothers and sisters in a trundle bed or a bunk of scaffolding against the wall. The founder of Tuskegee Institute never ate at a table or slept in a bed until after Emancipation.

When he went to the pig-killing, he watched the young men killing three to four hundred hogs a season. The old men were tanning leather, making hickory chairs, axe handles, horse collars, harness, shoes, fish baskets, rugs, and mats out of plaited shucks.

Men and women rose early in the morning and went to the cotton field for the day. The ante-bellum cotton plant bore forty to fifty bolls from late August to early January and field hands had to pick it three times over.

The child learned to eat fish and greens with sticks and his fingers. He watched the women at work. They cooked and cooked in swing pots over fireplaces. They washed clothes in homemade tubs or in running water where they pounded them with battling sticks and hung them on lines of vine to dry. They swept floors with sage brooms, shook up feather ticks on corded beds, boiled in the dye the cloth from sheep's wool, poured the tallow candles. The sewing women made dresses and sunbonnets, knit hose and shawls.

When the child was six he began his work. He ran errands, he carried dinner to the fields. He went along with a gang of boys to bring water in cedar buckets and to gather lightwood knots. His little sister would be watching over chickens or turkeys, his older sister stood behind chairs in the dining room, waving the peacock feather fan that kept the flies away.

One day a lady saw the little boy toting water and asked, "Does my little nigger want something to gnaw on?" That was the first time he tasted a buttered biscuit. But then he dropped the bootjack he was bringing to the white man and the man growled, "You little varmint!" The child understood these possessive tones. They were Master and Mistress. These two were the top. They became his parental figures.

As the boy grew older, Master and Mistress held a god's position over him. Now they gave dinner, buttermilk, and cloth; but they could also give the whip. They might sell him; might trade him for so many cotton bales; might send him down the great deep river.

Even in old age, a freedman could recall how Master and Mistress looked on horseback, what they ate, their Christmas gifts, their very words. He could love them as children love parents, or he could hate them or he could both love and hate:

Mistress was the best woman
in the world, but
Master was a terror.

Women often loved more; it was the women who hoped to meet Master and Mistress in Heaven. It was the men whose faces became overcast at the thought that

My father was my Master . . .
I had to wear a ball
until I was twenty-one.

Love could allow the slave to act like a protective parent toward the owner. One old owner when dying wanted to hear the bell rung and the conch horn blown as they had been in heyday. The bell and horn were gone, but the slaves, all crying, got a wagon tire and beat it under his window.

The ex-slave showed that he was a child without a cradle. He spoke of his parents in terms of facts; they worked, they had children, they died at about a certain age, birth and death never known exactly. He was not fed by them and he was not dressed by them; his clothing came in the allotments, as did his food. They could slap him, but they had not the final authority to punish. Unless his parents had been bitterly punished, he hardly spoke of them emotionally. His emotion was for his owners; they had usurped the parents' function.

He knew little about his blood relatives, but he lived in the midst of a clan big enough to make a town. This clan and the harsh realities of his life taught him how to get along. When, for example, slave dealers drove a gang from the upper to the lower South, he would notice that the gang walked chained together and that their guard rode with whip in hand and bowie knife in belt.

The bigger the plantation, the more he could understand sexual and occupational differences within his race. Authority came from the male, except for the rule of the women house servants. His masculinity was reinforced. At the summit of his society stood the powerful head man who gave out food and jobs. Next came the head drivers who walked behind working squads and directed the pace. Plow gangs and other adult groups had foremen; children's gangs had forewomen. The deer driver and the duck hunter were picked men; ordinary slaves did not go hunting and fishing. Dictatorial old men had the last word about the care of cattle, hogs, and sheep. Cooks, butlers, and children's nurses were slaves, but at the same time, they were domestic tyrants, not to be crossed. Coachmen, craftsmen, and house servants, with their assistants and families, held a high status. Status was reinforced by marriage between comparable levels of skill.

House servants possessed a wider horizon of vision and understanding incident to watching and listening to the master race. Mrs. Trollope, in *Domestic Manners of the Americans,* wrote that whites talked and acted before slaves as if they were not there. It offended her to see a young daughter of the house lacing her stays before a footman.

The average slave, when approximately 4,000,000 were freed, was a field hand who had handled only earth, seeds, seedlings, weeds, knives, hooks, and a hoe. He built the Pyramids over again in cotton every year. Depending on his age, muscles and placement, he was worth at least $800. An average girl of eighteen was valued at about $1,000; a youth of twenty, $1,500 to $2,000. If he would bring $1,200 in Virginia, he might sell for $1,800 in New Orleans.

The elders taught the young that a nigger could not have grand ideas. If so, the Master himself would take a hand in cutting him down to size. What the slave did not learn from looking and listening, he gained expensively through his mistakes.

The male could hardly step out of his routine of work, eating, sleeping, and "breeding little niggers for Massa." The very pass he carried to step outside his usual paths might be a trap; he could not read it. It was not safe to break rules; there were too many chances of being discovered. The life produced Negro informers, spies, court favorites, the jealous, and the envious.

The grapevine in the quarters swayed in the wind of the news. Everyone heard children twitting each other, "We got the same Daddy as you." It became known that the overseer settled a quarrel by making the two couples exchange mates; that August, the head driver, always walked all night Wednesdays; that a light-skinned child had appeared among the very dark.

The moral values of whites beat upon him so steadily that the non-white accepted them as his own. A cardinal principle was that the white did not work with his hands. If Fanny Kemble on the Butler Plantation lifted a hoe or a stick to show where to plant the flowers, her slaves objected, "You have nigger enough to do it."

When the non-person was small, he heard Mistress exclaim to her guests, "Ain't I got a pretty crop of little niggers?" He smelled burning flesh early; pigs, mules, cattle, and niggers were branded with a hot iron. He knew that he could be hired out for railroad building, public works, for work in turpentine forests, hotels, boats, and for public service. He knew that both white and Negro fathers had sold their own children.

There have been slaves who said they were happy. More of them were unhappy—the evidence shows it. The unhappiness of today reaches far back to an unnatural beginning. The slave lived subject to the fear, shock, and pressure that unhinge people now and send them to the mental hospital. His threshold for breaking must have been much lower than ours. Life in slavery was like that in war time, when populations bear as a group burdens they cannot bear individually.

A frontier culture, so quick on the draw, which permitted both dueling and freehand shooting was the background for shocks that ground into him when young. Shock struck through his body like salt in the mouth. Those who came from Africa had first the shock of the capture; then, unless they came from river country and were brought in canoes, the shock of the march to the sea; then the shock of the ocean passage. When they got to the auction block, they were already broken.

Among those born here, one man saw his owner take his sister and knew that seven slaves had had her before she was fifteen. He walked with a chain around his neck in the owner's migration to Texas; at night he slept on the ground, locked to a tree. Already he was branded on the breast and between the shoulders and was "no better than wild."

I can still see the auction block.
My mother was sold there.
I was sold there when I was eight
and again when I was thirteen.

I saw the Overseer kill my uncle.
He was a lead-row nigger.

On the march to Texas,
My mother dropped
When she could not walk any more.
The Overseer shot her and
left her where she fell.

The Negro's reputation for speed with a razor and a gun must have been nourished by these corrosive pictures. Once printed on the eye, burned on the eye, they never went away. The victim leaped to do a violent deed before it could be done to him.

The slave who saw murder experienced immediate changes in his brain, blood, adrenals; he felt complete cold prostration. The pattern in the brain became imprinted, and further shocks could make the sufferer relive the experience. "It is thus possible to have a broken-leg brain or a financial-disaster brain," said Dr. George W. Crile in *A Physical Interpretation of Shock, Exhaustion and Restoration.**

The slave had a shock brain. He saw floggings, the stocks, hangings, incorrigibles shot beside their waiting graves. His first experience with death might have taken place when he viewed

* *Oxford University Press: New York,* 1921.

a slave dying in the fields. Unless told to leave him to the buzzards, fellow workers split a plank, put the body between the two pieces and buried it. This kind of ending would make one afraid of even walking by a pile of planks.

Types of ex-slaves ranged from the almost vegetative to the superior. A few were so childish they might still have been on the Butler Plantation. Some were notable illiterates who seemed to have done as well without education as the rest of us had with it. A few had the stamp of dedicated higher education.

I knew so many like those recorded in the *Slave Narrative Collection* assembled by the Federal Writers Project and edited by B. A. Botkin in *Lay My Burden Down** that as I write I can hear them talking. These are very old voices. Eighty-two of 283 were over ninety and the median age was about eighty-six in 1937, so they were slaves only as children.

They were like other Americans in that they had moved around, mainly to the West. On a Southwestern trek, "A thousand walked together, fifteen to twenty miles a day, camping at night." Once they heard that Arkansas was the Promised Land. Dollars hung from trees there, to be picked like persimmons. Hogs lay around, already roasted. Fresh fritters smoked on the Fritter Ponds.

The freedmen went to work as farm hands at forty cents a day and became tenant farmers in cotton, cutting wood and splitting rails in the off-season. The wives had done cooking, washing, ironing, sewing, and the minding of white children. They had made a marginal living.

As survivors of slavery, they idealized childhood when they could run all day and never feel tired. Cornbread and pot liquor had tasted good and on cornshuck beds they had slept well. If only they could drink well water from gourds again and sit just one more time before the Christmas logs; three sweet gum logs lasted a week in the fireplace.

A woman of eighty-six said that after Emancipation she stayed on in the same cabin, sewing and cooking, while her husband earned money to go West. They reached Texas in the days of deer, buffalo, antelope, wolves, and wild turkey. The husband earned $10 a month as a farm or ranch hand, and

* *University of Chicago Press: Chicago,* 1957.

they farmed with sharp sticks and killed game with a bow and arrow. They bought land, built a house, planted an orchard, raised cattle, chickens and turkeys. The husband could read and he managed to work into a job as a teacher. Finally he founded the first colored church and became its preacher. She cooked, washed, and ironed for others and bore ten children.

The average former slave said that slave owners only did what they had been taught; the freedman forgave everything but cruelty. Maybe life or the hereafter would inflict punishment:

The worst on Master's place was
Solomon, his nigger driver.
He didn't like frolics nor prayers and
I seen him beating people in the stocks.
Solomon burning
In Hell to-day and
It pleasures me to know it.

Men were more bitter than women; they had been treated more roughly:

I got 250 lashes with
Massa looking on,
Holding a bottle of whiskey and
A box of cigars.

They frowned on the young as too lazy, too crazy to get to town and shows. An old Negro driver named Wasp said briefly that the young "ent wort shootin'."

Launched as they were on their own—knowing not much more than to start when the bell rang, to dig every weed out, to have manners and not to do the forbidden—even to live out life was an accomplishment. They had to avoid the Ku Klux, refuse to try to vote or to testify in court, keep out of debt, yet not appear too prosperous.

Time had bleached out much hatred and the old ones honestly thought that hatred was wrong, but somehow they inflamed the young just by telling how conditions used to be. Their grandchildren showed a violent hatred. It acted like dried blood; it was the organic fertilizer for ambition.

I knew an ex-slave, a surly and difficult man, pure African, a "Man so rough the Lord couldn't smooth him." I never saw him without a red necktie and a derby hat; they must have been the distinguishing marks of some overseer of his youth. He had been beaten so often and so hard in his native state that he left it as soon as he was free. Starting with nothing, he had built up a meat and fish business, chiefly among Negroes. He owned several houses, a horse and truckcart, carpenter's tools and land enough for fruit trees and a strawberry bed. He could not read, but one of his children earned her way to a college degree.

In his house, hatred was as visible as swamp mist. The wife, younger, free-born, pretty and complacent, looked down on him because he had worn chains. They lived in a constant broil. He was a saver, she was a spender. She was religious, he said he would never kneel again to anybody or anything. She said to me, "How can I save him from Hell if he won't kneel?"

The father talked about his chains so much that every child was sick of them, but when the mother said that she was, too, they all took the father's side. The children fought heartily amongst themselves and if separated they struggled with their own internal conflicts.

I remember a tall and splendid woman who looked like pictures of the Kikuyu. She had buried her husband and children, one by one—all victims of tuberculosis. Now she was washing, scrubbing and saving to send her two grandchildren to college.

As a church assignment, I helped to look after an old crone in her eighties. She lived alone in her cabin, did not know her age or how long her children had been dead, but she could still walk two miles. She had been a field hand, her body had been her strength and it still looked as substantial as a Percheron. Her hands were so leathery that she picked roses without feeling the thorns and she walked barefooted in the fields.

Living on handouts, she had become not much more than a stomach and a desire for warmth and snuff. A deep well of cunning could open in her obsequiousness. Carrying her no more than $2, a pound of tea and a box of peppermints, I came to understand, not what her slavery had been, but the methods she had evolved to meet it. She was too stout to wear any of my clothes, but was never done hinting about my hats: "so new

. . . so pretty . . . all roses." I would soon get tired of this hat, she told me. When that happened I should remember her. If she never got a hat with roses in this life, they could put it in her coffin.

As the economic scale went up, ex-slaves behaved like any people of their time and financial budget, except for their awful seriousness. I was friendly with two couples who were early college alumni, born around 1840, both husbands ministers, both wives teachers. As children, they had had no childhood, as adults they had had no fun except the very noblest. When their children were grown and gone, all they thought about was that they could now give more to their church tithe for others.

When I began traveling among communities, older people welcomed me with evident expectation. Someone had always controlled what they wanted and they were always hoping to secure their wants. I did not understand the meaning of this look—the dependent's look—at the time. It was directed not to me, but to something more—the AMA school—and I was not yet old enough to be more than a messenger.

The child who looked only to Master and Mistress and did not have father or mother or God from which to build models for himself, did not have the idea of justice through law. Whites destroyed his personality structure. The enslaved lost family, friends, environment, code of customs, and ethics. Members of the same tribe were separated by sales. Consultation with neighbors was limited; meetings of more than five exacted the presence of a white person. He lost his language. He lost his name.

Punishment lurked behind rebellion. Ordinary punishment might mean refusal of a pass or the withdrawing of consent to marriage or baptism, but it generally meant corporal punishment. Slaves could be confined in stocks or in the bull pen in the hot sun, could be branded on the face, forehead and chest, chained around an ankle, strung up with all the weight on their arms.

Flogging was done on the bare back, with leather thongs attached to a stick. The number of lashes was geared to the enormity of the offense. On one plantation of seven hundred slaves, a Negro driver was allowed to give twelve lashes, the Negro head driver thirty-six, the white overseer fifty, the owner, any number. Sometimes the condemned was hanged from a beam with feet just touching the floor. Salt and pepper might be rubbed into bleeding welts. Selling "down the river" was a punishment and the ultimate corrective was death.

The defenses the slave built up against the owner were those devised by the artful in all periods of history. He was deaf and blind as necessary; he never told more than he had to and the telling was done as slowly and grudgingly as possible. His group was one vast secret society; "never did hear what the War was about."

He thought of neat tricks. Field hands used to have a watchman on guard as do flocks of Canada geese. When Master on horseback came in sight on the hill, the watch sang, "Old hog round the bench," and Webster's *Blueback Speller* was hidden from view. Slave signals were like those of Indian days: field calls, whoops, hollers, a pig grunting, an owl hooting, singing. When Harriet Tubman ran toward the North, she passed down the cabin rows singing:

When that old chariot comes,
I'm going to leave you;
I'm bound for the Promised Land,
Friends, I'm going to leave you.

The slave developed skills in flattery and propitiation to fine arts. He talked as a child; a child is unanswerable. He spread the butter of courtesy; courtesy is diversion. As a diplomat, he found slyness and lying of great practical value—risky and punishable, but a good gamble. In turn, he swallowed the lies he heard. Yankees had a big horn on the head and an eye in the middle of the forehead. Eden was in Texas.

Interracial passion could be ended with the mob and the rope, but within his own group the slave resorted to ritualistic violence in feats of strength, fighting and sexual excess. When these outlets failed, hysteria carried him off. He ran away or revolted, even when death was after him.

I seen some niggers,
it taken four men to whup 'em.

The one who got 250 lashes for running away ran away again. Another brained the overseer who was trying to whip him with one blow from a hoe. A mother whose three children had been sold away from her killed the fourth as soon as it was born.

He took care of his health by allowing illness to run its natural course; his tempo by never hurrying; guarded his speech by being close-mouthed; disguised his folk lore with the cunning of animals; adapted his religion to his racial needs.

Despite the owner's masterly dominance, he could not control absolutely all of anyone. The human being, hard beset, can still reflect, if not express his identity. The slave must have held on to some slivers of himself—the days of health when it seems that the body can never die, the use of strength, skill in work; singing; the feeling for the landscape and the stars.

When I was studying history in school, I supposed that slavery was gone. It was not. After it was gone legally, the traces of it had to be assimilated by the individual mind. The civilizations of Greece, Rome, and the Middle Ages influence us, but slavery really happened here. It lingers fitfully, nearer to us than we like to imagine, as near as the Puritans and the Western migration.

Southern Compulsion 7

MY MEMORY OF the Southern compulsions of long ago must be like a Negro's.

I absorbed his fears, burdens, and uncertainties, I knew some of the visions that burned behind his eyes. The humiliation and outrage of his life come back to me unbidden; I have to stop to think of his pleasure in the sun. The white among colored people has felt their sirocco.

Their trouble began and ended with the fact that no one esteemed them. Outside their own homes, they had no voice. They always had to eat in the kitchen of the good things that belong to everyone—schools, churches, public facilities and pleasures.

The national history needs the grace of any saving remnant in our spiritual "way of life," for American whites are burdened with the fact that the Southern churches made no concerted private effort for Negroes after the War.

What the religious did was cut a strong stencil for our own creed of the Untouchables. The church separated itself from the alien race, even though it sometimes had permitted attendance and membership during slavery. Large Protestant denominations split into the Northern Baptist Convention and the Southern Baptist Convention, the Methodist Episcopal Church and the Methodist Episcopal South, the Presbyterian U.S.A. (Northern), and Presbyterian U.S. (Southern).

The word "South," cut into the church's foundation stone, meant that it was for white worshippers only.

I knew a small Roman Catholic church open to both races, but as the membership grew larger, a separate colored church was provided; I saw both races only at the Cathedral in New Orleans. The one Roman Catholic Negro institution to prepare for the priesthood I knew has since disappeared from the *Educational Directory* of the United States Office of Education. At the time I visited it, the Fathers were caught between the implacable theological disciplines and the implacable weaknesses of country schools: boys from the Deep South were not prepared for Latin and Greek.

At the time of my acquaintance, Paine College, Augusta, Georgia, under the auspices of the Methodist Episcopal Church South, was the only Negro institution of higher education I recall supported by Southern white Protestants. A few private high schools existed, but the gap in schooling was wide. Public education in cities stopped at about the seventh grade and cities which offered more were canceled out by towns which went no higher than grade five.

The Negro Land-Grant colleges, founded after 1862 by Federal subsidy, were regarded as vehicles of the practical slant. Politicians hoped to get cooks and carpenters out of them. Negroes thought of them as employment opportunities for the well-connected and saw their opening as the delayed patronage that comes to aid the drowning man after he has reached the beach.

The Southern vagaries about education of any kind were those of a martial society. Their war heroes became their governors and men of influence, and silhouetted against the image of the armed cavalier was the image of Venus in a high neck and long sleeves; they liked military schools for boys and "finishing schools" for girls.

The region was well under the influence of a distorted romanticism which came from depths that education and religion could not reach: the Ku Klux Klan.

The origins, distribution, methods, symbols and trappings of the Klan are a shocking giveaway of both races. Southern men competed long ago in jousting for a girl's favor and a revival of the medieval festivity after the War did something for good feeling. The KKK began then as an expression of good fellowship, especially among veterans.

The move into society began during the night when the Negro asleep in his cabin heard the rap on the door. The white-robed, white-masked figure standing outside asked in a tone of command for a bucket of water. When the householder brought it he saw that behind the ghostly figure stood his ghostly horse, white-shrouded and with muffled feet. In the rear, other ghosts on ghostly horses stretched down his lane, one with a skull at the saddle bow.

The apparition appeared to drink all the water and handing the bucket back said, "That's the first drink I've had since I was killed at Shiloh." Other deathly visitors displayed posters of a skull with crossbones and those marked with the dimensions of a coffin—2 x 6. "We that are dead and yet live are watching you." The Negro shook before the spirits of the Confederate dead.

As the sophomoric element of the fraternity reached the organization stage, the Klan grew to be one of the documentaries of the American character: den . . . tests . . . oath . . . pledge against liquor . . . realm . . . dominion . . . province . . . Invisible Empire; Grand Wizard, Grand Dragon, Grand Titan, Grand Giant, Grand Cyclops. Every Grand Dragon had the aid of eight Hydras, every Grand Titan had the support of six Furies, every Grand Giant had four Night Hawks.

The Klan has been pursued as a racket, bought and sold, gone underground, enlarged to be anti-Catholic, anti-Semitic and anti-Mormon. Newspapers reported a revival at the top of Stone Mountain, with the American flag, the open Bible, the unsheathed sword, the canteen of water. According to William P. Randel in *The Ku Klux Klan,** unbelievers have said that this "initiation water," sold at $10 a quart as a necessity for the establishment of each new chapter, is scooped from the Chatacoochee River near Atlanta.

In its various lulls, the Klan has been occupied with lipstick, whether people shall write love letters, who shall live where and the like, but it always comes back sooner or later as the messenger of Death from Shiloh. No one can grasp the nature of the Southern compulsion about the Negro without knowing it as the most powerful instrument of reaction in the area—the *anonymous* instrument.

The hard fact about the Negro who lived in this maze of the Invisible Empire was that the South did not admit that he was a man. He was kept as nearly as possible in the status of slavery. The public prosecutor in court felt at liberty to refer to "this nigger." The Southerner at the University of Chicago Summer Session wrote home, "There is a nigger in my class in Petronius." The feeling that the Negro was a subhuman, "a link between a human being and an animal," appeared in all orations. "Better off in slavery," essentially inferior in mind, body and morals; criminal, destined to remain a servant, peasant in an agricultural economy—all these were popular white conceptions. The very bad Negro was the educated one and the more education, the more of a menace he was.

The novelist, Thomas Nelson Page *(In Ole Virginia, Two Little Confederates)*, was wrapping up this doctrine in big words: "absolute and unchangeable superiority of the white race." Every level of white society furnished white spokesmen for these ideas. Women had little to do with them publicly. In the beginning they sewed the Klan regalia, but they had less guilt to assuage.

The white preserved his established order by liquidating the Negro personality. Except in domestic service, the Negro was effaced. The effacement did not need to cost money. Humiliation would carry it a long way.

The cleverest inexpensive humiliation was refusing the courtesy titles of *Miss, Mrs.* and *Mr.* To be addressed as "Mary" or

* *Chilton Books: New York,* 1965.

"Boy" by strangers is a direct personal insult, new every time. "Boy" remained boy, unless he became a minister and could be called "Reverend," until he reached "Uncle" in old age.

The code did not permit shaking hands with a Negro, or walking or riding with him. Negroes were unable to stay all night in certain towns and when automobiles were new, a colored chauffeur was forbidden to drive through on the highway.

Cities edged their minority into narrowed limits. The fun and pageantry and conveniences of city life were semi-forbidden. Within the limits of the little triangle in which the Negro could walk between home, work and church he was safe, provided he got off the sidewalk when meeting whites. Outside his triangle, being colored began.

He rode downtown on the streetcar, moving to the back. In railway transportation he had to go to the waiting room marked *Colored*, get a drink of water from the *Colored* fountain, use the *Colored* toilet, stand in line at the *Colored* ticket window until all those at the *White* window were served. I often went to the *White* window when the ticket agent left his line at the *Colored* window to sell to me. On the train, his was the *Colored* car; no Pullman accommodation would be sold him, no meal served unless possibly one table in the diner was separated from the rest by a curtain.

Trainmen exercised a peculiar power over Negro passengers. They acted like wardens or prison guards, or as military cliques have sometimes acted when they thought they were on top for all time. They used to throw in words like "nigger" for free, and if some drawling passenger offered a ticket for Tupelo when he had meant to buy to Tougaloo, they showed that they were glad that he was going in the wrong direction.

The first Negro travelers for Negro colleges and organizations had to put up with dirtier cars than the whites and had no hope of hotels. Carrying the everlasting box of fried chicken put up by the last hostess, they set out for the next overnight entertainment at a private home. Men might sleep in some room over a pool hall, noisy and brilliantly lighted. Women were afraid to do this; they said that crossing the continent in a covered wagon would be easier than their winter months on the road.

Being a servant canceled all these marks of disfavor. A valet, nurse, or attendant upon a white person had access to any accommodations his employer paid for.

An engaged girl had a miserable time shopping because she was buying her trousseau only by her eye and her measurements; she was not allowed to try anything on. She waited to make important purchases until she went North, or bought by mail. However, the head of any house was afraid of economic reprisals if he had too many purchases delivered by express.

As for more fundamental human needs, of course those who could not seek God in the church marked "South" very soon built churches for themselves. The hospital was "South," too, but building a hospital was beyond the Negroes' financial resources, skill, and imagination. Unless the hospital were large enough to have a separate ward, a population of 25,000 might have no facilities for non-whites at all. It could be a beautiful city with a genuine historic culture, but its racial philosophy put it under a long anaesthesia.

Those who defended the Negro's rights must have been more numerous than is known. Ministers sometimes said too much for their own good and had to leave town. I have read professional papers concerning racial issues by white professors in Southern theological seminaries who might have had to leave if the articles had been read by the average white person.

There were Southern women who looked after Negroes in old age, sickness, and trouble. Families would look affectionately after an old cook or nurse, sending her work, money, treats, and the baby's picture, taking her on a ride and teaching children to value her as a person.

In large cities, a few white men always spoke in behalf of education and justice. To do it, they had to be solidly fixed in the local society, at least to the third generation, but they were there—quiet men who did not run for election or get into the newspapers. On a lower economic level, men who would spit on the Negro as a race might go to extraordinary lengths to defend one who had worked for them. When the mayor or a planter or a college professor gave the Commencement address in our schools, they were always sympathetic and hopeful, blessing the graduates without going near them and saying what adults always say to youth as if they believed what they were speaking.

Early sociologists were beginning to study the Negro, but not without suffering for their convictions. Even after World War I parents forbade girls to enroll in those dreadful courses where they looked into Southern slums.

The only writer I knew about who stood up to the Southern Inquisition after publishing his opinions about race was George W. Cable. He had been brought up by slaveholding parents in Louisiana and he served as a soldier of the Confederacy.

Afterward, when he revised his inherited tradition, he proposed solutions that were remarkable in 1875–85; goals that are not yet attained. He was told that his 1882 Commencement address at the University of Mississippi "would not have been allowed five years earlier."

His region rewarded his thinking by destroying his ability as a writer of the imagination. *Old Creole Days*, *The Grandissimes*, and *Madame Dauphine* were written out of his New Orleans background, and when local disapproval destroyed his ability to drop back into the past, he could no longer write novels. He moved to Massachusetts, wrote about education and reform, published in *Scribner's* and the *Century*, went on lecture tours with Mark Twain.

His *Open Letter Club* about Southern problems had to stop because the white professional men who were contributing to it dared not lose their status and their jobs. His letters to the New Orleans *Picayune* were refused publication.

It is shameful to have forgotten the good people, but I have, because the ugly ones talked so much louder. What haunts me are the white troublemakers; they wanted the volcanic eruption. A high degree of Negro violence brought antagonistic whites into local prominence, and made all the symbols of white for purity, and red for blood, bloom along the highway.

When these flowers of the unconscious were concealed, and the regional good manners and courtesy lulled me into oblivion, something was always happening to bring me back to the colored allotment.

I knew a young alumna, traveling for an educational organization, who was injured in an automobile accident. The nearest Georgia hospital refused to admit her and she bled to death lying on the ground. This girl had been promising enough to be pointed out to me as a college junior and I can still remember her brown eyes, not dreamy, but sparkling with enthusiasm. A girls' dormitory given to her college in her name has kept her blood flowing over forty years. No student can have failed to know about the hospital which refused her.

Could this girl or anyone like her have used her town's public library? Certainly not, and she had to rely on Northern philanthropy for what her parents could not do.

Could she visit the art museum or the historical museum? Never. These museums were only in their early stages and she did not miss much, but she was made to feel unprivileged. If her little ghost could see the big rooms and the paintings and statues in these museums now, she would guess at once why all the chairs were removed about 1962.

Could she go to the free evening lectures on literature and science in the endowed institute? No. Private benefactors might have been willing, but a city ordinance would prohibit any mingling of the races.

Could she pay her way into the theater and to concerts? Part way. She could sit in the top balcony, the "Nigger Heaven." She would never think of going unless the artist were a great one—at this time, Paderewski perhaps—and no other opportunity of hearing him seemed likely. Her people felt like staying away from all movies; they told each other that "The Birth of a Nation" was incendiary.

Could she learn about Negro life from the newspapers? Not really. The local paper sneered or ignored. Not every family took the Chicago and Pittsburgh Negro newspapers, and the Main Street newsstand, already committing white girls to the vanity of contests for Miss State, Miss City and Miss Cotton Blossom, gave her only an impression of racial crime.

Could she believe with the innocence of the young in the great stone figure of *Justice* on the Court House? I think not. A girl who has mind enough to get into college can put random evidence together. She has heard about some colored man who struck or struck at a white man. He was immediately shot dead.

That was the end of it, except for teenagers like this girl, hearing of such a misadventure for the first time. They talked, they mulled over the issue: did he strike or did he strike at; what about all these accidents? "Did he fall or was he pushed?" Their impression had to be that the Negro was easily arrested, easily judged guilty, easily sent to prison for a long time. Yet a Negro who has an "in" with someone in the right place could shoot his wife and get away with it as self-defense.

Could she take her little Sunday School class to visit the municipal park? She could not. The city used to refuse permission to take missionary school children escorted by teachers there on nature walks and bird watching. Nature study almost had to be given up in our urban schools because it was impossible to go where trees, birds, rocks, and flowers were.

Could her younger brothers and sisters go to city playgrounds? Not then. Playgrounds were rather new, had not much equipment and were for white children. Men could go fishing and hunting, but women and children were confined to the streets and perhaps the dock front.

Could her father, a downtown worker, buy his lunch at any public eating place? Not even if he were Midas himself; he had to look for vendors of peanuts and sweet potatoes. A soda fountain was unknown to him, even drinking water was not readily at hand. Public conveniences might be found only in the railway station, at the end of a long walk.

Then there was little talk about "separate but equal" facilities. Before 1920—and I knew school buildings very well—it could be taken for granted that facilities were unequal. Anyone could see the difference, but it took a white Southerner to shatter this myth with the irreverent truth: "And he took the Dixie cups and gave thanks that they were separate but equal."

The effect of depriving Negroes of public services was that many lived and died without ever knowing what ordinary standards of excellence were. In health, scholarship, music, art, recreation, and science, they never knew unless they spent time in the North.

Generations of Southerners systematically starved the Negro's intelligence, upon which admission to a white school by way of the IQ and similar tests, now depends.

The only arts they had a chance to experience were architecture, gardening, cookery, manners, and those in certain areas of religion and music. The fine gardens around the most stately homes influenced small dooryards all over town. Both men and women bought and tended shrubs and flowers.

All had gentle manners, proportionately better manners than the rest of us. They had to have them or die, but that is not the core of it. In taking over good manners under compulsion, they found in themselves something that made them carry on with conviction. The elders punished "a no-manners child." Children soon felt guilty after they had been ill-mannered and would apologize of their own accord.

Their ungrudging good manners was one of their strengths. They had worked out for themselves Auden's saying:

No one can help them;
Walk on, keep on walking.

The oldtime waiters who urged patrons to enjoy their food were not necessarily acting. They knew compassion.

Passing from deprivations of the graces and civilities of life into the more desperate zones, I am not so sure that it hurts children to go to school in a building that looks like a baby tobacco barn. It does hurt, though, to have the largest classes, the poorest paid teacher, the shortest school year, and an acute shortage of books, paper, pencils, blackboards, and maps.

The free public or semi-public facilities were the post office, the railway station, the stores and the schoolhouse. Nothing else but the cemetery. The cemeteries were out on the edge of town, the graves marked with the granite or homemade wooden cross, or the blue cup and saucer. If the town shared a cemetery, a barbed wire fence ran between the races; "earth to earth, ashes to ashes, dust to dust," race to race.

The living, still in their pilgrimage, had to think more about the dangers of life, the ordinary economic and emotional problems, but as well of race riots, lynching, prison, and the chain gang.

Lynching was thought to be an inevitable occurrence. Between 1900 and 1910, nearly all the one thousand lynchings in the United States were of Negroes. I used to read the annual statistics published by Tuskegee Institute, usually knowing the area, and, once in a while, the city. About lynching, my students seemed paralyzed. Fear like the fear of thunderstorms swept through them; they could not even hear me discuss them. Usually they were eager to know the background which put their situation in perspective. It did no good to tell them that hangings used to be public holidays both in England and in our country. They always believed that mob leaders could never be found.

I thought that the fear might have risen in very early childhood, a specter taken in with taunts and warnings. The hold lynching has on the Southern mind can be seen in regional writing, even in that of the young who began writing only after lynching was over. Long before artists showed these scenes in painting and prints, short stories and novels described the deed in full detail.

About race riots, students had a normal curiosity, wanting to know what set off trouble and how it came to make such headway. I have the impression that citizens of large cities can overcome the feeling of fear and suspicion that riots give to Negroes. The citizen of either race wants to believe that his home city is beautiful, protective, above average. He argues with himself and says the flamethrowers were hoodlums, scum of both races.

In a small city wounds are kept open. Homeowners have an extreme love of place, they do not want to move away, and they screen off the present with the past. I have heard it explained that a certain man was not to be trusted. You had to watch him; his grandfather led the riot fifty years ago.

The chain gang was a terror so great that women who saw it remembered it in their nightmares. When convicts were singing:

Big boy, can't you line 'em well,
Big boy, can't you line 'em well,
Here we go line this track.

women were so terrified that they never even heard the chant or the tools ringing on the rails. They saw that the guard had bullets for eyes and that the bloodhounds could come slavering at command, but very likely part of their terrible reaction came from the strong impression of stark masculine force.

The outstanding contradiction in the Jim Crow pattern was the capacity for individual devotion between the races. It flourished and flourishes yet in both real life and fiction. In *The Sound and the Fury*, Faulkner's portrait of one feckless and grasping white family, their old cook is the only admirable character. Dilsey gets the lazy ones up in the morning, cooks the food, loves and looks after the mental case, brings the hot water bottle to the neurotic, shields the adolescent girl, orders the mean man around and interferes in his quarrels. Her own grandson—"You, Luster"—is merely a convenience to her white family.

The irony of Southern sexual patterns comes easily to the surface. The parentage of certain Negroes prominent nationally from 1770 to today is documented in Richard Bardolph's *The Negro Vanguard*.* The number born of Southern white business and professional men and Negro mothers long after Emancipation shows the male as holding a split sexual image of women. Each liaison added another cubit to the white woman's moral pedestal.

I have known some of these illegitimate offspring as adults. One of them, born about 1875, had the appearance of a Spanish grandee. For his whole working life he had an influential position in the state where his father was a judge. A few of these men have been such brilliant leaders that their lives helped to overturn their white fathers' pre-Civil War policies about race.

Children knew dimly about irregularities and were taught to make no comment. Only a poor little ten-year-old, fighting about his parentage, would say, "You can't scare me. I've got white blood in me."

The whole culture is so mixed up in its values that it is as strange as a race of unicorns. A bachelor, buried from his colored mistress' home, was a member of a city school board, and the white schools closed as a mark of respect. On the day of the funeral Negroes talking about him would begin by saying, "Of course, he couldn't help the way it was."

The cemetery's barbed wire was a treacherous mockery. The white man was always wanting to make his horizon larger, to extend his life by taking in the other race. He was the descend-

* *Rinehart and Co.: New York,* 1959.

ant of tradition and the plantation owner, idealized before the War as an impetuous and romantic type, a reader of Sir Walter Scott, a man of fantasy, acquainted with chivalry.

The transfusions and embroideries of the "way of life" have gone on for so long that a white Southerner born in 1921, living in a small farm and timber area, converted at a revival when he was twelve, can say that as a Mississippi high-school junior of sixteen, he learned that the South had lost the War. This 1937 war news about 1865 made him so rebellious that he had a suicidal impulse. At thirty-nine, P. D. East had the courage to tell this story in *The Magnolia Jungle*.*

I believe that the most monstrous of the Southern compulsions was not the obvious, not the mesalliance, not the deeds of blood. It was the explanation to colored children that they were regarded as inferior. Every parent and every teacher had to be ranged against every child. One child at a time, the adult destroyed something in the young. These Negro-to-Negro explanations were only half of what had to happen. On the opposite side were white children, white tongues, white explanations. One child at a time, the adult destroyed the young.

Outsiders would not be brave enough to listen to a tape recording of all the explanations over all the years.

* *Simon and Schuster: New York*, 1960.

Negro Resistance 8

THE CURVE OF a century in racial relations looks on graph paper like the curve of the stock market.

White compulsion bears down to force the Negro below the living level. The Negro resists enough for the curve to turn upward. Thrust and counterthrust, up and down, smile for threat and bow for blow, the excesses of one race bring about the excesses of the other.

> *De Buckruh had scheme and de nigger had trick*
> *And every time de Buckruh scheme once,*
> *De nigger trick twice.*

Resistance in the colored population worked like a tree cut down. The root sent up three or four new shoots; for a time it looked like a shrub instead of a tree. "They cut off the schoolin', cut a year right off the high school. My boy goin' away. I goin' send him to Oberlin."

After civic disappointment, the defeated acted obliquely. He occupied himself in some different way with his own fulfillment.

In the stream of history, it can be seen that the big problems of health, housing, and employment were too much a part of the larger whole for the minority to do much about them directly. Even in education, they had to resist by detouring. After a time, detours which seemed to go nowhere produced leaders who could transfer what they acquired in calculus to the solution of contemporary questions. When I asked Thomas J. Inborden, principal of Brick School, Bricks, North Carolina, where he learned the multiple approaches of a wonderful country high school, he said, "Studying Greek in college."

I recall a public health project that began because a youth, traveling to Chicago, read in a newspaper that Pushkin had colored blood. He was a Pullman porter, living by making berths and swinging suitcases. He wrote his mother after arriving in Chicago that he never even noticed the tenements beside the railway tracks. "I stood as tall as the Tribune Tower; I knew I was going to be a doctor."

My children aspired to moral greatness: "If Isaiah was so great, he was a Jew, do you think the Negro race could produce an Isaiah?" Boys were baptized out of their parents' admiration of character. I have taught boys named Isaiah and Isaac; Martin Luther and Luther; Crummel and Frederick Douglass.

Girls from fourteen to eighteen had only male heroes. The girls' names were romantic—Rose, Lily, Myrtle, Hildegarde—and their frame of reference about women was small. Ruth's Biblical journey with Naomi seemed fruitless, and the efforts of Harriet Tubman and Sojourner Truth far away. They said "Pocahontas had it easy," and they had a fretful dislike for Mary Todd Lincoln. "How come the President's wife could be so mean?" The only modern woman they had heard of was Florence Nightingale.

After Frederick Douglass and certain preachers, the dearest ideal figure clear to the largest number was probably the colored musician. Those musicians employed by colleges and valued by whites had reached the peak of secular education and even men who worked in barber shops or as valets would recite the facts that, following 1871, the original Jubilee Singers made $20,000 for Fisk University in the United States and $150,000 from two

European trips. They understood why trained musicians spent the summers traveling in the backwoods, loafing along the water fronts, listening in city hot spots. John Wesley Work at Fisk and Carl Diton at Talladega were putting their students through the conventional disciplines, but also rousing them to the exploration of their own heritage.

The reputation of singers in the conventional white tradition was also a matter of pride to Negroes. They filled scrapbooks with clippings about "Black Patti," "Black Swan," and especially Harry Burleigh, with whom they felt in touch because of his many arrangements for voice and piano. They included J. Rosamond Johnson and W. C. Handy, as well. Burleigh was singing at St. George's Protestant Episcopal Church on Stuyvesant Square in New York, and also at Temple Emanu-El. He had been a pupil of Dvorak, had a magnificent baritone voice, and both taught and composed music all his life.

The first young Negro singer I remember who could fill Carnegie Hall was Roland Hayes. He had to have the blessing of European critics first, but that was then the route of all young singers. His success had made him feel that his tenor voice was consecrated. He was a long way from today's vogue—he stood motionless and often sang with his eyes closed.

The average Negro of this period was proud of building his own ghetto. He was often young when he began and the issues appeared simpler to him than they are for his descendants. His family might never have lived in so good a house on so good a street, and that he could earn it and own it gave him a touchingly creative form of resistance: he was building "my home . . . my city . . . our city." Sociologists call the ghetto an unhealthy social form, and perhaps the Negro was not so proud of the imitative finished product, but while he was planning and building, he thought he had a hold on a self-contained life.

Thomasville, Georgia, was one of these towns with a section of Negro pride. It was a winter resort and a market for cotton, tobacco, and farm products, only about twenty miles from the Florida line. When General Eisenhower began to go quail hunting there, I recalled its winter warmth and luxuriance, and how

I had thought from several visits that it was a better than average town. The figures about the town-within-a-town there were assembled by Professor William H. Holloway, Department of Sociology, Talladega College.

In 1900, Thomasville had 5,322 people, with a division of about three Negroes to two whites. When I knew it fifteen years later there may have been 7,000 people and the same Negro-white proportion.

Residential and business areas were segregated. A Negro who had lived in the city for a long time was likely to own his own house. Three of the four residential areas were modern, with streets, sewers, lawns, trees, shrubs and flowers. Negroes owned 207 rental dwellings, ten of which were rented to whites.

In their business center, Negroes owned twenty-six enterprises: an hotel, three restaurants, several groceries, a drug store, a dairy, a butcher shop, a shoe shop, a harness shop, a shop of general merchandise, a woodyard, six barber shops, three drycleaning and pressing shops. An undertaker, a tailor, a milliner, a realtor, and an insurance firm were in business.

Eighty Negroes were in the professions: twenty-three preachers, thirty-five teachers, two doctors, two editors, two graduate nurses, a pharmacist, a dentist, and a musician. The four city mail carriers were colored.

Negro men had almost a monopoly in the trades, because they were the better brick masons and carpenters. A few were contractors, painters, tinners, plumbers, blacksmiths, wheelwrights, paperhangers, bakers, mechanics, pressmen, and carriage painters.

The women's "How to Live Club" offered literary programs and supported the colored ward in the city hospital. The Women's Federation was building an old folks' home. The drives for charities and self-improvement were like those women manage all over the country.

The Negro communities in cities such as Thomasville were provided with a unifying thread as soon as a local newspaper was founded and they were able to read news of their churches, schools, clubs, weddings, funerals, and social doings, never printed in the white newspaper.

The society page copied the snobbism but it was useful snobbism. Parents who had seen their Mary standing on a platform in a white frock receiving a diploma were satisfied with the *Commencement News*.

The importance of reporting weddings may be apparent only to women. The woman reporter left out nothing: the invitations, the wedding-gown, the veil, the bridal bouquet, the decorations, "Lohengrin" and "Oh! Promise Me," the ring, the buffet, the wedding cake, the maid of honor, the bridesmaids, the flower girl, the mothers' gowns, the going-away clothes, the wedding trip—there was no end to it. While the sociologists were urging Negro men in big words—become responsible, let the woman stay at home and keep the home—academicians never had a tenth as much influence as these social trimmings in shaping the marriage. There was a real need to wipe out the insults of the broomstick ceremony of slavery. A slave couple only had to step over a broomstick laid across a door, to the phrasing, "You will be faithful to each other, until death or distance do you part." A sale of either partner could un-broomstick the marriage. After the mate was sold, the one left behind was told that he could marry again. Sometimes this decision came through the church.

The city within a city was only a lesser version of the white man's city, but the Negro church was a resistance of mind and soul. The doctrines of the white religion were accepted, but the Negro church contained revelations of temperament and impulse and it began before the Negro began to do much about his city.

The churchless past brought the average slave only little pieces of God and the Bible. An early observer wrote that slaves thought the God they heard of was their Master and that His son, Jesus Christ, was their young Master. Many slaves learned much more. Outstanding slaves remembered today are chiefly those associated with religion. Itinerant evangelists walked and talked of the Glory Road, and the African Methodist, African Methodist Episcopal Zion, and various Baptist denominations were founded.

A slaveholding minister naturally told his hearers at the monthly service that they must work well and obey. At the worst, he preached, "Slaves are animals . . . you just like the hogs."

Negro preachers were dangerous—they might get carried away and say that in the House not built with hands, slaves would be slaves only of God. Prayer meetings were dangerous. Prayers might be offered for the unattainable: shoes that fitted, fresh meat—only Louisiana required masters to feed meat—all they wanted to eat, and no more beatings. What if God answered these prayers? Singers and mourners in groups were dangerous; ecstasy might ride on into revolt.

After Emancipation, the church was the first large building children were taken to. It was beautiful and its atmosphere made them understand the word *sacred*. The church had to contain almost all of Negro life outside of the job and the home. Organization, working together, learning, initiative, recreation, music, a hand in management—all began here. The discipline of self-denial outside the home began here. Almost before they paid all the pastor's salary, denominations began to found colleges and send money to African missions.

In 1908, the church was fostering young musicians and artists. They gave the musician his first concert, they came to the reading of the young poet who had paid for the printing of his first poems, and if he read well, the women would sell his book for him, since no bookstore was yet available.

I suppose it was from the pulpit that a taste for oratory was developed in the young men. The most inspired eloquence I ever heard from a Negro minister, the Reverend Henry McDowell, is still with me. McDowell was accepting his commission to go to Angola as a Congregational missionary. Africa was then far away; he was giving his life and his wife's life. Both were only about twenty-five years old. The Bible had formed his style and he spoke as a dedicated man. Tears ran down the faces of both races and both sexes in the audience—for themselves, perhaps, for they had lost the dedication of the young man and his wife.

Both white and Negro ministers used to lament that the Negro church establishment made such a show of religiosity, and that it was making a religion of race rather than of Christianity but they agreed at once that these criticisms were not limited to Negro churches.

The most elaborate institutional development I ever visited

was the First Congregational Church of Atlanta. Besides the spacious place of worship, the plant provided an elaborate equipment for group life. A lyceum, clubs, music rooms, social rooms, classrooms, a mission in the slums. The institution was said to be a realization of the minister's vision.

The minister, Henry Hugh Proctor, was born in the open country of ex-slave parents in 1868. His first schooling was a three-month session in a log cabin, but learning to read excited him, and he soon met an educated colored man he wanted to emulate. He earned and saved. He spent seven years at Fisk University and went on to the Yale University Divinity School.

I often saw Mr. Proctor in action as Assistant Moderator of the National Convention of the Congregational churches. He was a tall and muscular man, with the physique then hailed as the American executive type, the Bedouin tamed to society's conditions.

At a glance, I should have thought him a Methodist. He was the biggest man on the platform. He had great heartiness, he could sing, he was a man of practical solutions, he could have stood preaching in the fields in John Wesley's England. He lacked entirely the Congregational austerity, the Emersonian residue. Nevertheless I recognized his translation of the onetime New England faith. He came singing transcendentalism, and the vigor of his natural endowment gave him social acceptance from both races.

The mass denominations—Methodist and Baptist—were the outlets for the average man. Singing, shouting, and giving came out of him through them. The cooler traditions in the Northern pattern appealed to so few that they had to be partly supported with mission funds. The Atlanta church had a large city location and a minister who succeeded in uniting a vast emotional hunger and expressiveness with an ancient tradition.

Education led to changes in denomination, certain churches drawing the best educated; religious sifting and earning power led to social changes. Most were in the middle group and satisfied by having an upper class to look up to and a lower class to look down on, but still classes were fluid. A man and wife at the bottom of the heap had a version of the American dream. They never heard of Horatio Alger, but they would say slowly,

"Things are bad for the colored," and then add, "Jim and Alta Jones own their own home and their oldest girl is a teacher."

Everyone had some class consciousness, but caste was a more elaborate classification and provided the toughest resistance of all. I shall not be able to describe caste accurately because the requirements varied according to the locale—even in the same state. I imagine that men never knew as much about it as women. In operation it was the axe that "boasted itself against him that hewed therewith," a Brahmin separateness to make everything harder.

I had always been accustomed to Northern castes. But the stigma against the Irish, for instance, melted as soon as the approved standards of housing and education were met. I had understood from reading that the Southern white caste system was like the New York City Four Hundred, continuously exclusive. Negroes took over the white caste system and made it much stiffer.

The theory was that the upper class should improve the very lower. The top was royalty and was the flower of segregation.

The aristocracy was designed to advance the race by idealism and snobbery. The most effective way of getting into it was to be born there. Knowledge of ancestry and kinship with "name" Negroes advanced elevation, and education and a profession helped. Women could not always meet the maximum requirements. The society lived by birth, money, education, and conduct; it perpetuated itself by marriage. A member could be thrown out of its *Social Register* for a bad marriage, and would certainly be dropped for bad conduct. Conduct had to be measured against the superior life, not the ordinary.

Negro aristocracy even could be recognized in lonesome hamlets so small that only a few families were considered above the rest. Brains and unusual achievement might admit someone from the middle class, but making a splash with money would not. A middle-class boy who had done brilliantly in college and professional school would be admitted if he married a girl from the aristocracy. But he settled away from his family in order to hide his humble origin. Young couples were afraid of getting in with the wrong set and never being able to withdraw.

Appearance suggested that caste was drawn by color lines,

those at the top ranging from practically white through quadroon, the outsiders merely the darker. Yet, there was more to it than color. I also knew an exclusiveness of pure African blood and it was a disgrace if the young of those families even dated the lightskinned.

Color appeared mysteriously in everything. One glance at occupations or at church congregations would show it. The New Orleans *Blue Book*, a guide to bordellos published from 1897 to 1915, printed first an alphabetical list of white prostitutes, then octoroon, then colored; the unconscious listings in all minds seemed to follow this kind of order.

Light color was important for leaders. The AMA, in offering a man a high-school principalship, usually invited him to visit the school before making his decision. I remember a candidate who came back exhausted. He began talking as soon as he came in the door and for the moment he felt nearer to his white friends than to Negro. "I would really like the job, but the truth is, I am too black. That crowd has never had a dark man and they would set out to break me, perhaps end by breaking up the school. It makes me lose my self-control to think about it, but the principal there has to look white for a good while."

Despite this attitude, passing over to whites was regarded as betrayal. A man who as far as looks were concerned could have stayed at the best Northern hotels, had a racial allegiance that prevented his even entering them.

I know personally of only one Negro said by gossip to have "passed." He simply disappeared; his financial accounts were in order, he drew no money from the bank, he left a family and all his possessions. I have never been sure that he was not merely taken to a swamp or out to sea.

Caste made spinsters. Unless they could travel, women at the social pyramid's top had very little matrimonial choice. They told me that on trains they always kept their gloves on their ringless hands because some man was sure to be bold about starting up a conversation: "Good morning. . . . Is you married?" Perhaps the caste system also produced bachelors. A very dark stranger with gold teeth showing would not, even if well-educated, have been accepted by the aristocracy in the circles I knew. He was too dark and did not meet the standard of the porcelain crown. But if he had a Ph.D. from a good Northern university, adjustments would be made.

I thought of the caste system as expressing vanity and economic resistance to negritude, and as a more or less temporary phenomenon. Already I had friends who thought it was merely funny. A teacher of science, a black man, young, hearty, and equable, told me that he intended to make a specialty of putting his black foot squarely on the doorstep of all these colored women who boasted that his kind should never cross their thresholds. He said, "I could collect books—I like them; but first I am going to collect thresholds." He would have thought it rude justice that fifty years later "Porgy and Bess" popularized in Europe only the Catfish Row section of Charleston. Not much later Marcus Garvey, the Negro nationalist who promoted the Black Star Line Steamship Company, said that God was black. He offended every Negro except the very dark.

Those who felt themselves of the aristocracy had spells of adopting the white contemptuous attitude and word toward those at the bottom. They said that rabble would go on raising more rabble; they would never see the end of their brotherly responsibility. All this criticism was returned with interest from the lower groups. To this day there are New York Negroes who dislike Representative Adam Clayton Powell, without considering his record in Congress: "He has had things too easy; he has not lived up to his father."

Negro resistance has had a secret and left-handed weapon in the richness of Negro behavior. It has done something to cripple the white South. Servants used to perform the everyday tasks in a way that left the owner feeling free. The employer was the child in the sun; he indulged moods, laziness, and stubbornness as he would not with another Caucasian. Resting on the pull of muscles and the well of laughter, he ate meat and melon and was unreasonable with his servants if he felt like it. The demand on the servant's emotional resources was considerable and a primary social distortion of the roles in both races took place.

Woman, more than men or children, was the agent of this distortion. As burden-bearer and matriarch, she so filled the eye and imagination that it is hard to estimate her meaning and cost. The largeness of her nature enabled her to carry her own family and whatever came to her from her white family.

The comfort of being nurtured let people spare themselves effort, especially the effort of thought. The white South avoided its major social issue through religion, tradition, gold braid, rank, and similar monuments, to which all were required to carry stones.

Individual Negro resistance was rare. I knew girls who went home and cried after some salesman had called them by their given names; they punished themselves by never again going into shops. Cornered, however, some individuals put up fights.

A woman once told me that she was sent for from Chicago to attend her father's last illness in the South. They were Roman Catholics from slavery days; she sent word to the rectory that the end was near. She was walking up and down the living room in agitation and misery when the door opened without a knock and a young curate, a stranger, entered. He said, "Good morning, Fannie."

She replied, "Good morning, but I do not know why you feel at liberty to call me by my Christian name."

She indicated the bedroom door, he went in and gave the final rites. When he came out, no one spoke again.

Imagining the priest and the woman looking at each other across the elements for the Last Sacrament, I said, "Would you have said it if the priest had been an old man?"

"Oh, no, I would not even have thought it. I didn't mean to say it. My mind was on the boil and here comes this swollen-up boy, no more than just out of the seminary, about the age of my grandson. He need not think I will accept the lack of Christianity in his manners. . . . I used to be critical of the Church to my father sometimes and he always said, 'Don't you say a word—they're consecrated.' This belongs to my parents' generation, but I can't put away all the judgment I learned elsewhere."

The individual's safe weapon was migration. Every school had a few boys who could only be relieved of their misery by plans to leave for a Northern school and never to come back. From the moderately educated planned to go, saying that a good cook could get along anywhere.

I never knew a transplanted man who did not suffer homesickness for the landscape, the climate, hunting and fishing, favorite spots. Sometimes they were not sure whether migration had been a personal reward, but they were always sure it would work out better for their children.

It would be hard to identify the exact people who built the Negro section of a city, the church, the power structure, the ideals about heroes, but participation was widespread. It was a mass movement as white compulsion was a mass movement. The heartstring of belief which could be found everywhere was:

For I know Whom I have believed
And am persuaded that He is able.

They were always looking for visionaries. I once saw a boy named "Leader" poring over his multiplication tables. His parents were surely tempting fate with such a name, but there he was, a symbol that the race needed something.

The leaders who rose above the others were involved, in one way or another, in some field of education. Whites paid little attention to them and the world was so much simpler then that leaders had a dazzling freedom of initiative. Some of them shot up like rockets, seen in a blaze only after they were high in the sky.

Leaders and Patterns 9

TWO MEN OF two minds held the national leadership during my years in the South, Booker T. Washington and W. E. B. Du Bois. The people they were leading were chiefly Southern Negroes.

I often saw Booker T. Washington in the winter at New York's Grand Central Terminal Restaurant, eating alone, always at the same table, with the same waiter. Because of his reputation he might have been given hospitality elsewhere, but at that time he was in one of the two downtown places where any Negro could be served; the other was the restaurant in Pennsylvania Station.

He was a big man, well-tailored, preoccupied and inconspicuous. The fear of him among other money-raisers was almost comical to those not in the business. They could not tell as good a story as his, they had not spun a Tuskegee into existence; against him they had no chance. Yet because of curiosity, members of many boards of trustees had visited Tuskegee Institute.

On a hot day, the traveler who had passed by miles of red earth torn with erosion arrived at the green and flowering campus as at Jerusalem. They had not been able to believe the desolation and they could hardly credit the change to bounty. They almost took it personally when the choir sang, "Doubting Thomas, doubt no more."

Northern reporters might have some knowledge of crop rotation, but they understood that here was something they could not have done. A manifest fertility of earth and beast and man was here, brought into being by a man whose schooling amounted to three years at Hampton Institute from 1872 to 1875.

The fertility was so great that whatever the founder said or wrote was broadcast to the white South, Negro, white North. Young newsmen were so hypnotized that they hounded Mrs. Washington for the human touch and ended by saying only that she was dressed in violet and advised this and that for the mothers of the race.

The spectacular school he built has survived him, something that does not always happen. Mr. Washington was a great man of his period. I do not for a moment suppose that in his deepest being he chose a policy of affirmation and temporizing. He merely thought that to be alive was better than being dead and he would have shifted on any upturn. Speaking to an Atlanta audience was an incentive to such thoughts as "separate as the fingers, united as the hand."

"Drop down your bucket where you are" must have cost him something. He died at fifty-nine.

I never saw Du Bois. I will guess that very few of my Negro acquaintances outside of schools ever heard of him in those days. I feel sure that white enthusiasts for other people's plowing did not know of him and even the intelligentsia of both races who read him thought that his gift was for negation.

Du Bois was Massachusetts and Harvard, opposed to anyone's compulsory attachment to a plow, yet adroit enough to make his way with a pen until he was ninety-four. If he ever had much financial support for his cause, as Washington did, I do not know of it; he had the moral support of influential people and he went on tasting the aloes, never yielding to compromise.

After Tuskegee became known, the white South believed all Negroes had accepted the policies of Washington. The Negro upper class, however, knew that Du Bois was the leader. His book, *Souls of Black Folk*, helped the racial insistence on learning, character, and skill. Perhaps not everyone understood that he was against merely making the best of things. I knew Negroes who said that only Du Bois expressed their views, but they regretted his bitterness and thought he would have had just as much trouble with the world if he had been white.

All high-school students knew about Du Bois' views; *The Crisis* was the first magazine subscribed to at home. They were proud of Washington, but I never knew anyone who wanted to go to Tuskegee. Parents who could not read still understood the difference between the two leaders. They said the race needed Tuskegee, but, smiling, "Mr. Washington always know who he talkin' to."

After fifty years, the relative positions of these leaders has turned around. Washington's popular criteria have been reached and passed or modified by migration and the need for conferring college degrees. Du Bois is the contemporary prophet; college clubs of the 1960's continue his name.

Now that both men are gone, it can be seen that Du Bois had a choice in his life pattern and, in a sense, Washington had none. If they had exchanged environment and education, Washington from Massachusetts and Harvard and Du Bois from Hampton Institute and Alabama, their strategies would have evolved differently.

Popular educators who led the multitude toward Washington and Du Bois were local figures and never nationally known, even to Negroes. The South was spattered with them. They were Emancipation's magnolias.

Education cast a spell and to earn it the frail human body surmounted all perils. In this forgotten world, everyone was mad about education. A sick woman who was preparing for death once showed me her plans for a funeral and a grave, her will and some insurance policies, asking if I would look after everything. I asked if I should notify Caswell, her husband who had deserted. She said, "No, and if you ever hear from him, tell him I don't leave him even a good wish." She then produced something more steadfast. "When I am gone, no one will care about this envelope. Will you promise to keep it, so I will know I am not all gone so soon?" The envelope held her university credits, accumulated after attending night school and working all day.

Two local educational leaders, Richard Robert Wright and Mary McLeod Bethune, are typical. They were more successful than the average, but still representative. The man was born a slave; the woman was freeborn, although her older brothers and sisters were born in slavery.

Richard Wright, born in 1855, entered the Box Car School, made from a Confederate commissary in Atlanta, when the AMA founded it in 1866.

At eleven, he heard about John C. Calhoun's remark on the Greek language and the Negro: "Show me a Negro who knows Greek syntax and I will then believe that he is a human being and should be treated like a man." This gave him an obsession to learn how to conjugate a Greek verb. In his third year at Atlanta University, sent on a $50 scholarship from a women's missionary society and dressed in clothes from missionary barrels, he read three books of the *Anabasis,* four of *Cicero,* and four of *Vergil,* and studied mathematics.

He began work as principal in a missionary school in Cuthbert, Georgia, which was still receiving a small AMA appropriation. He went from there for long service as president of a Georgia State College. At sixty-five he moved to Philadelphia, took some extension work at the University of Pennsylvania and established the Citizens and Southern Bank.

Traces of early days traveled with him. He punished school boys by saying, "Take one hundred hours on the farm." His own eight children received vigorous discipline and were whipped when necessary. When they were young, one child had to read family prayers from the Greek, the second read the same prayers from the Latin, and two more read the French and German versions. When one daughter was at an age to want to do over the house, she asked him for oriental rugs and silk curtains. . . . "No. Plain living, but it's paid for." All his children were graduated from Northern colleges and some took postgraduate work.

At age eighty-four, the boy who had walked across Georgia to get to the Box Car School bought himself a four-passenger plane and employed a pilot.

The woman leader, Mary McLeod Bethune, was of the same stratum of founders, although she was born thirty years later and was aided by the progress of a generation. She was not scholarly, but evangelistic. Her education went only one year beyond Scotia Seminary, a Presbyterian U.S.A. missionary boarding school, and this year was spent in the Chicago Bible Institute founded by Dwight L. Moody. She was energetic and learned the technique of the soap box on Chicago street corners. Her biographer remarks that she did not "love nature." The glory of humanity apparently made her oblivious to other loves.

The likeness in these two lives came from the period. Both went to schools with white Northern teachers and received Northern scholarships. Both set to work at schooling their people. Each became founder, organizer, promoter, executive, money-raiser, diplomat.

Both threw off new organizations and buildings every year as easily as a child shakes the Fourth of July sparkler—a new campus, library, dormitory, hospital, recitation hall; the first local Negro fair, the county fair, the state fair; organizations for alumni, women, children, youth; homes for orphans, wayward girls, homeless men, the aged; civic improvement leagues, annual bazaars, choirs, Bible study classes; sewing schools, religious and social service in jails, lumber camps, turpentine camps; journals, publishing houses. This horizontal spread was necessary because their areas were so relatively empty of any cultural and social institutions.

Their checks were signed by state and federal officials, by the rich and by the self-sacrificing. They traveled to the state capitol, the White House, London, Oxford, Italy, Switzerland, Paris and Rome. They learned how to address the President, the Archbishop of Canterbury, and British nobility. They were assertive dynamos; they knew how to transform the long past into the American style of their day.

Richard Robert Wright chanced on his connection with a state school. Mary McLeod Bethune, after the early years, made her own way. Her perceptions enabled her to move her school for girls to Daytona, Florida, where Northern philanthropists wintered, and when the time came, she was skillful enough to meet the Methodists halfway, to merge her school into Bethune-Cookman College.

These two had raw courage when nothing else sufficed. They opposed their white boards of trustees and got ready to leave rather than give in. Mr. Wright was teaching Greek and Latin with state public school funds; Mrs. Bethune insisted on putting a high school on top of her eighth grade institution. They did not leave.

The man once scuttled around in the woods of Alabama in peril of his life; he was trying to find out for the United States Department of the Interior who was stealing the government's timber in 1885.

The woman was once expecting a visit from the Ku Klux Klan. When the riders came down the street, the school buildings were dark but the campus was brightly lighted. One colored man with a gun stood at the entrance. Inside the girls were singing:

Be not dismayed
God will take care of you.

When I knew Mrs. Bethune she was only a little over forty and much at home on the platform. I remember her passing some school data to President Henry Churchill King of Oberlin College, also sitting on the platform, as "busy work" while she talked.

When she was sixty-seven, a sufferer from asthma and heart trouble, trying to reduce from two hundred pounds, she declined to ride in the freight elevator of a Nashville Hotel. She walked six flights up to the office of the Southern Human Welfare Conference. When Mr. Wright was at what is now called "retirement age," some Georgia bank employee refused to call his daughter "Miss Wright." He moved North.

It was Mr. Wright who is supposed to have said, "Tell 'em we're rising," and Mrs. Bethune who is said to have offered prayer on the spot to a turpentine worker who brought her an opossum for Thanksgiving.

The early leaders were all of this quadruple weave: Southern residence, Northern education, the strong wire of resistance, and the devotion to multiple projects—a diversity of endeavors because they wanted to give everybody everything. I could name fifty other leaders, not as well-known and not as prodigious, but who fit the same pattern, and who acted with the same style. They did not get to the White House, or to Europe or to John D. Rockefeller, but they walked from the cabin into large initiatives.

The other kind of solitary leader who would build himself a house at Walden Pond and wait out his time was found most often in the figure of the musician. Most people, however, knew only of George Washington Carver. Slave-born, poor, orphaned, unmarried, his purity of aim seems to come from far back in the beginning of American life.

The little Iowa town, Indianola, where he went to Simpson College is level and open, the streets are laid out in a rectangular plan. Seeing it, I wondered if he began to paint flowers to get away from the simple geometry. If he had remained a painter of owers, he would still have been unknown. His experimentation with peanuts, soy beans and sweet potatoes brought him to the attention of the newspapers and produced profits for the white businessman. Fabrics and road-building material were some of the products of his experiments. Carver traveled to the back country with wagonloads of specimens in order to demonstrate his findings to the ignorant farmers. Women on the Tuskegee faculty told me that he was a great worry to the institution because he did not cash his salary checks.

Among the local leaders for two generations were some called Black Puritans because they were formed in the likeness of the first white New England missionaries. Children of ex-slaves, nursed in penury by mothers who thought that education was life itself, they saved their first fifty cents to buy an *Arithmetic*, learned orations as they chopped cotton, walked two hundred miles to enter high school and at twenty-five began earning their way through college. I knew more than one Jonathan Edwards, going around blasting sinners.

They were Stone Age folk, teachers shaping education with even relentlessness and never taking from students one word of what they called "back talk." Men and women were much alike, except that the women were unmarried. They were secular nuns caring for other people's children. Ministers and teachers lived in dignity on about $30 a month, plus whatever they could scratch from the soil. Their idea of a Christmas treat was to buy a book. Not a book for pleasure but a great book that many could use, a classic or a dictionary. The greatest extravagance in one woman's life, she told me, was getting her husband's *Pilgrim's Progress* rebound in leather for his birthday.

Once I had supper with an elderly Mississippi couple who might have been the Adoniram and Relief Dorcas of Colonial days. In a little town where loafers hung on every corner and girls in cerise dresses strolled up and down, they sat nightly at supper before the fire in their little house. Bread and butter and stewed plums and tea were on the table and the Bible at the husband's place. One read the *Outlook* and the other the *Independent* until bedtime. As he locked the door, she wound the clock and they knelt for long prayers. She called him Mr. Dorcas. She made his neckties out of black silk. They did not believe in song. When he prayed for "this wicked and perverse generation," she said amen.

I belonged to the generation they were subjecting to the judgment seat and I could see that they thought me too young to know anything until they discovered that I knew Boston. They wanted to know what the holy ground looked like. Did I know Faneuil Hall? They must have been the last two in the world who cared about the corners Sumner ran around and the hot spots of abolition days.

The Black Puritan was sternly composed, passionately clean, industrious, just, penurious, self-sacrificing to the core—and sustained by something from on High. This stern leader taught that hardship fattened the Negro treasury.

The rigid formality of African carving is somehow related to the Negro prolongation of Puritanism. The last Puritans may be black, their bones stiffened with the tribal designs.

The simplicity of a system in which only two national leaders, Washington and Du Bois, could dominate was one of primeval innocence. This early stage of "race men" passed away and a new period began. Organizations paid workers to do what volunteers used to do; specialists in urban life, rural life, history, labor, scholarship, womens' interests, and religion carried on.

Departments of sociology began studies of the contemporary at Fisk, Atlanta and Howard universities, and Talladega College. The NAACP organized in 1909, the National League on Urban Conditions in 1911. Dr. George Edmund Haynes' *The Negro at Work in New York City* dates from 1912. Carter Woodson founded the Association for the Study of Negro Life and History and the *Journal of Negro History* in 1916.

The cotton boll weevil crossed the Mississippi River in 1910. The mechanical cotton-picker began lumbering in a few selected places and people who could pick only 250 pounds in eight hours began to talk and worry.

City population changed in its psychology. College students and musicians studied the spirituals more and more, but an urban refinement that did not wish to be reminded of the past was looking for other kinds of inspiration. Migration to the North was noticeable by 1915. Negro songwriters entered Tin Pan Alley and turned the trend away from the sentimental ballad. Jack Johnson won the heavyweight championship. I knew women who became interested in prizefighting when Johnson defeated Jim Jeffries in 1915—not because he was the winner, but because he won while the fans were yelling "kill the nigger."

The Black Puritans did not like the fact that the young were becoming known for music, jokes, and dancing. "No more than any loafer can do," they declared. In their time, they had walked as though fed with the Sacraments. They turned a steely eye on the new race leadership—not hard enough, not noble enough, not dedicated. Everything was too ordinary, too common.

The old ones regarded the emerging names as being from the spiritual middle class. Their baptism had been merely on the forehead; it lacked immersion because they never had to break the ice. They had not taken the two-hundred-mile walk to school; they had always worn shoes.

The new pathfinders I knew never went beyond high school under Southern auspices. The national leadership was passing to organizations which emerged in my apprenticeship. Resistance to white compulsions centered in the Urban League and the NAACP. I knew best Walter White and William Pickens, both of the NAACP.

At one time, Mr. Pickens let himself be thrown off trains in order to test the laws in transportation. Tall and of fine stature, he appeared in command of his body and had a fierce alertness. Except with arms or sufficient help, any opponent would have hesitated to touch him. He wore a Phi Beta Kappa key earned at Yale; in Texas it lay with him in the dirt beside the railroad tracks.

He was late beginning his education, but he could have fulfilled Calhoun's specifications about being a man. He first became a professor of classics, although in his schooldays, Greek was passing from the college curriculum and had to be learned in the North.

Mr. White, a man paler than I, told me what it was like to investigate lynchings, first as a white man, then as a colored man. He said he could never forget lynchings, except when writing or at home. I grieve that so many men like Pickens and White had to wear their lives out fighting. They were not in danger just once; they led fairly long lives taking their chances.

The North began Negro schools and colleges in the South out of the same conviction which gave birth to Harvard when Massachusetts was the frontier and which sent the Iowa Band from Yale to Iowa when Iowa was the frontier. The Negro was the frontier again in a later century's culture.

Mass Creation as Resistance 10

THE COTTON-PICKING MASSES who hardly knew of the prophets and pacemakers were full to bursting with contributions to racial identity. A large majority unconsciously held an individuality in substantial resistance to white culture. It would have been frightening to see them all together at once.

The wild, the alien, the inexplicable, the flighty—these qualities which others tried to cover remained in them and flourished. When they got together, they had the trick of becoming molten. They flowed into one and their collective endowment emerged as easily as their breath. Language, religious experience and translations from words to music to motion stood out in African likeness. The strength in the racial reserves could then be conveyed by any concert of spirituals sung by backwoods public school children.

Stout determined girls in white muslin stood in rows, singing, "What kinda shoes you goin' to wear?" In those tones were tenderness, harshness, fear, rebellion, the screech of the unreconciled, sorrow and its acceptance. They were fourteen years old and already they knew what was to be.

When I began to look for the things the Negro had created in spite of resistance, his modifications in language were of more than surface importance.

After I had left New York, where passengers pacing the station platform said "Here comes the eight o'clock express," I saw little clusters of Negro men leaning against baggage trucks and what they said was "There go the Cannon-ball—Woosh!" A man did not know the difference between an express and a local, did not know the time, was not going on that train, but his comment was on an essential: speed. He had not enough breadth to trim and contrive, but he often got at the content.

In James Weldon Johnson's sermons (*God's Trombones,* Seven Negro Sermons in Verse), the poet was close to what happens. Preachers casually evoked poetic visions every Sunday. The congregation, too, had poets who could come up with lyrical improvisations, mixtures of Bible talk and slang.

The language of daily life was pungent and lavish—"Liquor talk mighty loud when it get loose from the jug. . . . When the spoon want anything, it have to go to the bowl." Few were Catholics, but they had their own equivalents for "Believe in the Virgin and run."

In speaking about themselves they usually said "colored people," or "the colored"; if they wished to be precise—as in writing—"Negro." Never Afro-American. They were afraid or self-conscious or dubious about Africa, and intellectuals especially were contemptuous because they thought Africans were made static and indolent by the climate. Ministers prayed for "Mother Africa," apparently out of some tenderness for the land. Congregations thought they should send money, the Word and medical missionaries.

I never heard an oath or any talk commonly supposed to be vulgar in the bad sense. The notes passed around surreptitiously in the schoolroom were about school affairs or crushes along the line of "Roses are red, violets are blue." The sexual symbols of adults were derived from nature, tools, important features of life, such as trains, or household utensils—"I got the stopper and you got the jug."

What I heard was conventional for the speakers, differing from the norm in the way Old English poetry now differs from modern English. Howard Odum and his associates, looking up folk songs at about the same time, said that some of their material was unprintable. The double meaning and the symbolic were racial delights. So much so that when teenage girls found out that "cabbage" also meant "greenbacks" they became wary of using any word that might cause a laugh; they called cabbage "that vegetable like collards."

An account of the speech of long ago is easily available in Joel Chandler Harris' *Uncle Remus*. Harris, a fatherless little boy, was sent to live and work on the Turner Plantation in 1860 when he was twelve years old. He was lonely and in his free time wandered to the slave quarters to listen to the old folks talk.

He had a writer's feeling, and he wrote down what he had heard. He said he wanted to preserve the tales exactly as told. Much later he wrote to the *Folk Lore Journal* of London that "Not one of the stories is cooked."

The Uncle Remus world is chiefly American: horse, cow, bull, goat, pig, ram, dog, goose, chickens, guineas; fox, opossum, wolf, bear, deer, alligator, snake, wildcat, mink, weasel, terrapin, buzzard. His stories have three acts: (1) animal meets animal, (2) conflict, (3) one animal overcomes the other.

The animals have mates and families, and it is clear, especially considering the year of authorship, 1860, that life is full of marauders and tests of skill. The victim suffers terribly from fear. Children and women are held sternly in check. The courtesies are fully observed. Music, liquor, and goodtiming are approved, if not used to excess. The victor is always male. It is not prayer that wins, nor speed, nor beauty. The winner knows tricks.

The old voice, rising and falling in calculated suspense, says that Bre'r Wolf "talk mighty lovin' " but a river can drown him. Bre'r Terrapin is silent, slow-moving, hard-shelled, long-lived, determined—but these are the virtues of one who wins second place. Bre'r Rabbit, the swift and suave, the agile and wily, is the King.

The basic principles in these stories of animal life and problems were still applicable to the lives I knew in the early twentieth century. Threats from the outside kept on coming. The victim was always running away. The woman and child were considered politely in the Southern manner—after the man. Tricks still had vital uses; diplomacy paid off in well-being, maybe even in saving life itself.

Uncle Remus tells one good ghost story. Certainly the dead woman's husband, alone in his cabin at night, is frightened. Why not, when she comes slipping and sliding in to get the two silver dollars he took off her eyes?

My friends lost a certain confidence in me when I said I had read Joel Chandler Harris. It was nothing to them that some of his tales have been traced to Africa, Jamaica and Europe. He was a white man making a lot of money out of dialect, perpetuating slavery. To talk about it made it come back.

Harris spoke more than once of the Negro's "curious exaltation of mind and temperament, not to be defined by words." Those who had this endowment thought he was making fun of their crudity. If I cared about them, they said, I would not read him.

They were so used to street cries they never noticed them, but they were a walking edition of an early stage of Harris. Any hawker slid from language into song. He could not just call "Oranges!" He sang, "Sweet oranges, sweet, sweet, sweeter than the honey in the comb." The words alone convey little, but the singer's embroidery on the tune is one of the small prettinesses of Charleston, Savannah, New Orleans and smaller cities.

Tomatoes, tomatoes
Fresh and fine.
Three baskets,
Three baskets,
Three for a dime,
Red tomatoes.

Flower, fruit, and vegetable sellers, knife sharpeners, icemen, umbrella menders, old iron and junk dealers, fish peddlers, and chimney sweeps walked and drove around, jangled bells and sang from season to season. The small songs of the vendors were worth listening to. They explained how the folk songs and spirituals began. In the big gatherings, the crowd itself developed the songs further.

Dissociated from whites on the deeper level, the Negro was living in man's earlier day when religion concerned most of his life. His religious experience was, from childhood to old age, male and female, practically universal.

The broad policies, administrative devices and beliefs of the major white Protestant denominations were taken over deliberately and with devotion. Then on the borders and around the edges came changes due to cultural uniqueness.

Similar changes occur whenever an American denomination breaks away from the parent. The breaking off releases new leads of thought and social status. An outpouring of expression comes from the formerly voiceless. This happened in the East as the denominations shaped themselves to the new country; when Virginians went west over the mountains; when rural emigrants from the South reached industrial cities.

Any church service I ever went to was a revelation of some kind. Away from the big churches on the important street corners, leaders who had heard a "call" put up a religious tent out in the palmettos. Even though the leader might be a malcontent, nomadic, poverty-stricken, the congregation came. The downtown church seemed too fine; the poor surroundings made the poor feel at home. The outpouring of their urgency and despair modified my experience in an historic church with stained glass windows; the tent generated a fearsome energy which shook the leaded panes of tradition.

The content of church services was drawn chiefly from the Old Testament. Preaching was literal about Hell, rhapsodic about Heaven, practical about daily life. It revolved around duty, education, the rearing of children, Biblical ideals and lives, justice, community problems; it hardly touched social questions or the world outside.

Punctuality was a repeated topic. I remember a sermon announced as "C.P.T." (Colored People's Time) in which the text from Ecclesiastes was minimized for the sake of the punch line:

Lost—one golden hour,
Set with sixty diamond minutes.
No reward is offered, for
It is gone forever.

To adults who have no clock or watch and cannot tell time, this verse was food for thought. So were the evening series of sermons on Charles M. Sheldon's novel *In His Steps*. This old book was published in 1896, but newcomers hearing the sermons based on it used to try to decide questions by asking "What would Jesus do?"

Almost any church service is a kind of art. It hints at a mystery beyond the apparent. The easy swing into ritual comes out of faith; the seeker can truly get in touch with God.

The credulous were at the mercy of the wearer of the tiger skin who had music in his throat. Once I just missed seeing Rabba, the Flying Prophet of the Judgment. He was a tall fellow in loose white robes with fanaticism coiling through him, drifting down the seaboard, preaching the end of the world. For "Judgment Day," when the heavens would open, women cut and sewed the prescribed white garments and men built a scaffold twenty feet high. At noon on that day, the Prophet and some attendant Angels jumped from that scaffold.

Almost before the bones broke, the man in white was out of town.

A few years later I walked on the street where the scaffold had been and talked to both believers and unbelievers. The latter said just what might have been expected, "Fandangoes! I hate to be colored!" They also said that religious excess was like lynching; mobs got together because they were so bored.

The believers were more complicated. The whole build-up had happened before their eyes, and afterward they had talked it threadbare. They even might have contributed to medical care for the injured fakir. Yet the raw magnificence on which the fakir had worked was still there, waiting for Truth. They said that the Prophet and the Angels had fallen because they, the people, had not had the true faith. The Lord delivered Daniel. Christ raised Lazarus. They had to say to each other "Oh! ye of little faith!"

They practiced the usual forms of reverence. Worship began with the folded hands, the bowed head and perhaps kneeling; then came singing and the responses. Beyond this, the eccentric or the elect literally rose over the rest, the whole body involved. The individual had an uncanny talent for yielding himself up to the crowd. The unity which enfolded all was stronger than I have ever seen in white congregations.

The Sunday morning service was unbelievably slow, delayed from the very beginning. An eleven o'clock meeting might not stand up for the Doxology until noon. Women came late and later; they had to cook dinner for their white folks, start a meal for their own families. Perhaps for these practical reasons, worship was the routine of hymns, Scripture, prayers and sermon, with no variation except in the taking of the one or two collections.

The givers marched up and down the aisles, letting their silver ring on the table and waiting for change from a bill. In order to keep the purse strings open, a medley of song, entreaty and response was exchanged between minister and congregation. The man on the dais leaned over the lectern, pounded hard on his spoken phrases, glided into a hymn. The listeners answered with shouts of encouragement or snatches from the same hymn:

Everybody . . . Who will be the first?
"Let the lower lights be burning"

> *"Let the lower lights be burning*
> *Send a gleam across the wave*

Bring your dollars, bring your dollars,

> *"Some poor, fainting, struggling seaman,*
> *You can rescue, you can save.*

Give . . . give . . . give
Give out of your abundance.

> *"You can rescue, you can rescue,*
> *You can save."*

Dissenters in other churches said that this marching up to the table with money was exhibitionism. Looked at by itself, it was a ritual—deft and poetic, not ended until it was effective.

The real song-answer communication between minister and people belonged to Sunday evenings, in the relaxation after the day. Everything pointed subtly toward the revival which is the peak of the evangelical method, but the degree of heat turned on depended on the season, anniversaries, the need for money-raising, and local events.

The speaker began: "People are asleep in Sin. They must wake. They must be churned into the foam of Repentance. The Spirit of Light and the Spirit of the Avenger are here."

Out of the audience the equivalent of choral groups emerged. Leaders, soloists and acolytes improvised entrances and exits, songs and responses, with clarity and appropriateness. The anonymous provided the supporting structure of drums—hand-clapping, jumps, shouts, foot stamping. While the mass was simmering, the slow heating passions thrust up volatile participants. They displayed abnormal behavior: mysterious movements, incoherence in voice and gesture, perhaps a trance or swoon.

The ritual reached an emotional climax and read like a crude new song. It was not rehearsed, not planned beforehand, it simply fell into place. Steady intoning from the pulpit repeated beloved Bible verses; it took on the solo of the percussion instrument, insistent and merciless. The audience acknowledged with a cadenced murmur. As the murmur swelled soloists began. Abrasive sopranos pierced the heaviness; women were the strings, men came in as saxophones or as new drums.

The preacher was a man with a voice, often a big man physically, a shouter, a fighter. His trombone ran up and down the scale; faster and faster, louder and louder. Hypnotism was so easy that he had only to shout:

In the Beginning was the Word

The crowd in front of him shouted back in abandon that reached the roof:

It's so. . . . It's the truth.

When he said something soothing to let the people rest, as:

We are the Children of God

their echo grew mild:

Do, Jesus . . . . . You tell 'em

The only white person in a sea of colored folk, I lost the feeling of self and of neighbors and went back to being a tree in a forest. Crowded in space and drunk with green growth, the wood was alive with bird calls and insects shrilling before a storm. The fronds of tropical creepers lengthened. In the darkness of the imagination somewhere the earth was shaken. The sermon's thunder, half-sung, half-shouted, rolled over the trees:

They look like men, they look like men,
They look like men of war.

The clue to the feeling of the supernatural is that the preacher's words were redolent with images from the Bible. Those who could not read had no other way of hearing the great words. They suffered from a starvation and this was their food. This was how they finally learned verses by heart.

Bearing the Cross

Yes, Lord

Between two thieves

Between two thieves

Father, forgive them

Forgive . . . forgive

Days numbered on this earth . . .
sin . . . tomb . . . tomb . . .
Satan waiting . . .

O! Lord . . . Lord

Gasping under the weight of sound, the trumpets blew:

Ride him . . . . . ride him . . . . .
Roll that stone

The horns of lightning darted their forked tongues:

Daniel . . . . . . Glory . . . . . . Glory . . . . . .
Jericho . . . . Jericho

The wind of voices moaned and cajoled. Old oaks of men jumped from standing straight up, jumped again and again until they groaned, swayed, interlaced branches.

Women grew conspicuous. They looked as if they had left this world. A praying mantis of a woman worked herself into a sing-song shuddering recital; possessed by the recital she cried aloud, ended in a spasmodic seizure. When tension was still rising, I saw middle-aged housewives walking the backs of the benches.

A recess came. A voice sang sweetly:

He's the Lily of the Valley, the bright and morning star,
He's the fairest of ten thousand to my soul.

Quiet came with the hymn, but soon the air fluttered again with purple birds. A woman gasped for breath, louder than an asthmatic, faster; others jerked as if in the beginning of a fit. A girl like a young oleander stood up, choked, screamed incoherently, "Ah . . . Ah . . . Ah . . . ," crashed to the floor. Her neighbors became nurses, fanned, crooned, helped her to the mourner's bench. Other women went limp and fell to the floor.

When the sermon turned to the rousements about Heaven and Hell the tax on the nervous system was severe. Even if only one in ten displayed the extremes, and the other nine were a moderate chorus, the observer tended to exaggerate; he was confused by the volume of sound and the unusual prostrations. Gradually, the preacher toned down his enticing; abruptly, he broke it off. The end was silence; the boundless forest in stillness again.

Songs are made out of these services, both "sweet gospel" and "hard gospel." The outsider feels his wounds from them. The service is a song. He is in the song. He believes, he feels reverence. I never got over the feeling that I was in the midst of great poetry that came out of the life of the soul. At the same time the soul's mold was earthy. I was watching a professional spellbinder helping people climb the fence to the abnormal. His magic could sometimes be calculated in terms of the amount of money to be raised and some of them had it worked out to a dollar.

My students were shaken and puzzled about the loss of self-control in "getting happy." They forgot that I was white and talked with anxiety. "Do you think they are sincere? . . . Could it be a spell on them? . . . Are there really spells? . . . I think maybe the Devil got 'em. . . . Don't pay them any mind, they old; they getting happy. . . . Let the Devil take 'em, why not? . . . Isn't this like voodoo?"

When I answered, I knew that their parents might have been among the dancing dervishes of the night before and that what I said would go all over town. I tried to put revivals in perspective. I said that revivals did not originate here with Negroes. I had heard that in my great-grandmother's time, about 1815 in rural Maine, a sermon on the Day of Judgment had made people fall to the floor fainting and crying, "What shall I do to be saved?" Tracing on a big map the westward movement across the United States, I said that revivals had moved along with the frontier.

To know that white people had had revivals with abnormal behavior confused them more. They returned always to, "No matter who does it, isn't it all a lie?" I did not think it all a lie and we talked about rhapsody in the poetry they were learning, and in tribal music and dancing where rhapsody first appeared in the individual. This was more intelligible; they said, "I see it, but it's not for me."

In revival season, I used to be awakened by crowds going home from the meeting house singing, "Hallelujah, Thine the glory." They were like tired merrymakers getting off the Ferris wheel at the Fair. Daily routine was so dull that the fear of Hell was one of their special recreations.

Revivals opened almost as wide a gulf as crime between the intellectuals and the lower class. Men were put off religion, sometimes put off by the tendency of women to be too easy. They asked why women could be so blinded by fakirs who just ran in and out of town for chicken dinners and the collection money. They did not credit the cries of "I am a sinner"; more likely the sinners liked an orgy and wanted to backslide so they could get saved again.

Women of the intellectual class were vaguely afraid of the crowds and felt lost to such religion. They said that the convulsions must be sexual and they harshly criticized me for taking any interest in revivals. The sexual element was undoubtedly close to the religious manifestation, but there was a component an outsider could not define. It seemed not unlike that attributed to Eastern religions, a trying to transcend the Self for the Not-Self.

In the background was the change in the body. People who went to extremes appeared oblivious to their surroundings, might believe they could not walk. The skin turned grayish and the faces took on a look I have seen in hospital beds. The succinct expression and swift changes of this ritual seemed to move in the same direction in both city and country. In spite of the commercial aspect, it conveyed the triumphant and contained the elements that defined Negro style.

At certain times all in the congregation had complete sympathy with historic gospel hymns. After religious storms they liked quiet; all churches sang over and over:

Strong Deliverer, strong Deliverer,
Be Thou still my strength and shield.

It could be seen, however, how the masses kept the race from getting white too fast.

At the same time that the upper classes and castes were whitening rapidly by means of savings bank accounts, home ownership, college degrees and mathematicians the equal of any, the masses were revealing casually the curled-up fragments of their essence and creating a luminous image of non-whiteness.

This artistic essence served as resistance to whites and to Negro aristocracy. The small portion, the will-o'-the-wisp of the essence that outsiders understood, gave the Negro his definition in music, poetry, theater, and dance for the next fifty years.

Northern Resistance 11

AGAINST THE CHAINED endowment of the tropics and the heat of our own South, powerful opposition by the methods of peace began from the colder North. It intended to open the national cultural aims to all people.

The money spent, when all the religious denominations and all the years are included, has been a staggering amount, but the leaders were the real wealth. They came first from New England, then from New York and the old Northwest Territory, later from across the North as far as the Dakotas.

In my time, first came the self-confident men—the Old Guard. Born in the 1840's and Civil War veterans, they came out of farm life, classical education, and disciplined religious purpose.

Dr. Lucien Calvin Warner, the chairman of the Executive Committee of the AMA, was Old Guard. He was tall, thin, aloof, distinguished, living at the Hotel Vanderbilt, retreating to Egypt in the winter, absorbed in philanthropy.

He was brought up on a farm, "living frugally but not often

in hardship." More than half his studies at Oberlin College were in Latin, Greek, and mathematics. He fought in the Civil War. He was desolate at Lincoln's death. He was graduated from the Medical School of New York University and practiced medicine for seven years. During that time he invented a piece of medical apparatus that was still selling in drug stores when I knew him. He did not patent his device; he gave it to the public.

When he began to travel and lecture about health, his thoughts passed from sickness to prevention. He had many women patients and he soon believed that their complaints came partly from tight lacing and half a dozen layers of clothing about the waist. He and his brother, also a doctor, began to experiment with a health corset. It gave me a start to recall that I had seen this corset in my grandmother's rooms—Warner Corsets. After this manufacture was going well, he branched out into chemicals and other interests.

He was fearfully sharp about managing money, but did not really seem to care about it and decided early not to go on accumulating. He provided for his children, began to give buildings to Oberlin College and retired at about sixty "to return to the world what education has done for me."

He looked impersonal and cool, as if everything but mind and will were draining away, but he told me that he had sung at the Moody and Sankey Revival at the New York Hippodrome in 1876, and that it was the last true religious revival.

What could such a man have known about Negroes? I do not know, but the individual did not seem to be his approach to anything. He fled the single patient early, while retaining the doctor's approach to humanity. When he spoke of his travels in Europe, Asia, and Africa, what had impressed him was whole cultures. When he joked about his charities, he said organizations only wanted him to pull them out of the red.

The itinerant preacher, already on the prairies at the time Warner the farm boy was born, might have thought that this man of money and affairs lived too comfortably. Dr. Warner was then what people call old, but his eye was always on the future. He had a knack for understanding and utilizing people very different from his own tastes. He would have looked well in the British Lord Chief Justice's wig and robes. He was as much a symbol of justice as any man I ever saw.

While Dr. Warner was at least recognizably like other men, the chairman of the Missions Committee was not. Dr. William Hayes Ward was then editor of *The Independent*, an Orientalist who had in 1885 directed a Babylonian expedition and was said to be the only American who could read certain Assyrian tablets. In 1912 his associates used to laugh at him because the ferocious amount of information he had about the Middle East was so useless.

At eighty, he remains in my memory as the most adroit and impressive chairman of a committee I ever saw. He turned off long dockets with speed, wit, and forbearance. He acted free from any interest in money, reputation, or social approval. What others yielded to these factors, he devoted entirely to the idea of freedom. Before obstacles to liberalism, he was a fierce and uncompromising fighter; he had the mental equivalent of the swift chopping blow, and he kept at his post from 1882 until after World War I.

I have no idea what he knew about Negroes, either. He would have been capable of never noticing that their skin was different from his own. It was about Negro rights and fulfillment that he was a tiger, and I have heard him tear apart anyone who spoke of "the Negro mind."

The next generation in the committees consisted of the men born in the 1870's—the average a Congregational minister in his forties. Historic ties with churches continued; I remember the ties with Brooklyn's Church of the Pilgrims where Henry Ward Beecher once auctioned from the pulpit and set free a nine-year-old slave.

The younger men were no longer so rock-ribbed. They were tamed, polished, diffuse, men with Phi Beta Kappa keys, veterans of postgraduate study and European travel, chilled to the point where they preferred the system of three alternatives to choose from. If a blunt opponent said that an expenditure was "no more needed than an Eskimo needs ice cream," the men of alternatives began softly, "My friend underestimates man's capacity for ice cream."

Women's societies gave a great deal of money, so there was

always one woman on the committee, white-gloved, velvet-hatted, and furred. The one Negro, Professor Lewis B. Moore of Howard University, was so able that his attitude never once suggested that he represented a minority. He once jokingly told me about a white man who said he would give a substantial sum to Negro education as soon as it could produce a mathematician; he had to part unexpectedly with the money on the evidence of Kelly Miller's career. I only knew Kelly Miller as a speaker; he was later the Dean of Howard University.

All committee members had to be interpreters of missionary education for the churches. The average church member was living in the past about minority groups. He thought of Negroes as figures sitting by the fireside of knots in *Uncle Tom's Cabin.* He preferred the Southern white mountain people to be poor and picturesque, "our own kin and Lincoln's." He thought about Indians in terms of the feathered headdress and the galloping horse. He recoiled from Mormons, "those polygamists," and he did not want to hear one word about Mexicans and Cubans; they were too new. It seemed to him suitable that underdeveloped people should have underdeveloped facilities. He wanted to be torn, his purse opened wide for disaster.

I do not know when this clinging to the past began, but records say that 1899 was the year of "growing public resistance to appeals for human rights." When the United States *Survey of Negro Education* praised AMA schools, donors who had been willing to sacrifice ten dollars a year to lessen illiteracy and poverty stopped giving. They were aghast to hear that missions supported music departments and colleges, luxuries they could not afford for their own children.

A wealthy possible donor, cajoled into visiting a college to see if he wanted to make it a gift, met a young couple in a hack at the edge of the campus. He told his driver to take him back to his hotel. "I have seen all I need to see. When they can ride in hacks, they can pay for their own education."

Women's societies practiced a sort of Christian cannibalism. Granting a girl a scholarship meant getting hold of a loved object to dominate and to follow for the rest of her life. Women became alienated from the AMA, deciding it was "soulless" whenever they heard a school had been released for operation to the local community. This made the women's societies ripe for the plucking by anyone who could wring a good story out of hardship. Saying that "Mary McLeod Bethune began with $1.65," they wanted to give their money to whoever was starting a new school on an abandoned farm with a capital of $5 and one pig.

The cherishing impulse overlooked the longtime educational policy. By 1869, the AMA was saying publicly that the lower school system intended "not to preserve itself but to diminish itself in favor of public education." I saw all the elementary schools, except those needed for practice teaching, turned over to municipalities, after their continuance was arranged. Pilot and experimental projects might be carried on, but in general, all funds were destined for colleges.

Committees were occupied with matters of relocating, amalgamating and developing institutions, but were prompt and generous about the few personal questions: "Did this teacher get pellagra because the dining room fare was poor, or was it because she was a food faddist? . . . Shall this alumna, supported all through college upon her pledge to go to Africa as a missionary, be required to return any of the money, since after graduation she married and settled down in this country? . . . Is the college water system all right because the town says it is, and did the professor get typhoid elsewhere?"

The decisions came promptly, without argument. The bride did not have to repay the money, the sick teacher was paid her salary over a long convalescence, the school fare came under review, and technicians from a New York laboratory went to test the water.

We had few serious troubles; the greatest were from hurricanes—one typhoid epidemic, one death. Pensions were decided upon individually. I never knew but one pension to be refused; the missionary in question had accumulated a relatively large amount of land in the vicinity of his charge, and this was contrary to the policy of the AMA.

Talk went on annually about which hotels in which cities would entertain Negro delegates to national conventions on the same basis as a white delegate. Suave proposals that Negroes ride in the freight elevator and have their meals served in their rooms got short shrift. It seemed shocking to me that so many organizations only came to this policy after 1945.

Missionary agencies had to take account of other funds in the South. The George Peabody Fund of $2,000,000 for whites dated from 1867. Rockefeller gifts for both races amounted to $53,000,000 before 1910. The Rosenwald Fund was spending its principal to build country schoolhouses at the time the AMA ended its supplementary grants to public elementary schools held in Negro churches. The Anna T. Jeannes Fund was aiding the education of teachers in the grades from 1907. The Interchurch World Movement and the Federal Council of Churches had active departments of Race Relations and the YMCA and YWCA supported Negro secretaries on traveling circuits.

The AMA committees were assembled as a composite, man of action balanced against mystic. Their ability to compromise was so expert that they never had a schism. They differed most about the support of Congregational theological education in the South, but about schools and colleges they were single-minded. They were impartial as to sex on every point except women's salaries.

The difference between the committees and the staff was that the latter were personally involved with the minority groups. The Old Guard of the staff were twice-born: they had already worked in the South—just after Emancipation. They were not mortal like the rest of us—they preferred the high altitudes.

Miss Delia Emerson left New England for Virginia as soon as it was possible after Appomatox. She had to pay artificially high room rent, could not be sure of buying food, was socially ostracized and barred from some churches. She received the shock that makes for dedication. She never married, and she never left work with Negroes. It was no accident that she impressed one with her constitutional strength; she lived almost a century.

When I knew Miss Emerson, in her seventies, she looked like the pictures of her cousin, Ralph Waldo Emerson. She was thin, austere, white-haired and handsome; everything looked gone from her except her spirit and her magnificent dark eyes.

She was the money-raiser for women's societies from 1883: money, scholarships, house furnishings, hospital equipment, books, pianos, barrels and barrels of clothing to sell secondhand in school thrift shops. I worked until one o'clock on Saturdays but she who had lived on $20 a month in 1865 worked on the rest of the afternoon.

She dealt with women's groups all day and every day for thirty-five years. What could be left for her to learn? She could have invented the Trojan horse. When her *frou-frou* of lavender scent, black silk, chiffon and lace met male opposition, she knew before he knew every move he would make.

Another of the same group was Henry W. Hubbard, lawyer, Civil War veteran and mathematician, the treasurer since 1876. He stood for forty-odd years of law, order, regularity, memory, and money. Looking around the office conference table, he had the air of the father who is a notable horseman, but who has raised a crop of little boys afraid of horses. He habitually viewed the world with alarm. His office made me make out a voucher for one lead pencil; he held fast to every penny, where would we ever get another? Henry Hubbard was a bachelor, portly and well-tailored, living at the Madison Square Hotel just around the corner from his office and wrapped up in wills, annuities, bequests, appeals and endowments. Walking alone down the hall, he was singing, "We are living, we are dwelling in a grand and awful time."

He died the perfect death for treasurers: death in an instant from a heart attack, as he sat in the bank vault clipping coupons. The pallbearers' feet thudded as they carried him up the aisle at Broadway Tabernacle; the choir sang to music of Ralph Vaughan Williams a hymn that was mysteriously like him:

Thou wast their Rock, their Fortress and their Might;
Thou, Lord, their Captain in the well-fought fight;
Thou, in the darkness drear, their one true Light,
Alleluia!

We had no rule about traveling expenses, but I was told that I was not to travel hard or economize about hotels. Men cruised about every which way, giving up Pullmans during the day, sleeping on the floor on the Indian reservations and in a huddle among white families in the back country.

Our salaries—in the offices and for teachers—were set by general principles; after the worker reached the standard pay for the job, there were no increases. Fees for public speaking and writing were turned over to the organization—not to gouge the speaker, but to keep him from dissipating energy. We invited to lunch or dinner, at our personal expense, teachers who chanced to call at the office and we took to our homes for the night those who would have trouble getting hotel accommodations.

The oldest member of the office force was the editor of *The American Missionary*, Dr. Augustus Field Beard. A member of the class of 1857 of Yale, he became an AMA executive in 1884 after twenty-five years in the pastorate, the last in the American Church in Paris. Dr. Beard had lived through the Siege of Paris; he had eaten animals killed from the Paris Zoo. He was French for so long that the mask of Voltaire had fitted itself over his Connecticut face and his French cynicism, plus his retirement into editing, had removed him from everything but his real interests. He appeared stone deaf to salesmen, and at least hard of hearing to some of his brethren. Deafness, he told me, was an advantage, if a man knew how to use it. I asked him once what had bored him most as an executive and he said, "Listening to rich men in committees."

He was a conversationalist, a letter writer, a polished after-dinner speaker, a gourmet in a delicate way, an omniverous reader, and a connoisseur of men and of scholarship. He was also complicated, contrary, witty, unexpected, sweetly tyrannical, and as sharp as a good trial lawyer.

When I shared his office and ate with him, I noticed that he made everyone feel like talking to him. I used to hear stout middle-aged men shouting their secrets to him. His unique position was that he knew the life story of most of the Negro leaders. They were few then. He had known them as boys, picked them for Yale scholarships when they were in short pants. Trustees, calling to ask his advice about candidates for a college presidency, used to get little psychographs as good as any Gamaliel Bradford ever wrote. He looked off into distance until his memories brightened, then he began to speak rapidly, always recalling the candidate's high-school Latin and mathematics, the IQ measurement of his day. For his one-hundredth birthday, he chose for his present a plane ride over Norwalk, Connecticut, his native city.

The Old Guard was literary in taste, prone to sacrifice, more religious and more concentrated in purpose than anyone I now know. Their secretaries and clerks were shaped in their likeness: pale, single, walking on tiptoe into board rooms, deeply sunk in duty.

The New Frontier was an executive, Dr. H. Paul Douglass. His three assistants thought of themselves as new frontier too, but they were young and two of us were working only as technicians.

Mr. Douglass had been a student of both James and Royce in the Department of Philosophy at Harvard. He was graduated from Andover Theological Seminary, but left the ministry when he could do nothing to stop a lynching in Springfield, his Missouri town. In his thirties he redirected his vocation.

He was an educator with the enrichment of avocation that marked the modern period. He could build a boat and sail it, build a house, and design and execute a formal garden. He was knowledgeable about farming, construction, and mechanics, yet could quote endless poetry. He followed the development of modern architecture, painting, sculpture and dance, and had resources in music.

As a mystic, he made long-term plans; as a practical man he drew the vision on into the act. As a spender, he could make one dollar do the work of two. He was always direct and he was a tough antagonist. He made no obeisance to denominational politics and I have heard him say he never tried to "sell" any project unless he could do it by beginning cold before the full committee. In other words, he never invited the key people to lunch to sound them out in advance.

He was thirty years younger than his colleagues and the generation's difference showed in his thinking. The Old Guard at first regarded him as a dangerous radical. He employed married women as teachers long before it was a general custom, although his opponents said it would break up the home. He was against conducting missionary schools in a Mormon environment and the pious thought this was treason to Congregationalism. He proposed integrating faculties and turning faculties from white to Negro before his associates thought the time was ripe. He pressed turning schools over to local authorities while others thought it a hazard. He helped get both Southern white men and Negroes on the boards of trustees of Negro colleges, against the opposition of both races.

As time went on, he became the bridge between the old and the new. When the AMA was going out of existence as an independent entity, he became the spokesman for the heritage.

Mr. Douglass' commitment to the Negro was extremely outspoken. He believed in the eternal values buried in the unfit. Asked if the white race must not save itself at all costs, he said that such salvation was a matter not of authority but of moral taste. For himself, he did not accept one law for the individual and another for the race. He would rather die with a huddle of colored folk than save his Anglo-Saxon soul alone, and he quoted, "It is better for thee to enter into life maimed, than having two hands to go to hell."

He was a visionary who never believed in literal fire and brimstone. He used to teach philosophy; he spoke the language of his first vocation.

Around the big conference table in the old-fashioned office with pansies in the window boxes, the staff sat from time to time, visibly separated and invisibly united. The young with quick step and unmarked faces were discreetly speechless. The elders had taken the measure of each other professionally and were schooled to endurance. They did not have to pretend they wanted to see each other outside the office and Dr. Beard was the only one they wanted to lunch with. They lived in the simple uterine comfort of their own affairs.

Privately, the Department of Support thought that the Department of Education spent too much. The Department of Education thought that the Department of Support should get out of its easy chair and hustle for money. The Treasury thought that Education and Support were a couple of financial ninnies.

In all piety, everyone had located his neighbor's jugular vein.

He would never puncture it unless there came a supremely desirable time. Geography affected feeling; love was for the neighbors in the same room, family feeling for those in the same department; recoil began with those at the other end of the hall and avoidance with those around the corner.

If, however, the routine of peace was threatened, life rose in these separate cells in a great wave. They stood by each other. Each flowed over his own edges into the others and they became a collective that was young-old, male-female, practical-prophetic all at once.

All these men and women were older than I, and I am more alone because they were all dead long ago. I went to the funerals, grieving that their long and generous adventure was at an end.

Looking back, I see between the Old Guard and the new ones a likeness to today's gulf between science and the humanities.

The seniors were the humanities. They went South with their Bibles under their arms and the grandparents of the present Negro leaders came at once into the climate of religious idealism. In the face of the evolving curriculum after World War I, they mourned for what they called "character education."

The younger element, trying to help the schools toward national standards, symbolizes the systematic science of the day.

Schools 12

WHEN MEMORY DRIFTS back I hear the school bells and a man's voice urging that the underprivileged study astronomy because their lives on the ground would bring such disillusion. I see six-year-olds in pink frocks running on the playgrounds and heroes of the multiplication table writing uphill on the blackboard:

$$9 \times 7 = 63$$
$$9 \times 8 = 72$$
$$9 \times 9 = 81$$

My grandparents' generation was genuinely interested in ideas of education presented in such a book as Edward Eggleston's *The Hoosier Schoolmaster,* written in 1871. Since their time I have distrusted the layman's zeal for the details of education.

Schools were an admitted necessity in the Northern plan of resistance to the perpetuation of Negro dependence. Even the very religious who would have preferred to give money for missionary churches recognized that the church alone could not affect an illiterate culture before Kingdom Come.

The South loathed and flouted as much as possible these

marks of opposition to its atmosphere, yet for three or four generations the Northern schools worked into the environment so discreetly that they lasted until public education assumed their support.

When I began as Assistant Superintendent of Education, after three years as a teacher, the AMA supported about seventy schools, plus many Oriental Night Schools on the Pacific coast. These last were taught by Chinese and Japanese and were supervised by an ex-missionary born in China and in command of the language; the New York office had little to do with them.

Schools for the disadvantaged were scattered: in the Southern mountains and lowlands and in Utah they were for whites and were chiefly high schools; for the Spanish speaking in New Mexico and Puerto Rico, grades one to nine; in Florida—for Cuban cigar workers—they were for adults; among Indians, the one high school was in Nebraska; while Montana and the Dakotas had elementary schools.

I used to visit white schools in Grand View and Pleasant Hill, Tennessee; Saluda and Lynn, North Carolina; Joppa, Alabama, and Piedmont College in Demorest, Georgia. The students were old for high-school work—eighth-grade boys had to be excused from school to go home to vote—and they came from pockets in the hills, underprivileged in work, transportation, health, and education.

Women's societies used to be bewitched with them as our surviving ancestors. My impression was never of poverty; it was of a different way of life, and for the men, anyway, strong and interesting. Girls and women were, in my contacts, acquiescent and subdued: "No, I don't know the names of the mountains. I always lived here and I been drug over 'em so much, I ain't going to give 'em a name."

The AMA doctor in Harlan, Kentucky, acquired there his first experience with gunshot wounds. He used to write in his monthly reports the history of neighborhood quarrels that ended with guns. One of our executives got off the train one morning and climbed up the mountain to the school, just for the walk. He was told that he had taken a great risk of getting shot. The owner of a still thought every stranger a revenue agent and might fire from ambush.

The mountain life brought out all the obstinacy in human

character. Children still in the grades might watch water flowing uphill, but denied it while they watched, "No, downhill." Still, their rural life was similar to that in other rural places, and I thought that between migration, and changes in transportation and industry, it would be modified for the better.

The rural character I remember was more substantial than that described two years ago in *Night Comes to the Cumberland* by Harry H. Caudill.* The draining away of the able population has left voters who threaten the "Welfare" for more money and choke the mountain streams under the laurel with refuse. It may not be true, but the white schools impressed me as holding fiercely to their isolation.

Negro schools were interested in other places and countries, at least as much as any children were at the time. I once saw a thirteen-year-old girl standing on the platform at Commencement, cradling a plaster cast of a statue: "We, the Freshman Class of 1914, in token of our great love for the Greeks, give to our school this statue of the Venus de Milo."

Thirty-four schools plus a few odd grants were for Negroes and they carried the bulk of the enrollment of all AMA schools. We supported in full four colleges, Talladega in Alabama, Straight in New Orleans, Tillotson in Texas, and Tougaloo in Mississippi. All had large secondary schools for boarders, but real college promotion was waiting for more money. We also paid the salaries of one or more professors at Howard and Fisk universities and Piedmont College and at two theological seminaries, one for each race.

The high schools ranged from Cappahosic, Virginia, to Bricks, King's Mountain, and Wilmington, in North Carolina; Charleston and Greenwood in South Carolina; Savannah, Macon, McIntosh, Albany, Athens, and Thomasville in Georgia; Athens, Florence, Marion, and Mobile in Alabama; Lexington in Kentucky; Orange Park and Fessenden, Florida; Meridian in Mississippi. We contributed to, without administering, certain school budgets—Cuthbert and Forsyth, Georgia, and Mound Bayou, Mississippi.

Elementary schools for boarders survived in Lawndale, Troy,

* *Little, Brown: Boston,* 1963.

and Beaufort, North Carolina; Marshallville, Georgia; Cotton Valley in Alabama; and Moorhead in Mississippi. These schools were survivals from long ago, the more rural ones for the overage. I have seen boys at such institutions who appeared like leftovers from the Civil War. A month or more after school was running smoothly, they would appear—walking, penniless, baggageless—saying, "I wants to work my way thru."

Schools might be in the Negro section of a city, river town, or cotton center, or in open country. No neighborhoods wanted a colored school. Looking over any area with a realtor brought letters saying, "We cannot believe that you would break up our happy white homes." Buildings were never aggressive in appearance. Only the pointed church spire, a few smokestacks and the looks of Main Street joined the schools to the outer world.

We had not one single Gothic building. Ours was an architecturally sound poverty of red brick and yellow frame buildings, the rectangles spare and plain outside, the interior muted in green and white and gray. Slave carpenters had built a few of the buildings and in them their grandchildren had earned baccalaureate degrees. One school plant was cunningly located inside a Civil War fort.

The AMA architect, Arthur Holmes, worked in the office every day. He planned the new buildings, directed repairs, restrained local desires for the cupola and improved the landscape design. Campus grounds were large and had old trees. The schools looked very much like average Southern facilities of the period.

Today's young would regard these quiet and stately grounds as prisons. There were no athletics, games, or sports; no book store, snack bar, radio station, no means to go anywhere, and walking downtown was discouraged. The only organizations were college choirs, literary and music clubs, debating societies, YMCA, YWCA, churches, and the beginning of honorary societies. The reason the life could be accepted without the outlets of academic excess was that all students everywhere were more confined to the campus then, and besides, our students had no money to spend at all.

Our city high-school program was academic in spirit and purpose, sound, in an old-fashioned way, except in the department of science. It had to be slanted for those wanting to go to college or to teach in an elementary school. We offered household arts and carpentry, but no languages, except French in New Orleans.

Our agricultural high-school program was evolved when more people lived in the country. The country child entering them was set down in the midst of the ingredients of good farm living. His school had 1,000 to 2,500 acres of land, mules, cattle, pigs and poultry of pedigreed estate, thousands of dollars' worth of machinery, tenant farms, a farm co-operative, a farm manager graduated from a first-rate agricultural college—all this along with all the buildings and standard equipment of any academic institution. One of these schools had two thousand peach trees, two hundred apple trees, several acres of strawberries, one hundred cattle, one hundred swine and seventy sheep; in an average year, one thousand bushels each of corn and sweet potatoes would come to harvest. The student body numbered five or six hundred, the budget was relatively large, and the administration required accurate judgment of student ability and character.

When I was visiting, bells rang in the dormitories in the morning dark, breakfast was at six o'clock, plates of ham and eggs were brought to the teachers' table, buckwheat honey dripped on hot buckwheat cakes. Morning worship brought everyone to the chapel by eight; the day moved on, bell to bell, class to class, with military precision.

Even those accustomed to snatching food in the hand liked three meals at the table. The food was like the students' home diet, with the addition of milk, oatmeal, salads, canned fruits in the winter, eggs, if there was a farm, more vegetables. The diet contained more meat than poor homes, fewer sweets than the middle-class home. Colored faculty members told me there was more food and more variety than in the homes, but I used to look at the tables and think miserably that I should starve.

Teachers taking turns in presiding at student tables ate student fare there, but received a supplementary food allowance. This always made trouble, because some declined to eat anything students could not have. They knew that student food was subsidized by the school; children were eating more than they ought to be asked to pay for, but it seemed to them gross to be different. They declined the food money as a matter of conscience.

Junior and senior girls used to take turns managing a housekeeping cottage and every girl lived there long enough to get housekeeping experience on a higher scale than she had known at home or in institutions. They planned, bought, cooked, cleaned, took care of the linens, and entertained guests of the college.

Tenants on the farm were buying their homes with, I think, no security except their agreement to improve their livestock and their way of using land as the college advised. Except for the garden, cotton grew to their very doors. I recall a tenant who put a son through Cornell University and a widowed mother who gave her daughter a summer session at Columbia before she began teaching.

All agricultural schools had side lines for adults: Farm Credit Unions, Farmers' Day, the three-day Farmers' Institute. The last was a mixture of Chautauqua and county fair, with talks, demonstrations of plowing, seeding, canning, food preservation; exhibits of the latest in poultry houses and care of swine; the showing of pedigreed animals; grain, vegetables, fruits, melons, jams and jellies, pickles, flowers, quilts, rugs, children's clothing, furniture made in the school shop. Girls who had been "off" to college to major in household arts presented the best part of the production.

I have forgotten the cost of boarding schools, but the student always paid in work if he could not pay in cash. Average high-school tuition in a day school was about $15 for a year of thirty-two weeks. School lunches cost three cents; a school outfit from the thrift shop cost about $5. The current rate for student labor was twenty-five cents an hour and at that rate a girl who worked for the institution two hours after school on Friday made an ample return for her year's tuition.

At first, the amount of teaching and necessary supervision of new student labor was horrendous. Girls from the barest homes knew only how to wash and iron clothes and scrub floors well. The martyrs who drew work on the floor-scrubbing detail at five o'clock in the morning did it at once without oversight.

They had everything to learn about cleaning, cooking, kitchen and dining room care. When the novices cleaned a room, they dusted first and then raised clouds of dust. The boys from this economic level knew only about cotton and chopping wood; they had to learn slowly about the care of animals, gardening, painting, and minor building repairs.

The school paid a matron to take a girl from the backwoods who could not tell the time nor set a table, and start her on the road to housekeeping. Around a stove, both her hands were left ones. In the beginning she bawled, "It in," loudly enough to be heard in the teachers' dining room. That meant that she had learned the feat of putting the egg into the boiling water, but could not yet tell the time. When someone else told her the three minutes were up, she said, "It Out." From the egg, she went on learning, and after a year, she could very likely go North with a group of girls in June to earn next year's board and tuition. The school maintained its Northern contacts for summer work through a church or the Urban League.

Country schools usually had about twenty-five young men who entered without a cent. They came from the inaccessible back country, sent by their ministers or discovered by the men on the faculty as they explored remote places. The school would take them just as they were. They lived in the dormitory, worked all day on the farm, went to night school in the evening to two classes—no more, because they were sleepy from hard work and had to get up before day. The following September, they could re-enter with board and tuition paid for the year, or they could transfer the credit to any brother or sister. A girl could come on the same terms, doing kitchen or laundry work for the first year.

These late comers could be over twenty-one when they finished the eighth grade, but school must have been the best life they knew about and anyway, they had nothing to lose. Once in the groove, they hung on until high school graduation and some actually went on to college.

Our country schools were operated successfully by both white and Negro men and by one white woman. I do not see how a Northern woman got the necessary farming experience and the judgment to select good tenants, but women were sometimes intuitive about fitting into the locale. After a white woman gave one of the addresses at a farm institute, the principal wrote me that an old colored man came up to him and said, "I wants to ask you, is that lady white or colored?" The principal commented, "This was a great compliment to her address."

I spent many weekends in isolated rural atmosphere. The dancing of adolescents on the playground was crude strength in sinuous waves, with rigid halts of fear and sacrifice. The spirituals went as slowly as the plow, the sound of rain came out of the voices.

Once I talked all evening with a school principal and his wife, mostly about skyscrapers and tarantulas—the tarantulas out of their life, the skyscrapers out of mine. "The American Radiator Building is black and gold." . . . "There was one old red fellow that was fairly human." . . . "An elevator is just a little room that runs up and down on cables." . . . "We had him for a pet after we lost our pet deer."

These two lived in a cabin in the midst of cotton fields as their neighbors did and worked to instruct the whole community, a community in a state where the law permitted a girl of twelve to marry. They hardly knew what took place outside of a ten-mile radius of their home.

In a similar place in another state, a place so rural there was no way to leave but by walking or muleback, I once saw a minister teach an illiterate congregation Addison's hymn:

The spacious firmament on high,
With all the blue ethereal sky,
And spangled heav'ns, a shining frame,
Their great Original proclaim.
The unwearied sun from day to day
Does his Creator's power display,
And publishes to every land
The work of an almighty hand.

He stood lining the hymn and he defined every word. Then he sang, repeating and explaining as if he were teaching an oratorio. This was a slow method, but when it was done, the words were spoken correctly, and Haydn's music carried the people along.

Boarding schools had two Sunday services, a Wednesday evening prayer meeting and grace before meals. The religious framework was intended to enlarge the ideas of those who knew only more primitive shouting ritualistic form. Institutions were deeply religious only in the sense of teaching brotherhood. Their strength was in respect for the individual and the fostering of personality.

Morning chapel was like that at many private schools. A child struck some chords on the piano and the assembly began to sing:

> A *mighty fortress is our God,*
> A *bulwark never-failing;*
> *Our helper He amid the flood*
> *Of mortal ills prevailing.*

Bible reading followed, then the Lord's prayer and a second hymn.

A school had no revival meetings, asked for no local gifts, invited no ministers in for talks, offered no propaganda. Day students had their own churches and attended the Congregational church only during Commencement week. Children were fond of "Old Salem on the hill," but probably forgot at once the name of the church connection.

The school's atmosphere was sharply different from that of the child's world outside. The skies fell on the one who was tardy, the one who let a piece of paper flutter on the campus, the one who did not sweep under the bed. Unnatural demands for order, cleanliness, and punctuality stalked like wolves in waiting. Crowding was not permitted and a pupil entering the first grade learned that his school led straight on to college. Every high school was able to offer the units for entering a college of good reputation, accredited for teaching, at least in his own state.

The feeling of masculine direction was strong, but women shaped the more intimate life. The discipline of day-to-day living was established by Yankee housekeepers before I was born. They were an imposing group of women—built amply, like opera singers, never thin like librarians. Either their own children were grown and gone or they adopted all children as their own. They did not require blood ties in order to expend energy on the young. They were as well-educated as other faculty members, brisk and active, patrons of the library and the musicales, influential and outgoing. They taught adolescents whatever mothers teach in the home.

Every September they welcomed a group of students who had never ascended a staircase. I first noticed the staircase fascination when I was calling on a housemother after three o'clock and saw children streaming up and down the stairs. "Why? Well, they think the stairs are exciting; they keep running up and down for a fortnight."

Along with the stairs, they had to get used to time schedules, order, definiteness, organizations, the terrible exactness of teachers. All had to grasp new approaches to books and study, all had an hour's tasks to perform on the campus every day. Some had to get used to differences in eating, sleeping, housecleaning, bathing, and mending. Boys resisted having to take care of a room, the first they had ever shared with only one roommate. Table manners, evening study hours, and strange foods were more difficult for boys than for girls.

Housemothers had to do the detective work if a dormitory had a thief. They had to satisfy cranks, children, and teachers every day and had to judge when life for the children was so difficult that there had to be food treats, relaxation, and a party. This was a pre-lipstick, pre-high heel, pre-hairstraightening period, but the coeducational parties every Friday evening took stamina from adults then as now.

Housemothers, all of whom made the supervision of youth appear easy, were paid more than high-school teachers and had a suite of rooms instead of one. They were hard to find and I dreaded having to find replacements.

I helped to find teachers, nurses, social workers, and doctors for all institutions. The educational requirements were fixed and relatively easy, the fringe exactions were not. Workers had to be able to adapt to this special way of life. For instance, when the Indian Normal School at Santee, Nebraska, lost its experienced art teacher, Michelangelo himself would not have been a suitable replacement—he was too devoted to his own work. The big *ifs* about an appointment were always about unknown qualities: would the person grow in his own specialty, would he fit into a cooperative undertaking, would he be able to understand the temperament and living conditions of another culture?

My functions were those which were performed in any position of supervision: overseeing the teaching staff, the budget, the courses of study, records, publicity, pilot projects, surveys, teachers' institutes, and the buying of school equipment. I was a special trouble-shooter for women's problems.

The Virginia elementary schools at which Miss Delia Emerson taught in the 1860's survived for fifty years, but while she was still alive they were the first to go. In my first year all the AMA three-month grants made to lengthen the five-month term of the rural public school were discontinued. About thirty of them had been meeting in the Congregational church, costing the town only the teacher's salary.

We began to work intensively on programs for the remaining elementary schools in preparation for the day when all except model schools for practice teaching would become public institutions. We enforced various regulations. Any principal who, for the sake of the tuition, accepted sixty children in the first grade was reminded of the rule not to exceed thirty the moment his monthly report arrived. We provided the first printed courses of study, more music teachers, one teacher of arts and crafts, quantities of books, pictures, maps, globes, things to see, and things to handle. Our monthly *Round Robin Letters* for first-grade teachers were written by two of our most original teachers for beginners, a Negro woman in Alabama, and a white woman in Georgia. Other teachers were planning letters about geography, arithmetic, eighth-grade English and so on.

As soon as the programs for lower grades appeared improved, and at a low cost, the committees discussed changing policies. They had not understood that a beginner can just as well read twelve primers in the first school year as read his one primer over and over. They began to wonder how much we could improve reading ability by pouring in more content. Long discussion was carried on against the background that local communities, both white and Negro, must soon begin public support of the schools. It was reaffirmed that we should concentrate on bringing high schools rather than elementary schools nearer to contemporary standards.

We never had real disciplinary problems. The grave issue was always retardation. Around 1916, a brilliant graduate of Fisk, Howard or Atlanta University could earn a master's degree in one year in an excellent Northern university. Talladega graduates entered Yale as seniors and were graduated with the A.B. degree in one year. Our other colleges, all smaller, did not yet send students North; graduates began teaching in their own states.

At the top of their high-school class, brilliant students were able to transfer to Northern high schools without loss of credit; I taught a few of these every year. The average student was retarded from one to three years.

Retardation began to make a difference by the time the child reached the third grade. Reading and number skills might be fairly good, but by the time he was nine, a child had other problems. Outside of school, where was he to make the contacts which would orient his thinking to the modern world? His home did not feed his mind; his city did not feed it. His school books did not concern anything he knew. We developed reading aids and illustrative material which drew on the pupil's own experience, but we were disturbed by how little we could cover. At the same time, the child was learning what it meant to be a Negro. His teachers were grown people outside the school who taught him through fright.

Retardation was the problem behind all our school drop-outs. Family desire for education was so intense that even if the possibility of improvement was slim, a retarded child who wanted to continue his education would be allowed to go on. The parents would have said, "Seem like he having a little trouble," and let him go on repeating grades. Once in a while, retardation was a challenge for excellence in teaching. Teachers foiled in one direction sometimes worked out new and effective approaches.

Almost occult skill was necessary in putting together a teaching staff. A group would not fuse without certain ingredients. At least one person had to have originality; it was desirable that another be a scholar. Without at least two exceptional people, the group was dull. No matter how good the educational preparation, unless someone sparked the others even a weekend seemed as long as a winter. On the other hand, in a small faculty which had to live together in isolation, there could not be two off-beat individuals unless the two were married; two separatists could split the whole into two factions.

We used to wonder at the gifts of a teacher who could communicate sensibility to students by the force of his personality, as great art expresses itself before it is rationally understood. The very substance of life was apparently conveyed to children by such a teacher in ways that could not be explained.

I saw early that an illiterate child could find meaning in poetry that appeared too difficult for him. A silence would follow a reading, then the child would say, "What do it mean?" The look, the tone, and the desire to pursue the subject showed that the poetry had already meant something. I had children who learned by heart Gray's *Elegy Written in a Country Churchyard*. The poem was not forced upon them, they just liked it. Gray's poem was within their scope of understanding. They also liked Blake. It was astonishing to them that a man who could write "Tiger, Tiger, burning bright," and "Jerusalem," also made engravings.

We had no access to original paintings, sculpture and noble architecture, although we had pictures in quantities. Children who were not allowed admittance to the best churches in town were enthusiastic about Chartres and Mont St. Michel and imagined sculptured figures on the prows of vessels on their local rivers. I often showed the children pictures from the past, and they enjoyed them. They would have understood primitive lines in modern paintings—as, for instance, in Hartley's "Fisherman's Last Supper."

One of the signs of student resistance to education was their immediate disposal of corrected papers, examinations and notebooks. Their mothers who stated, "Why, I've got every algebra exam I ever wrote," could not understand their behavior; the children were "hard-headed." The dark meaning of, "I don't want to be done good to," was explained. Hands that had once supplicated were beginning to push the help away.

Teachers 13

THE FIRST COLLEGE teacher was a white man, perhaps a mathematician or a classicist, strong enough in the faith to Christianize the prickly long-leaf pine.

Within fifty years the last teacher arriving was a Negro man with perhaps a Ph.D. in Economics from Harvard or Columbia.

The white man with the Phi Beta Kappa key across his gray vest became a dean. After he withdrew into the shadows, his name remained on the campus carved over the entrance to a library, or in the rooms that began the art and music collections, the college archives, or the botanical collection.

The Negro at once began his research for a paper to be submitted to the *Journal of Economics*. He used the Brazilian quotation, "A rich Negro is a white man and a poor white man is a Negro." He soon left the South for the national arena, the YMCA, NAACP, the National Urban League, or Government service. He wanted to be in line for the early surveys of Africa.

The teaching staff was like that in other schools across the country. A college degree was required for high-school teaching, proportionately more for colleges, and two years beyond high school for the elementary grades and special subjects. A three-day Teachers' Institute held every two years gave everyone the feeling that he belonged to something, and the policy of offering transfers and promotions according to individual interest was well known.

Teachers knew in advance about the difficulties of isolation. Salaries were advertised as making possible only a bare living:

> *We are pleased to offer you appointment to missionary service as teacher of History at Ballard Normal School, Macon, Georgia, at a salary of $200.00 for the school year of eight months, with room, board, laundry, and traveling expenses from your home and return.*

In 1908, these terms were the equivalent of $500, or about $100 less than city salaries for beginners. Salaries were set according to position. They were not affected by race, but they were by sex, because the facts of supply and demand necessitated giving a man at least twice as much cash as a woman. Male college professors and administrators had substantial houses on the campus and salaries that may have reached $2,000 or more. The principle behind this varied salary scale expressed by representative donors and churchmen was that "Missionaries should make a sacrifice."

One reason the AMA retained teachers until World War I was possibly because teachers were so comfortably situated. They had the luxury of space and good working conditions with no responsibility whatever for the mechanics of living.

I lived according to Victorian standards in a fine old brick residence. Nine adults lived in the house and to take care of them five more lived there: a housekeeper, cook, waitress, chambermaid, and a handy man for the fires and the yard. The last three were students working for their board. Laundry was sent out and housecleaning was done by students working out their tuition. The cleaning was of an excellence long gone except in expensive shops. The laundress, bringing the wash in a basket on her head, used to ask for more frilly blouses, because ironing sheets was dull. The cook had a fine hand; roast beef and fried chicken came flanked by rice, green peas, collards, popovers, and, at last, ice cream and custard were served. Young teachers who married and left the school could never make shrimp gumbo and beaten biscuit taste right in their own homes.

The house was built for solitude. The bedroom or bed-sitting-room was large, with sun coming in at three or four windows. The desk, bookcases, study lamp, and armchair were designed for a student. A basket of fat pine kindlings was at hand; on winter evenings a fire flickered in the fireplace or shone through the isinglass of a tall stove. As mere "living expenses" long ago, such comfort was common enough to be taken for granted.

With small salaries and room and board provided, teachers lived an almost moneyless life. No one read the advertisements, months went by without the need to buy more than toothpaste. Everyone walked instead of taking the trolley, and amusements did not cost money. Checks were taken intact to the bank to save for excursions to Florida or New Orleans during the holidays, for stop-overs at Niagara, Philadelphia, or New York on the way home or for summer school.

The average teacher was a white woman. We always had from one to three men in high schools, but the minute a school had to pay what was called "a man's salary" every school wanted a man. Besides male teachers, we had agricultural extension agents, treasurers, craftsmen, printers, and superintendents of buildings and grounds—the men provided a sense of solid structure.

The period was still that of the tall executive. The average man was tall and of good physique, reasonably able in his specialty. He was married, had two or three children and went in summer to a home maintained in the North. He seemed like any other professional man.

Men's hearts did not bleed over their jobs. They did not give in to ostracism as women did, perhaps because they did not experience it. Some were purchasing agents; in a year they spent a lot of money among local white men. They also knew the Negro leaders of the community and attended meetings at night.

The length of their stay depended on the age of their children.

If the children went to the white public school, their schoolmates called them "nigger-lover" and threw rocks at them. If the mother taught them at home, they lost class advantages and were lonely. As they grew beyond the elementary school stage, parents either sent them North to boarding school or left the work. When they left, they became school superintendents, deans, professors, or specialists in rural life.

College presidents were promoters; secondary school men were tied up with administration. Only professors were scholars. School life was as dependent on both sexes as a marriage. Men were the architects, women contributed most to the inner life.

The footsteps of women were lighter and fainter on the earth but children were named for them. Wives of teachers or other employees, unless they had small children, needed work to lessen the impact of ostracism. They were librarians or managed dormitories and teachers' homes. The AMA willingly employed one woman as a college professor and five as school principals at a time when New York City was still fighting their promotion and right to marriage.

Women on faculties fell into two groups. There were the brisk attractive girls of both races, not older than twenty-five, who had come to stay "maybe three years." Girls from Radcliffe, Mt. Holyoke, Oberlin, Barnard, Brown, Teachers College, and the University of Wisconsin, Fisk, Howard, and Atlanta Universities and Talladega College were enchanted with their specialties, their life plans and their discoveries of self. Students copied their clothes, manners and speech. The contribution of the younger teaching group was in their style and their ambition. Pupils knew that they had often gone to college on their own and that they planned to undertake postgraduate study on their own.

The other women were white old-timers who had begun in the late nineteenth century—an occasional one in the 1870's and 1880's. The winds which had bent them were only small breezes now, but among them were those who had been called to the door at night by the Ku Klux Klan and told to leave town. One woman left Mississippi. Another stayed on in Alabama even after she was shot at through the window as she sat at her desk. The one who was told she would be put on the train by force remained in Texas.

These were single women, interesting because they had stayed long enough to let the way of life stamp itself upon them. They had taken deep root in their isolation. Not one lived where good newspapers were published, so their contact with the world was made only through weeklies and quarterlies; news was old when it reached them.

They were like all teachers. They had struggled so long with the immature mind that when they said "Shakespeare," they added automatically "English poet and dramatist, 1564–1616." In the early evening, they went to the music room to listen to the young teachers singing, "I dread the day you will forget me, Marguerite," and "I dream of Jeannie with the light brown hair." Their evening hands were never still, knitting sweaters, crocheting baby caps, stringing chinaberry beads for the church bazaar. All were "great readers" and they talked about books. Later in their rooms they would correct student papers.

Close around them lay the litter of their compensations: their houseplants, canaries, goldfish, collections and photographs of the nieces and nephews they were helping through college. I remember a woman who owned 5,000 books. The panorama of English and American literature ran floor to ceiling around her bedroom and overflowed to her schoolroom.

Any woman of the Old Guard would have suggested a character sketch for Arnold Bennett or Theodore Dreiser. "The Founder," for example, as she was called behind her back, had in her vigorous youth founded, built, and operated a country boarding school. Upon reaching the age of retirement, she gave the school to the AMA. The pebble under the mattress was that they had to accept the giver with the gift.

She stayed on in residence, judging those who had replaced her with inscrutable eyes—those very pale blue eyes that give nothing away. She was outrageously healthy and agile; day after day she bounded from classroom to dormitory, farm to kitchen, teacher to teacher, leaving a long trail of admirers, rebels, partisans, and potential executioners.

Non-founders were a milder type, usually completely wrapped up in children. I remember one who taught eight miles from anywhere, out where the swamps had alligator colonies. She began her summer travel in a black Gainsborough hat drooping with crimson roses, and she abounded in chiffon scarves of an earlier period. She used to like seeing prints at the old Anderson Galleries on 23rd Street in New York and would say that she especially enjoyed lobster Newburg at the Waldorf Astoria when it was at 34th Street and Fifth Avenue.

I never could fathom how she fired fifth- and sixth-grade children with ambition. She had helped forty-five through high school and five through college. Down there among the pines and swamp cypress, this feat was equivalent to putting them on the moon. She had to select the child and test him by her own methods. If she judged he could make it through high school or college, she roused him, made him do extra work, called on his parents and persuaded them to allow him to go away to school, begged the scholarship and the clothes, arranged for the departure, sometimes even the ticket. Her parting gift to the voyager was a copy of the Psalms or the New Testament. She was not pious—she told me that she never prayed with these students—but at seventy-five she said the extra schooling of fifty children had made her a good life.

I have never forgotten the ending of another of the non-founders. She went South as a girl soon after the War and stayed at the same school until she reached the stage of wearing a wig and a little wool shawl. She became a power in the community; she surely revealed a great deal about women and about kindness. Dying slowly of cancer in old age, she asked her pastor to write the AMA for her. She wanted to confess a sin.

In nearly fifty years of teaching, she had begged from Northern channels enough barrels of clothing to dress a city. Bending over a barrel to unpack it, she sometimes found cracked spectacles, old parasols, crushed tulle hats and sets of false teeth. She had unpacked every barrel, written every note of thanks; she knew to a dot what foolish and useless things Christians will sacrifice to the poor.

Now in her painful days, the sin that haunted her was that she had sometimes kept out clothes for herself without saying anything to anybody. "Tell them I stole; and now . . ." The man who answered this letter got up and stood looking out the window toward the East River a long time.

The old-timers were as much my introduction to life as any of the minority groups. Women did not go as far as men, but they were as odd as Oxford dons. They were very able workmen; outside of work, they flourished by their eccentricity. Their skirts were long when other women's were short; their sleeves and hair were puffed when the mode was for the severe.

The quirks by which they shaped themselves into a distinctive type gave missionary schools the core of their character. They were shellacked in duty and eaten by sacrifice, but somehow when they communicated with the young, the faith and ambition of their generation were transplanted in full bloom. The stigmata of their calling could make the "normal" look small.

I doubt if they responded to Negroes informally or as friendly equals because they began as teachers at a time when adult illiterates roused their protective feelings. The parental feeling never left them. At the worst, it turned to condescension, but most of them were humble. They had given up their own lives and were dedicated to others without being conscious of the fact.

Since the veterans influenced Negroes so profoundly, did Negroes influence them? Yes, and always in the profound way, not in trifles. They left their own area of the country for a lifetime. When uprooted from their schools they had no niche to return to; friends and relatives were dead or had moved elsewhere. They came to old age deracinated as Americans. I know, because I prepared the data for their pension applications.

They were possibly disqualified for marriage rather early because the Cause was nobler than the suitor. Let a young man say "nigger" before his girl and she was through with him.

I imagine that their religious beliefs must have been as shaken by their experience as if another Darwin had come. No matter how inspiring the Scripture and music and prayers every Sunday, sermons planned for the illiterate become hard to bear. The hundredth repetition is guaranteed to make any listener review his own religious position.

Now that these schools are gone, I can think of secrets they took away with them. One is that the industrious apprentice learns from all sides that the living could never be as able as the illustrious dead. It is better not to be too good and better not to live too long.

People grew in response to the difficulties and complexity of their work, at least up to the point that mortals could bear. A ferny and pine-needled obscurity far from a railroad made people religious and introspective. Big urban schools brought more out of teachers than small-town schools; the clash of minds and living stretched everything farther.

Schools for girls never brought out the most in women. Their bright and chintzy atmosphere had a dullness intellectually. The male added something to a woman's thought and this was true even when the males were no more than schoolboys.

Negro schools brought out more in white teachers than white schools did, but perhaps not more than Indian and Mexican schools. The essential for growth was immersion in another culture.

The mysterious and aspiring quality of the schools came partly out of the intense personal difficulties of the teaching staff. I believe that the most penetrating and original contributions were made by the single white women, veterans of long service, and by very fair Negro men. Other faculty members experienced the pleasant scattered round of living—these two groups did not. Outside school, the Negro men did not function in society as men, nor the women as women. Both of them were a kind of foster parent. The women were another version of the matriarch; they gave and gave and gave. The men were philosophers, subtle and powerful intermediaries in the culture. They were like the naturalized Americans who came here from Europe; they could refer to two cultures, two histories and two lifetimes.

All the men were Southern by birth and Northern by education, married and with children. Sometimes the whole family could have passed as white. They were like whites in schooling, travel, and tastes and whites went to them to find out how the masses would react to various projects or ideas. They knew, but not by association. The black man would only come to them in a pinch. They were what would now be called "adjusted" personalities. Some did it by compassion, others by becoming benevolent tyrants.

I came to think that property takes undue possession of the mind. School men had never had as much responsibility for property and those of both races and all types of preparation became absorbed by it. It destroyed scholarship and made for greed; in about twenty-five years, every teacher, every field and every picket on a fence became the administration's personal property. A wit on the Missions Committee, hearing how plants swallowed men, made a parody on a hymn about it. "Sit still, O men of God! you cannot do a thing."

Yet, despite the bureaucratic snarling, an unearthly breath of a humane tradition filtered down, generation to generation, person to person; the influence of one on another. The late Samuel Coles says in *Preacher with a Plow* that he received the dream of his life from his dormitory matron, Miss Ida Hubbard. Coles had been a field hand, a track hand laying steel rails, a woodsman in a logging camp and a blacksmith before he entered Talladega College at twenty-four. He was such a tall young man and so skillful in the blacksmith shop where he was working out his college bills, that I remember him well. He said that Miss Hubbard told him the story of the Scottish missionary, Alexander M. McKay, who set up a forge and machine workshop in Africa around 1875. It was at her suggestion that he later studied agriculture.

He spent thirty years as an agricultural missionary in Angola. When he got there he was told that superstition forbade men to farm the best land. That land was left as the home of ancestral spirits and the living farmed the poor land. Mr. Coles first made a plow. Then he had to persuade a few men to defy the superstition. He defied it first, plowing while they watched. Later they plowed and planted with him. He then made more plows and lent them as if they were library books. Every borrower promised to help someone who had no implements.

A friend who arrived at Angola to visit the mission thought he must be losing his mind. Surely the buildings in front of him were those of Talladega College; surely the very spacing was as he remembered it in Alabama? Mr. Coles had borrowed the blueprints, taught the natives brickmaking, and reproduced his Alma Mater.

The fine individual life, which was the central motivation of the schools, was a true projection of the character of such individuals as Miss Hubbard and the men at the top.

The only men I cannot find duplicated on the field were

William Hayes Ward, Augustus Field Beard and H. Paul Douglass. They were the prophetic and fiery advocates of the Negro, and they never gave in. This untameable element was withheld for a reason from the field. Under the Southern compulsions, either a man had to leave the South or his fire was quenched.

Integration 14

IT NOW SEEMS odd that our question about integration concerned an aspect more advanced than the public is yet able to cope with: the integration of teachers from minority groups into community schools.

Men were accepted easily enough; they were few and taught special subjects. Indian, Mexican and Puerto Rican girls did not fight for education long enough to become public school teachers. In both white and Negro schools, the minority group did not want to be taught by one of its own.

Parents felt sure they at least knew something about the teaching of reading and arithmetic. A white school in the mountains made trouble for a local girl who applied for a teaching vacancy in the second grade. She was a graduate of the AMA high school with two years of further study in the North but the patrons' contempt for what was near at hand excluded her—"Old Si Slocumb's girl—the whole family is ornery!" Local opposition was not a small incident; it derived from old feuds and was likely to reopen them.

Even though a Negro community might work itself to the limit to educate its children, when the schooling was done it did not want even one as a teacher. Publicly they said that white teachers knew more; privately they said, "My child shall not go to school to a nigger."

The AMA tried to unite the representatives of these two Negro cultures that did not want to be united. Executives used to ask local committees if they did not think it right that some of their well-schooled young receive positions as teachers. The answer was always, "Yes, but let her go somewhere else."

The AMA employed both races from the beginning, but I do not know at what point mixed faculties in Negro schools began. The policy was so long established that I heard no discussions of it in committee meetings.

Any candidate of adequate educational preparation, with the usual backing of personality references, might be appointed to any vacancy for which he was suited without regard to either race or sex. Three important conditions, however, had to be met and these were matters beyond the applicant's control. Housing, whether for an individual or a family, would have to account for racial separateness sufficient to conform to Southern custom. The candidate had to possess a personality which would fit well, or complement those of other faculty members. As well, the community in which the school was located had to be sufficiently stable racially to accept a change or changes in personnel.

In about 1916-1917, of thirty-four institutions, sixteen were staffed by Negro faculties, the others were under white management with mixed faculties. The latter had little trouble with the white community. The political tribesmen everywhere knew, of course, that in the Negro school, adults of both races joined in chapel services and teachers' meetings, but all that took place within the buildings. Behavior had the decorum proper to a school and other Southern customs were duly observed.

Looking back now at the degree of integration in these faculties, I am struck by the adamant Northern determination to prove that Negro faculties could be equal to the white standard of the best AMA institutions. This determination was demonstrated in three of the four colleges. Negroes were in pivotal positions, influential in policy. Those of professorial rank had homes on the campus; salary and tenure were determined by requirements of the job, not by the characteristics of the man. Three of the high schools with the best plants, educational facilities and an experimental point of view had Negro faculties.

These institutions, as well as others less notable, were all that could be staffed with superior candidates. It was not anticipated that the AMA be limited to Negro faculties, but only that there be a continuous search for the highly qualified. I heard discussions about young Negro men who would be prepared as candidates for the office of dean or president, fully seven years before the change from white to Negro was made.

We could find only two or three men a year who could be considered for positions which would lead to the top in scholarship or administration. The requirements included experience in Southern living, Northern postgraduate degrees, gifts in speech, writing and personality, a wife who would fit well into college atmosphere.

The other schools were less demanding; they served the limited educational aims of the area. Some with Negro faculties were small and far back in the country, and were not included in plans for major development. They served the very simple and poor, and the principal might be the local Congregational pastor. Years would pass before the town or county assumed direction of the schools; the white schools of such areas were also inferior.

Some of the schools with mixed faculties, but with white direction, flourished because the same care which was lavished on finding exceptional Negro teachers and administrators was expended on finding exceptional whites. The Negro teachers, although not influential in policy, represented the opening move in the Northern campaign. As well, the AMA did not want the Negro community to forget their own. There were women teaching in the elementary grades and the department of music; men teaching woodworking and printing.

Silent warnings about going too fast with the integration of teachers came from the community whenever a white teacher was replaced by a Negro. Enrollment fell off when this happened, even if we had arranged for the teacher to receive special training the preceding summer at the Columbia or University of Chicago summer sessions. Most of the piano lessons stopped abruptly when a white teacher was replaced.

The effort and strain of turning the operation of a private school over to a town was great, but converting an all-white faculty to a complete Negro faculty was greater. Everyone concerned did not dispute the final wisdom of such a move, but everyone wanted more time—"too soon, they are not ready." The Missions Committee doubted if even the extra aids proposed would keep up our prestige with colleges. The Executive Committee was willing to step heavily on the fine points of philosophy; how could an expensive plant be kept up by people who had no experience with property?

The white faculty, told about the prospect confidentially before anyone else and offered transfers, did not want to be transferred. They wrote in protest to their home churches, and their ministers began to write about our harshness with devoted missionaries.

Letters from the Negro community began with bitter reproaches. Their Harvard was being taken from them and they were being pushed back into the log cabin school. This was a second Reconstruction, totally unchristian and soulless; it brought complete disillusion about the words "American" and "missionary." Formal petitions from the *Committee to Save Our School* had hundreds of signatures.

At some point, the newly hired Negro faculty heard that they were not wanted. Once, they all resigned before they even began to teach.

I hate to remember even now the difficulties with some of these programs designed to break down caste and prepare people for the best professional level they could attain. Obviously, the AMA was turning to new groups for financial support. The appointment of local teachers of both races made for a loss in Northern support. This policy of local appointments was a bridge leading to a more realistic educational program since it arbitrarily did away with the sacrificial element in missionary service and called for greater support from parents and the community. At least married women teachers in the elementary grades were rooted in their own lives outside of the school. They had homes, families, church work, and did not entertain the idea of contributing their whole lives to the schoolroom and the unprivileged. They said that Johnny should pay attention in class; they were gone as soon as the last bell rang.

Our campus feuds were about college matters, not about race. Dramas about position and money enliven all academic life. In AMA colleges or secondary schools I never saw the internecine warfare that raged in similar white schools, but it could be that a strong common purpose dampened private interest. As a traveler I soon learned where the sensitive points were; I was not to ask the theoretician anything about the practitioner, or the money-raiser anything about the money-spender. Presidents and treasurers remained closed books to each other and the wives of administrative officers never appreciated the housemothers and managers of the dining hall. The farm manager monumentally managed to survive although on the outs with all the professionals. The one who divided the faculty was the daughter of a painter, brought up in France or Italy.

Although professional jealousy was not so much a problem as management, it came into view as soon as professors with thin hands and penetrating eyes began to show their old age. Visiting alumni were roused by the condition of their venerable mentors; they wanted to shower them with presents and help them upstairs or down the narrow paths. The young professors, the heir apparents, trembled in the shadows, willing them to fall down.

Young Negro men fresh from Northern postgraduate study, and believing secretly that those over thirty were finished, found the dedication of elderly whites quite a bore. Promotions and the dignity of homes on the campus would be opened to them as soon as the elders vanished. When one of an old couple died, the survivor usually left.

It was the single women who blocked so many dreams. The grapevine pushed out long groping tendrils about these plain drones who had for so many years eaten oatmeal on gray mornings before they left home carrying the green flannel bag or the black portfolio. I once saw a letter written by one Negro to another—"If that old bitch from Massachusetts would ever die or get through here, I could begin to live." It would have been the same if she had been a Negro woman, but he was too young to know that this tedious devotion is not peculiar to any one race.

I wonder now what was achieved by these early attempts at integration. Among mixed faculty groups, I believe that professionally integration was harmonious and successful. All were teachers; they were co-operative and had regard for each other. Differences of opinion were traceable to age and sex, sometimes to specialized subject matter, but not really to race.

I observed social relationships only in day schools and friendships were few. Teachers appeared to trust each other in professional matters and might exchange letters on such points in the summer, but a sharing of personal matters presented too many difficulties. Conditions of urban life pressed on some, problems of rural life on others; after they had kept a few children after school, there was the need to begin the long walk or the long trolley ride home.

Going beyond the mechanical difficulties of keeping in touch, I think that both races were governed by the Southern compulsion. Interracial relationships were under so heavy a taboo that people were conscious of it all the time. The sensitive reacted as the South intended. They left companionship when closing the schoolhouse door.

Students 15

AFTER I LEFT the intimate small city setting of Wilmington where I called my students *Mary* and *John,* I called everybody *Miss Smith* or *Mr. Jones.* I thought the formality might help fire their ambition. In my childhood, when I was eleven years old, a young man, a new teacher, called all of the girls *Miss.* The honor all but overwhelmed us, and our secret society voted in a meeting that we had to prepare right away for further study. I vowed to elect Greek in high school.

I lived with my own students as with a flock of birds, listening to the song and watching the plumage. In early years I neither wanted to nor could objectively study their behavior. Later, as a supervisor, I made various studies, usually with reference to particular skills.

After I had left the work altogether about 1926-27, I studied one group of high school alumni. I had visited the school in question year after year and once had taught there for part of a winter. I went back and called on everyone and his family. Fourteen years after they had left school, I wanted to see how the quality of their lives compared with their school report cards —A through F, meaning excellent to failing.

My sample school was typical of those in small cities—the community not too poor, not too extreme, with no recent race trouble. Around 1912, my one hundred students came from only seventy-eight families. Nineteen families had two or three enrolled at the same time. The cost was $12 per pupil for an eight-month school year.

In our small schools, every student had to earn almost the same sixteen units for graduation:

ENGLISH	4
MATHEMATICS	4
HISTORY (ANCIENT, AMERICAN AND STATE)	3
SCIENCE (BIOLOGY, AGRICULTURE)	2
HOUSEHOLD ARTS OR MANUAL ARTS (LAB)	2
PEDAGOGY OR BOOKKEEPING OR MATH	1
MUSIC (CHORUS, TWO 40-MINUTE PERIODS PER WEEK, NO CREDIT)	0

Parents enforced the home study hours well, but they would have liked the curriculum to provide for foreign language study.

One quarter of the students had lost one parent; fourteen mothers and eleven fathers were dead. The average child was one of four children, but three came from families with more than twelve and one had twenty brothers and sisters. My report on one child read:

CLASS OF 1915

Rose Annie Martin: eighteen-year-old Junior, middle-class family, Methodist, *B* student. Tall, slender, dark, pure African, face lighted by wonderful eyes; moody, strong-willed, explosive, resentful; intelligent, industrious, executive ability, dramatic sense, natural leader; easy flowing speech, but slow to get the sense of a printed page.

She had fifteen years to live; learned to look like a fashion plate, supported herself as dressmaker for children's frocks and for evening dresses; tried Chicago for a year, but returned to live with parents; one engagement, which was broken.

When I saw her she said she had been happy and ambitious, bitter and rebellious by turns. She died of tuberculosis at about thirty-four; never able to use her unique gifts of personality because of reading difficulties and perhaps family restraints.

When I knew a child's home address, I could almost predict what his school marks would be. An *A* student could come out of a hovel and an *F* student from a good modern house on the best street, but these were the exceptions. Normally, a good neighborhood meant good marks and a bad neighborhood meant bad.

Thirty-seven homes were in the center of the city in excellent old neighborhoods mingled among the white. They had been home owners for some time. Pupils from this central area received rows of *A*'s on their school reports.

Forty-seven lived in the first two ghettos settled; the houses gray, the conveniences crude, much crowding, six in three rooms, perhaps no lamp for evening study. *B* was a good mark.

Six country boys and girls who were working for their board were poorly prepared in reading, but mature in their intentions about learning. They were able to earn *B*'s and *C*'s.

Ten lived "across the tracks," in ramshackle housing inaccessible except by walking. Their early schooling was always poor and they were doubtful risks for graduation. Their parents were relatively unskilled labor, perhaps domestic servants. The sixty-four living fathers included five professional men, seven craftsmen in carpentry, printing, cooking, and cobbling, two each in farming, business and mail carrying, and forty-six who were porters, valets, gardeners and odd-job men. Sixteen mothers did full time work outside the home, thirty did part time work. Twenty mothers worked only in their own homes. The last group were the "leaders" of the community; they knew more about the world and their children were likely to be the most articulate of the group.

All the students belonged to a church. Children could hardly remember when they had not heard the sonorous tones of morning prayer:

Oh! Merciful Father,
We thank Thee
That in this morning light
We are spared
To be on pleading terms
with the Gospel.

Eighty-five students were Methodists and Baptists; fifteen were Congregationalists, Episcopalians or Presbyterians. The young appeared confident in religious faith, although they did have some questions about revivals. This doubt was the first grave difference with parents.

Next to the church, the pervasive influence was music. Piano teachers could make a living, boys played guitars and harmonicas, everyone sang. A home with a piano and a child who could play gave the family status. Twenty-seven students frequently played in public.

The former students I was studying were within the age limits of twenty-eight to thirty-six. They would have more marriages, more children, and more changes of residence, but their occupational pattern was probably set.

CLASS OF 1916

Moody Marston: seventeen-year-old Sophomore, middle-class, C+ student, Methodist.

Very light mulatto, tall, thin, nervous, fast-growing, jerky, never still. Youngest of seven, all brilliant in school and conservative in thinking, he used to fight his brothers from the radical side; they would have liked Greeks and Italians deported; he thought that an outrage.

Conspicuous for playing tricks, hated routine, at times surly and defiant; wrote badly, talked well, knack for debate, obsessed with reading newspapers, magazines, the dictionary and encyclopedia.

When I called on him he sent for all his five children to show me; postman, held office in his church, owned his house; favorite reading politics, knew about the political machines in New York and Philadelphia.

Seventy-three out of one hundred had been graduated from high school. Those who dropped out did so in the first two years, and included seven who had left town and might have gone to school elsewhere.

A new factor shocked me. I had never thought that in fourteen years fourteen would be already gone from life. Eleven were dead, two in mental hospitals, and one was wasting away in a tuberculosis sanitarium.

I had expected to find that many had migrated. I could almost have picked out those who would be gone; movement could be correlated with good scholarship. Of the eighty-nine living, more than half had left their native city for Chicago, Detroit, Boston, Philadelphia, Pittsburgh, Buffalo, Denver, and small Southern cities:

DEAD BEFORE THIRTY	11
LIVING IN THE CITY	41
LIVING IN THE STATE	14
ELSEWHERE IN THE UNITED STATES	26
SOUTH AMERICA	1
RESIDENCE UNKNOWN	7

Those who had pursued some form of higher education were, as expected, those who had received family support, but the town was not well-to-do. I was surprised at the number—the first in their families to get through high school—who had gone on. It had taken every summer session and some Saturday and evening work for ten years or more to get through college.

Ten had gone to college or beyond; seven attended professional schools. Eleven others were close to earning their advanced degrees or teachers' certificates; eight from college, two from business schools, one from an art school.

The occupational level was higher than the parents' had been in terms of status and money, and they more clearly realized their professional aims. Twenty-one men were occupied in work that they must have liked: doctor (3), dentist (2), minister (2), mail carrier (2), machinist (4), and one each as a lawyer, druggist, musician, commercial artist, soldier, undertaker, and baker. The men in law, medicine, dentistry, music and art had planned for their vocation since high school; the undertaker and baker had each inherited a family business. The two ministers were brothers, both of whom had withdrawn from the Baptist church and became associated with more primitive evangelical groups in the West.

The husbands of the former female students were similarly

employed, except that one was a college professor and another a laborer.

The occupations of the fifty-nine girls were divided as follows:

HOUSEWIVES, SOME PART-TIME WORK	25
TEACHERS, ELEMENTARY SCHOOL	20
PRINCIPALS, ELEMENTARY SCHOOL	2
NURSES, GRADUATES OF NORTHERN HOSPITALS	2
DRESSMAKERS	3
STENOGRAPHER	1
COOK, IN THE NORTH	1
WAITRESS, UPSTAIRS WORK IN THE NORTH	4
CARING FOR OLD PARENTS AT HOME	1

In the old-fashioned school records of achievement, the students fell into the ordinary groupings of any one hundred people:

SUPERIOR	(A)	26
GOOD	(B)	27
FAIR	(C)	23
POOR	(D)	18
UNSATISFACTORY	(F)	6

The superior students, the top quarter, exhibited an ability in every subject. They were a little further along in the cultural process than other students; half the fathers and the older sisters or brothers were in a profession or a trade. All the members of the Congregational, Episcopalian and Presbyterian churches were found in this group. Half of the good students of piano were here. All could have gotten on acceptably in Northern high schools. As anticipated, this group contained all but one of those who went to college immediately after high school.

In the fourteen years, fourteen of the "superior" had gone North and only four remained in the city. These four filled the more influential teaching positions.

What I had never expected was that twenty-six of the superior were to provide seven of the dead. All but one had died single in his twenties. The group had not yet reproduced itself, perhaps because the men did not marry until they were established in their occupations. So far, there were only ten children.

Ernest Smith and *David Crocker:* these were chums from the same street who had been thick since childhood; everyone called them "David and Jonathan"; both were seventeen-year-old Sophomores, middle-class, *B* students; one Baptist, one Methodist.

"David" was a stocky, brown-skinned boy, played baseball, worked afternoons; sunny and well-balanced, industrious and decisive; could sing, liked people so much he always wanted to know about the lives of authors, hoarded general information; talked well, wrote atrociously, would not take time to conquer the defects of early poor schooling.

"Jonathan" was athletic, fine tenor voice, thought in terms of history, responded to ideas and abstractions.

The chums were representative of good family backing, may have been happy because they complemented each other.

I have not seen them since they put on long trousers. They went to college together, then separated for professional schools. The meditative one became a doctor, the jovial one a dentist. Both are married and settled in Northern cities.

The two middle groups rated "fair" to "good" were the uneven students, often briskly capable but foreigners in the land of books. Once was never enough for them to hear or read anything so it took them longer to come to the stage of reflection. They always had one weak subject, usually math for the girls, English for the boys. This was not the result of low mentality, but of uneducated parents and poor schooling when they were little. Sometimes mothers understood these problems and made up with tenderness and ambition their own poverty of education and means.

What these middle-of-the-roaders had accomplished was a small miracle. The minds that had to be coaxed and cajoled began to set the local pattern. Maybe they had accomplished just enough to please both whites and Negroes. They moved into most of the teaching jobs in the area and they had forty-one of the total of sixty-three children. Girls who had been unable to put a subject and predicate together when I knew them came to see me dressed in dark green silk with a tiny white design and white gloves. They had conquered both number and tense and complained pathetically about country dialect and fried food.

The progress of the middle group made me wish I could have another chance on behalf of the lowest groups, rated "poor" and "unsatisfactory." Twenty-one of the twenty-four had come from poor neighborhoods. Seven had lost one parent. The average father had no stable occupation.

Now, four of the group could be counted as lost, three to tuberculosis and one to a mental hospital. Of twenty living and active, eight had gone North, six had moved to the country, six lived in their old homes. They had only six children, the least of any group. Only two surprised me: one was a jazz pianist with his own orchestra, the other was a doctor.

The reason for the low rate of reproduction was again economic. Young men of their group were too poor to marry; ten of the girls had never married. After their brilliant classmates had gone, these girls, quiet and well-behaved, found a few city teaching jobs and others began to teach in the country roundabout.

Launched on teaching careers, they were forced to choose between marriage or the social status of their job. First earnings were plowed back into summer school until they received a teaching certificate. Next they tried to earn a higher certificate or modernize the family home, or, if they had rented, buy a home. By the time the occupation and home were settled, their more harum-scarum schoolmates had gotten all the men in their age group. In a small city they rarely met men who could equal them in courage and character. After one or two short trips North for pleasure, they fell to spoiling their parents or educating nephews and nieces.

CLASS OF 1917

Sweet-Alyssum Ware: sixteen-year-old Freshman, poor family, poor neighborhood, *C*— student, Baptist.

Dark fat girl, waist laced small under faded gingham, swishing walk, untidy, careless, awkward; childish behavior for her age, face alternating between delight and obstinacy; irregular school attendance; silent in class, tardy with papers, illiterate in both speech and writing; hard-shell to coaxing, explanation, reward and punishment: "I'm never goin' to be nothin'." Curious way of clowning and laughing, slapping her knee and going off into gales of laughter, she could make the whole room laugh.

When I saw her, she was married, but had no children, had been teaching the third grade for years, spoke correctly. Her peak of experience had been visiting relatives in Boston and after that riding the cog railway up Mt. Washington. She was afraid to go, did not even like mountains, but did it to please her husband; she never before had had any idea what the United States must be like, would like to go up Pike's Peak.

The "unsatisfactory" children, as teenagers, were hurrying toward the dubious distinction of being social misfits. They were good-looking, well-dressed, not stupid, and did not have the obvious home or money problems. They were cut-ups, poker-faced, deaf and dumb to school. They were deaf to family blandishments too; their mothers worried, "He don't never crack a book." All the boys who flourished knives on the playground and the one who displayed his revolver came from this group.

The last element of my study was color. It was then a quick practical index of status which gave clues about the possibility of higher education and jobs.

I did not associate color with brains but, rather, with behavioral factors. A fair skin went with better living conditions, more chances for reading and some travel; it might mean a wider view, but not really a better mind.

I had had to see the downward trend in achievement among upperclassmen before I realized the role that color played in the male rebellion against the world. Girls were more petted and sheltered at home; they seemed less affected by color. A boy's indifference to school sometimes meant that the color business had actually curdled the brains he had started with.

Six children were so fair that they could have passed for white. Thirty were full Africans. Thirty-four were mulattoes. Thirty were quadroon to octoroon or less. These girls had long straight black hair, faintly dusky skin and mysterious grace.

Two of the most difficult boys in school looked white. They had stable homes in large families—all of the other children had done well—but as the youngest, they were fierce rebels. Both were loners, saying, "What's the use?"

One pale boy with straight blond hair lived in an almost complete isolation. When he was twenty he said to me, "I have wasted my life thinking how bad everything is." He died before he was twenty-one. The other was a captivating sinner, lively and two-faced, and with a complexion like an English schoolgirl's. He spoke and wrote well, was unfailingly polite, but at fourteen he gave no adult any hold over him. As soon as he was old enough, he went North and disappeared. His mother told me his whole life story and said, "After bringing up Lissa and Hale and Jack all right, what did I do wrong about him?"

I learned that economically secure parents could be more anxious about their children than those of the lowest economic grade. It might seem that high-school seniors in the "superior" group were in an assured position; they had brains, family support and a head start. It did not work that way. Those who could read rebelled; they were the first to feel the rhythm of a better world.

All were pleased to discover the weaknesses of American whites in history. They kept reminding their teachers of "The Trail of Tears" and the fate of Indians. It fortified everybody to read *The Scarlet Letter* and to realize that Puritans had thrown dissenters to the dogs. About Salem, they sighed with satisfaction, "Ah! I thought witchcraft was only for ignorant people." A boy would turn ugly about "America the Beautiful," —"I'll never, never sing it." A girl was more likely to say, "I'll sing it anyway. It's my country."

The gods gave a reprieve to children of harsher poverty and poorer schooling. Their worries still concerned meat, shoes, spelling and examinations. Going to high school was splendid, it gave them standing at home, in church and in their neighborhood. They could not read and write well enough to catch on to the subtle, but their minds had made their own discoveries, they could feel themselves growing. For a bit, they were on an elevation and the storm was withheld from them for a while. Perhaps they could not suffer the despair of the race beforehand, but had to wait till the door was slammed in their faces.

Better students could see that college was their one chance, yet even if they received a degree, their city was too small to give the one sure job, teaching, to everyone. The more they thought about barriers, the more unease and indignation invaded their final year. They had coasted happily through the earlier years. Suddenly they were almost grown up and needed more schooling and sure prospects of a job. Without the job, how could they meet marriage and the desire to help their parents? If they ever forgot their iron spikes some Pharisee came along and reminded them. I listened to several baccalaureate sermons based on the text, "Ye are bought with a price."

CLASS OF 1914

Berenice Castleton: seventeen-year-old Senior, upper class and caste, A student, Protestant Episcopalian.

Slender and pale, straight fair hair, green-blue eyes, look of weariness; lover of learning, omniverous reader, gifted in Math and Music; sarcastic and aloof from both races.

Before she had begun college, fell in love, married, husband became a college president.

When I saw her she had grown happy; devoted her time to college students, Open House, Sunday suppers, helping those of limited experience.

These one hundred former students had become average adults. All had work. Usually they had a mate and children. They had homes with fireplaces and treasures, living comforts and ambitions. Some of them asked me to guess how much money they had in the savings bank and then told me. Their youthful fears had gone; other fears had replaced them, but they appeared comfortably normal.

No one at all had gone bad. Two of the girls' husbands had skated on the thin edge, but their problems were concerned with property. Crimes against the person had not occurred; so far the wives had been able to hold them in check. Marriages had been on the same status level and children were carefully raised. Homes that I could remember as barrack-style in their parents' day had electricity, a bathroom, a clock, a radio, books and magazines and newspapers on the table. No one but the doctors had cars, but most had taken at least one trip to a big Northern city.

If I could have seen all of the alumni instead of only the two-thirds who remained in place, my outlook might be brighter. The death of the youthfully gifted was hard to forget. I had hounded them about buckling down to work, but now, every name crossed off my record book in blue pencil reminded me that it had not paid them to be superior. They might as well have been mediocre and stayed alive. I was given a second chance to judge the mediocre. How long would it take for them to replace the more sensitive who faded out and were replaced? I would have liked to know how far the mediocre advanced and when they became the leaders.

When I began teaching, the South had less than five thousand Negro high-school students and only 1,100 of them were in the Deep South. I sampled the education of nearly one-tenth of them. The small number in these schools was above the masses in achievement, but did not yet have a good education. Yet they were the carriers of racial hope. When I left in 1919, the AMA had flocks of high school students, but if Fisk University and Howard University were excluded, only about five hundred students had been in college. The first two had AMA appropriations only for special departments. Talladega was already a small college and the next one in line for concentrated development.

The degree of character and effort that went into earning and spending for higher education among these one hundred alumni spoke well for their homes, school, and church. Their teachers had given them materials and methods which enabled them to fit into occupations in their environment.

When it came to preparation for jobs outside of teaching and problems of health and well-being, the school had accomplished little. The older ways of the home and Southern traditions held sway. My onetime students were already afraid of the new—and they were only thirty-five. The period of apprehension—the point of high-school graduation—had so thoroughly vanished that some of them could hardly remember the time when it was a chasm.

The Landscape and the Voices 16

WHEN I LEFT New York on the late afternoon train I often went straight to Florida, then made brief stops along the coast to New Orleans; thence north to Jackson and across Mississippi to Meridian, finally to the web of schools in Alabama and Georgia. I worked on memoranda about the school I had just left, took pictures, made drawings of buildings and sketches of landscape and learned the indigenous flowers and trees. But most of all, I just looked out the window. I read little, I could never get enough of looking.

The Southern landscape made a deep mark upon me—more than the Rockies which do not speak of man, more than the desert, more than any American region except New England.

The railway maps were etched in my mind and I rode the long rails of the Southern, the Seaboard Air Line, the Cotton States Special, the Yazoo and Mississippi Valley, the Central of Georgia, the trains called "Shoofly," "The Owl," Number 14, Number 47. Bells clanged at junctions and brakemen called

Tupelo, Catawba, Palatka, Sylacauga, Mobile, and Spartanburg. Cut off from yesterday and from tomorrow, on board these malicious trains that left before dawn or after midnight, my sleeper rushed through the darkness and I thought, "This is now."

I arrived at and left hotels at all hours of the night. I put scores of Gideon Bibles into the top right-hand bureau drawers. I became a connoisseur of eggs, chicken, spoonbread, waiters, hackmen, and arguments about God and Daylight Saving Time. The race question was beyond me—I had no background for thinking about it. The South is bewitched land. It has always had the Klondike's power to take possession of people.

I felt a wild love for the landscape. After the New York rectangles, relaxation came in its curving lines, its tropical breath and its garden quality. I accepted without dispute its waste land and its desolation. Riding all day through swales of palmetto, I still watched as if every spike were the first arbutus. I became enmeshed with the looks of the earth, and the tawny rivers with Indian names became as memorable as the blue rivers I first knew.

The mountainy thickets and the great open spaces like the sea moved me more because I could communicate only with the landscape. I had no contacts with white people, and none with Negroes on this level. The grassy silence looked to me like the mind of man. Landscape alone explained items in the history, the occupations and castes, the economic status. The Old South spoke in those mangrove colonies where trees take root, spread, enlarge, replant themselves, take root again, until the dark and watery beginning becomes the solid shore.

A ride between walls of scented yellow jasmine on spring evenings goes a long way toward an understanding of Southern romanticism. The gun, the duel, chivalry, and the unwritten mottoes of men flourished here along dirt roads in the moonlight.

The Southern fiction was of the past and the Northern writers who wrote about the South were few. I put Dixon's *The Leopard's Spots* and Ray Stannard Baker's famous line, "The problem of the twentieth century is the problem of the color line," away together, and I began to read about the Civil War.

I had always known veterans in blue. On Peachtree Street in Atlanta on Confederate Memorial Day, I first saw veterans in gray. Standing among the graves of a Virginia churchyard that overlooks the battlefield of Bull Run, I became able to hear the guns. The Gettysburg battlefield where my ancestors fought for the North tore me both ways. At Washington and Lee University where Lee spent his last days, I saw him as the great figure my grandparents had shown me. I saw so many pictures of Traveller that I should have known him if I had met him on the road.

One of the soldiers of my family died in Andersonville. I had been taught that time forgives and I was astonished at the blistering inscriptions cut into ugly little Georgia monuments. In Montgomery on a hot spring day I shrank away from Northern tourists babbling about the Lost Cause. The horse in St. Gaudens "Sherman" on the 59th Street Plaza in New York offended me; his hoof was above the Southern pine.

The social panorama came alive in endless mansions, courthouses, churches, cabins, morning markets and Main Street Saturday nights, the orchid thrusts of the catalpa, the scent of chinaberry trees, the razorback's rooting nose, the smell of turpentine, the look of the pellagra patient, the skeletal lines of the malnourished, the man and the mule walking the red soil, the woman standing in the open door. Enigmas fluttered across every view at earth-level, man-level and church-spire-level, and the undercurrent sucked all of them into oblivion.

The impact of the area was still of a rural and small town atmosphere. Out in the brush, twenty miles from where the express train rocked through, the force of gravity bowed farm people toward the earth. The children making ready to be bowed in their turn walked eight miles a day to school, lunched on a cold biscuit, read haltingly with long pauses between the words. They knew how to keep out of the way of rattlers and alligators, danced like the burning bush and fled to the woods at the sight of a stranger.

Life stretched back into Richmond and Mobile and all the little cities named Rome and Athens before the War. I spent weekends in Birmingham, Atlanta, Jackson, New Orleans, Tampa, Savannah, Charleston, Nashville, and Norfolk, exploring historical sites and museums, walking through Negro neighborhoods, and attending their churches.

Negro business streets—with displays of goods, clothes, food, pawnshops, saloons, street hawkers and bands, the odd misspelling on the signs—were as foreign as streets in Chinatown. Toward dusk they echoed with the rough, plaintive, early blues of the lone singers. In the Yamacraw section of Savannah I met grown women with their heads tied in blue handkerchiefs who had never been outside the neighborhood.

In Memphis, not far from the levee, I remember in Hotel Gayoso, the murals of De Soto on the Mississippi; nearby a half-lighted street lined with little frame houses in the pattern of homes, an area of prostitution. In other cities I remember rows of such houses, one of them with girls of both races loafing on the piazzas, within two blocks of a large City Hospital.

Negroes in the largest cities had sometimes inherited property from free ancestors. It was said that 262,000 free Negroes lived in the South in 1860 and that they had a life of their own.

New Orleans Negroes still had it. The aristocratic tradition had taken them over bodily. French to the core, they looked down on robustness and on Mississippi and Alabama. Charleston Negro society, too, looked only into its own mirror. Grandparents had owned slaves, Sheraton and Hepplewhite furniture, heavy silver tea services from England carried on silver trays, portraits done by itinerant painters, gardens behind walls, lots in the cemetery for the fair-skinned caste. In a crumbling empire, descendants remained Royalists, holding to the forms: "No black teacher, no black friend, no black graveyard."

With the years, I saw the reverse of the slow, drowsy symmetry: illiteracy, child labor, tenancy, share-cropping, peonage, usury, malnutrition, tuberculosis, venereal disease, maternal mortality, boredom, and violence. As the boll weevil ate its way eastward, the empty cabins of migrants in the bottom lands stood with doors wide open. The peasant mentality in both races stood with arms akimbo, saying, "Man better not go foolin' with God's work."

The soft and smiling South was also as hard as nails. In my first year I heard that Georgia made a profit of $354,853 in 1907 on the leasing of her chain gangs. They stretched their blue and white cross-stripes across rock quarries and along the roads. The convict's leg dragged the ball and chain, the white guard with the gun kept an arsenal in his eyes.

Once I arrived at the Albany, Georgia, school the morning after a midnight lynching, when a man had been burned. During my years in Negro education more than seven hundred lynchings took place. From letters and talk I heard about thirty-two in the vicinity of AMA schools and churches:

ALABAMA ..... MOBILE, MONTGOMERY; ANNISTON, SELMA
FLORIDA ...... OCALA, "NEAR TAMPA"
GEORGIA ...... ALBANY, ATHENS, CUTHBERT, FORSYTH, FORT VALLEY, MACON, "NEAR SAVANNAH"; VALDOSTA, WAYCROSS
LOUISIANA .... NEW ORLEANS; NEW IBERIA
MISSISSIPPI ... JACKSON, MERIDIAN
TENNESSEE .... MEMPHIS, "NEAR MEMPHIS"

These cities were too large to be representative. Lynching was more likely to have taken place at the crossroads. Counting the places of the seven hundred deaths, I noticed six hundred hamlets so small that they would be known only in their own counties, or at most, their states.

In about two-thirds of the cases, the supposed cause was a murder or an attack on a woman. The remaining third were attributed to quarrels over property or a miscellany of accusations hard to prove: "alleged cattle-stealing, well-poisoning, robbery, killing a horse; being a desperado" and "enticing a servant."

I cannot find particulars of the Albany, Georgia, lynching I came upon, but it could have been similar to the one the late Walter White investigated in Georgia, his native state, in 1918. A Negro's gambling debt of $30 was paid by a white man and the gambler set out to work it off. Later the white man beat him. He resisted, killed the white man and wounded his wife. During a week's search for the criminal, the mob lynched nine Negroes.

One was a wife who insisted too loudly that her husband had nothing to do with the killing. She was pregnant, and the sight of the pregnancy inflamed the mob. She was hanged head downward as more convenient for the disembowelling. The corpse was later set on fire with gasoline. After this rehearsal of the dominant point of view, five hundred Negroes left the vicinity of Valdosta.

In the same year, a Mississippi lynching braided a malignant interlacing of five lives. Five days before Christmas, four Negro young people—a girl of fifteen, a boy of sixteen, and a young woman and man, each twenty—were lynched on suspicion of murdering a white man. Both the girls were said to be pregnant by the white; the young man of twenty wanted to marry the fifteen-year-old girl. The white man had warned the boy away from the scene of the dispute.

I heard old stories about lynchings from Negroes; perhaps they were already becoming myths. The NAACP Report of 1919, *Thirty Years of Lynching in the United States,* says that Georgia, Mississippi, Texas, Louisiana, and Alabama were the five first states in lynchings—1,680 people from 1889 to 1918.

Once a lynching happened, tales about it lasted. In any city where an AMA school or church was located lynching was always nearby. No year went by without my getting letters:

> *First they cut off his ears, then*
> *they cut off his fingers and*
> *sold them for charms*
>
> *they carved up his sexual organs,*
> *said they wanted them for love powders*
>
> *500 bullets fired into her body as it hung . . .*
> *chopped the tree to pieces to get souvenirs . . .*

These impacts from the morning mail gave me a lynching image. The body's tightening makes vision acute and in the fanciful landscape behind my eyes, I began to see the live oak bearing fruit.

Lynchings were done from bridges and from various trees, but I have thought most about those from the live oak. It is a monumental tree, slow-growing, long-living. South Carolina had the Washington oak, Georgia the Lanier oak, Louisiana the La Fitte oak, and the average city also had these members of the tree nobility, always green, with twisting branches in a great spread and roots to be imagined as spreading as far as the branches. Among the fine dark leaves I began to see the swaying body of the pregnant Mississippi woman, disembowelled and dishonored.

I had before felt the live oak as much a pledge of life as the stars. I imagine that the mob, too, carried these after-images, because hack drivers used to begin to tell the stories when they came in sight of the trees.

The Ivory Coast masks of the thirteenth century were made to answer ancestral terrors, but I felt their chill as contemporary. The Congo, Gabon, Sudan and Dahomey figures recalled some of my first impressions. The Benin masks of the fifteenth century made me recall how colored faces had looked before I could separate them as individuals.

When I was alone, the voices I heard in the lovely landscape were never the sounds of beseechment, but the raucous voices of dissent, the fox, the chase, and the riders.

Local politicians still had on the walls of their offices the intent and flaming face of John C. Calhoun. Calhoun's disciples were unceasing, going about turning the lower classes against the aristocracy, the uplands against the lowlands, the farmers against the merchants, the granite against the clay and sand. All these turnings were the second twist of the screw; the first was against Negroes.

The politicians who impressed me most painfully were Senator Benjamin Tillman of South Carolina and Senator James Kimble Vardaman of Mississippi. They were conspicuous for what colored people called "niggering among poor whites."

According to Hodding Carter in *The Angry Scar** Tillman was one of a family of seven sons, six of whom came to a violent end: the first died of fever, the second and third were killed in the War, the fourth and fifth were "killed in personal encounters"; the sixth killed a bystander in a gambling quarrel and went to jail for two years. The last—Benjamin—became the ranting fury who gripped South Carolina for twenty years. The Negro, Tillman preached, was not a man but an animal, a

* *Doubleday and Co.: Garden City, N. Y.*, 1959.

savage, the missing link, best off as a slave. His education would bring on race war. "If you want to rise, keep the nigger down." This "Pitchfork Ben" talk made him Governor. After he controlled state politics, he went on a Chautauqua circuit over the United States, talking about the missing link and saying that the 14th Amendment should be abolished and the 15th nullified. He addressed a Democratic National Convention and tried for the Presidential nomination.

Senator Vardaman did not rely entirely on the rabid tongue; he might have invented the Hollywood trappings. When the "Great White Chief" took to the open spaces of Mississippi, eight yokes of white oxen drew his eight-wheeled lumber wagon. The candidate wore white clothes and a white sombrero and his jet black hair hung to his shoulders. As Governor of Mississippi, he reduced Negro education to the vocational level and closed state schools.

The last time I saw the name Vardaman in print was when Faulkner gave it to the boy in shock in *As I Lay Dying*. Vardaman was the boy who struggled with the fish cut up into pieces of not-fish. He keeps saying, "My mother is a fish."

The rural poor of Senator Vardaman's state accounted for a vocabulary of contemptuous names: poor whites, white trash, rednecks, peckerwoods, whickerbills, barkeaters. Suffused with their alleged superiority over the Negro, they could be diverted from other issues.

The ravishers of politics were many. Senator Tom Watson of Georgia was once a Populist who urged unity among farmers and the Negro. He lived until 1922, too long for his liberalism. He became a turncoat. His newspaper defended lynching, railed against the Jew, the Roman Catholic, and the Negro. The Negroes called Georgia a benighted state in my earliest days, because, they said, the 1906 state elections led to the Atlanta race riot which lasted four days.

They also said they had not gotten over "Uncle Tom" and now here was "Cotton Tom." He was Senator Thomas Heflin of Alabama, an orator from the time he entered the House of Representatives. Governor Theodore Bilbo of Mississippi, later a Senator, centered his vilification on Negroes at the moment when Leonard Ayres of the Russell Sage Foundation ranked his state last in the nation in an educational survey. He lived into World War II and died while under Congressional investigation for anti-Negro campaigning and accepting bribes.

Negroes had bad luck even trying to read about politics. The only newspapers easily at hand were full of Tillman and Vardaman.

All kinds of people knew about contemporary gossip, but even the well-educated knew little about history. The early college had to stress subjects nearer at hand. They knew there had been slave rebellions but did not recognize the names of De Vesey and Nat Turner. The name of the politician who said, "As Governor, I would have led a mob to lynch . . ." was known but they ignored the views of Cable, Wade Hampton, and the best contemporary newspaper editors. They felt that no white could be believed—indeed, he might change his mind—therefore the whites were of no concern to Negroes. When I was pleased that the United States Supreme Court declared unconstitutional the "grandfather clause" in Southern state constitutions in 1915, they told me to wait and see. A new way of getting around the law would be found.

Jonathan Daniels said in *Tar Heels** that the Wilmington race riot which "choked the Cape Fear River with corpses" was the aftermath of an election year. Ten years after this riot, the consequences were still being brought home to me.

In the circles I knew, men appeared to have no thought of voting. They said that even if they paid the poll tax, they would be told they could not interpret the Constitution. If they attempted registration, they might lose their jobs. Everyone joked about an old man allowed to vote once by passing his ballot in a cleft stick up to a second story window. Afterward he said, "Seem like a vote change party goin' through the air."

The voteless produced their own politicians, for whom they had scurrilous proverbs: "Fattenin' hogs ain't in luck . . . Watch out, when you're gettin' all you want." The fattening ones were those who had gotten state or public school jobs through white politicians. Whenever men gossiped about how crooked these educators were, on the white man's behalf or the Negro's, it was

* *Dodd, Mead and Co.: New York,* 1941.

said that they were double-crossing both races. The state colleges were not in general favor yet, so the political spoon was stirred quietly.

An observer could see why Negroes never believed in justice before the law. Ordinary talk seethed with threats of reprisal against families, exportation to Africa, castration, whipping, death for subscribing to Negro literature, and the ugly practice of giving a mean Negro a couple of dollars to kill another, then handing him over to swing for it. Old laws no layman ever heard of could always be produced when they served a purpose.

If I explained that New England had these legal maneuvers, too—for instance about keeping the Sabbath—they reminded me of the law which allowed planters to add three-fifths of the slave population to the free population in order to determine Congressional representation. They said that even murder cases could be thrown out of court as not important enough for the cost of the trial.

The small-town white rich man who appeared to run everything had to know all the subterfuges, but unless he was disagreeable, he was a respected and popular tyrant. He owned the cotton gin, the turpentine works, the cotton and tobacco warehouses, the biggest general store. He sold plows, seeds, fertilizer, machinery, fencing, poultry and livestock feed, patent medicines, food and clothes on credit. He operated tenant farms taken in foreclosure. He was a director of the bank, an official of the school board; he knew his state's Senators, Representatives and Governors.

He lived in the best house, the white one with the coveted pillars and the paths outlined in boxwood around the specimen trees. I knew of one who was a deacon in the church and the director of the church choir. The young of his family were in evidence; sons and nephews were moving into control of the textile mill and setting up automobile agencies. The wives supported the country club; the daughters had to go to New York to the hairdresser's every two weeks. Because the setting was so small, this entrepreneur was seen easily. He has been repeatedly described in fiction.

The traveler, condemned to stay overnight in some hamlet at

a hotel—opposite the railway station—which had not changed the sheets since the last guest, could hear all the gossip about this richest man in the county. Men lined up in a row of rocking-chairs across the veranda below and argued about the steps of the rich man's development. As the evening grew late, they left him for religion, repeating the same sentence three times and beginning, "Now you take Ham." They often wound up with Noah, wondering why God had not taken care of the race problem in the Ark.

The Negro entrepreneur was beginning to rise. I knew one, the late Isaiah T. Montgomery, founder of the town of Mound Bayou, Mississippi. He was a tall man; in his seventies he still looked like a tree in its prime. He had not the look of an executive, certainly did not look like a businessman. Something else in him was behind his drive, he suggested the explorer.

Mr. Montgomery was born in 1847 as a slave of Joseph Davis, Jefferson Davis' brother. He was brought up on Hurricane Plantation. All his family were taught to read, and as a teenager he was taught accounting and kept the plantation accounts. As a youth he was valet and bodyguard to Jefferson Davis. He was in the War as a gunner's mate before he was seventeen and his ship was in the bombardment of Vicksburg.

After the War, the Montgomery family—father, sons and cousin—acquired Hurricane Plantation for $30,000. Their cotton won prizes, but legal restrictions caused them to lose the land. The Mississippi Black Code of 1865 imposed additional restrictions on Negroes. They had to hire out to former masters, to have licenses to trade, preach, and to carry arms; they could not rent or farm land except as they were chosen for that purpose, and loitering was grounds for arrest.

At first the Montgomerys tried to get around the legal fences by securing a substantial white protector, but they could not do anything to challenge the sophistic claims that Isaiah had been too young to sign the purchase papers. The Montgomerys took the money offered them and let go.

With his share of the money, his part ownership in a sawmill and his assets of experience, Mr. Montgomery bought many acres of swamp and marshland from the railroad and founded

Mound Bayou as an all-Negro town in 1887. When I asked him why, he said, "I wanted to make a place where Negroes would not have to get off the sidewalk for anybody."

The migrants who bought the land cut the logs for their cabins and the settlement grew. The founder and his cousin threw out buildings and projects rapidly: a commissary, a sawmill, a sorghum mill, a cotton gin, a dock, a warehouse, a lumberyard, a feed and fertilizer store; a school, a church, an assembly hall, a funeral parlor. The founder employed the first teacher of the public school and he guaranteed the salary of the first preacher. The cousin's wife complained that Isaiah always got the larger profit. He was reported to be the only Negro in the United States who could put down $50,000 in cash within the hour.

What I heard about his financial methods from people long gone was possibly not accurate. Commissary supplies were said to be marked up twenty per cent or more, in line with state practice for tenants. He was alleged to have asked fifty per cent interest on loans; he collected first mortgages; he leased state convicts at $15 per month.

He was the Mayor and chose the three aldermen. He named the colored deputy for the town and the county's white sheriff appointed him. He cut a deep groove. Settlers had to bring a marriage certificate. An unwed mother was banished with her illegitimate child. Gossip said that he called people down if they shopped out of town.

When I visited Mound Bayou it looked like any other little Mississippi town of about four thousand. It had the same Cherokee roses in flower and trash in the gutters—the beguilement of nature and the carelessness of man.

I stayed in Mr. Montgomery's house; perhaps it was also used as a guest house. I noticed that he delegated nothing. He escorted me to every schoolroom, every industry and, I think, to a bank. He sat beside me at every meal and he put me on the train. I met only his family and the school faculty. He was too experienced in life to give any hint that my visit might have some connection with the AMA school appropriation for the next year. He appeared to be completely indifferent to the practical and acted as if I were going to write a history.

He was an impressive and likable man. I wish that records

would permit the study of his complicated personality by a modern biographer. No Negro has been more thoroughly hated by Negroes since his death. I have heard the young say that he was a dictator who robbed the poor and who sold them out at the Mississippi Constitutional Convention of 1890, a meeting which disfranchised the Negro.

He was the only Negro delegate at that 1890 meeting. His explanation was that the Negro could not "fight a cyclone," so he voted with the whites. If he had not, the contemporary can understand that his horse might have come home riderless that night. His reasons for voting against his brethren would hardly have come from anything so easy to comprehend as fear. In addition to the problems of the environment, I think that fate cursed him. His superior mind knew that not too much progress could come in one generation. He was completely cynical about whites; perhaps he extended cynicism to inferiors and expected nothing.

His background gave him two hearts. The first heart, the original, was non-Negro and bore Jefferson Davis' name. Hurricane Plantation where he started out in life was an imperial vision of five thousand acres. The President of the Confederacy was the hero of his youth. The first time I met him in New York, he left the AMA office to go to call on the widowed Mrs. Davis. This was fifty years after the War.

Mound Bayou was only the second heart, smaller and meaner in blood supply. It began only when he was forty and had made his adjustment to what is thought of as reality. A town was an outlet for his indescribable air of command, it was where his height topped other men. But still it was a town of the poor who began by cutting trees for their log cabins.

If he had forebodings that there was nothing anywhere, they came true. The cousin who was his partner was murdered. His son-in-law was murdered. His daughter, who kept his home, was shot by a white sheriff.

These three brothers under the skin, Tillman, Vardaman and Montgomery, are not to be forgotten. Listening in other times and places for the warning rattles patterned after theirs, I have sometimes heard rattles when no snake was there.

I heard the Booker T. Washingtons of education, religion,

mathematics, and agriculture as they came along and I met the younger composers and social scientists. I listened to the latest esthete from Harvard, a boy hot with ambition to rewrite Negro history from its African origins. I held in my hand a piece of the last slave ship to enter Mobile harbor.

The print of old books ran through me and my fancy crossed the savannas and rode down the tropical rivers of Africa. Incantations and narrow paths came out of the distance and slipped into my awareness of American Negroes. I learned that when Stanley lost a man on the brink of a cataract, his bearers scattered and acted just as my children used to act when the weather turned cold.

The voices of the young Negro money-raisers who felt such righteous scorn of "Old Man I. T." of Mound Bayou were rising in solo and in chorus. Doubled up with laughter at the Old Marse tactics which worked as well in Vermont as they did before Southern legislatures, they said, "The bastard finally parted with $10,000, but I had to Old Marse him to the sky for it."

These up-and-coming young men were already permanently separated from the land. Simpler people were not; they turned back to the aboriginal comfort of the landscape before the eyes. They might be hostile to Southern whites but when the preacher prayed for "our Southland," murmurs of "Amen" came from all over the church. What they blessed was not man, but nature.

The land lay there, a pure marvel before the eyes. In the presence of the sun, the rivers and the ocean, the trees big enough to worship, and the small serenities of the honeysuckle, it must have been enough at times to live only in the eyes and in the senses.

The Negro was not long away from ancestors who felt a mystical bond with the land. When his hope in God and man was still in chains, nature must have been a fertilizing power of whatever he imagined to account for his life.

In the time of World War I, the Southern area which is neither forest nor prairie still carried in spots the untamed and limitless look. All its art from both races is formed in its brooding image.

The Rhythm of Death 17

BEFORE THE END of my first year and long before I had seen much of the landscape, I had some communication from the other world. I recognized here that death walked along with life.

In my New England background, death only looked for old people, about eighty-five; sheaves of wheat stood on their coffins. In California, the population was so young. I did not even know where the cemetery was. Now I was in this community where the young were the illustrious dead and the flowers on the coffin were roses. People talked as if death dropped from on High and nothing could be done about it.

People I had liked and been proud of were taken. A June graduate of my first school died before the end of summer and a classmate of his died within the year. A third boy died within two years. Two boys who died while working their way through college were the most brilliant and original students I ever taught; they went at seventeen and nineteen. Ivan Crawley of

Wilmington, and Crawford Wilson of Memphis; I resent it to this moment that these boys are only names on a page, forgotten as boys must be forgotten. Both died of public mischance before they were old enough to die of their own faults.

The younger died in a student rooming house where a defective gas-fitting asphyxiated him. An outcry followed, the Board of Health condemned, but the active mind, the good body and the satirical wit had already gone away. Ivan would have cited from the Book of Acts, "But I found that he had committed nothing worthy of death."

The older boy was, considering his age, a serious student of history. Crawford remarked in class once, "I think a *man* can do anything," and at another time, "I believe in the future; it may not be mine, but our moment is only a pencil mark on the ages. We have to help the world unfold." He went to Wilberforce University because it offered military training and he thought it the duty of every man to be able to bear arms for his country. He died of typhoid while on a summer job in a Southern city.

These two boys were not far enough along in life to feel certain about, but I had regarded them as my opportunity. I mourned for the men they had not yet become.

I have a long list of those I knew who died young before 1920. Going back to the same schools year after year, I used to miss both young children and young teachers. When I asked, I was told they were out in the cemetery on the hillside.

The living with whom one was trying to make an engagement always put themselves in the shadow of death. They said they would come, "If I live and nothing happen."

I supposed that the circle of little girls running and singing were playing "A Tiskit, a Taskit," but when I went nearer, the words were different:

Aunt Katie dead
Yes ma'am
Is you been to de buryin'?
Yes ma'am
Did you git some cake?
Yes ma'am
Did you git some coffee?
Yes ma'am

Did you git some tea?
Yes ma'am
De, shoo, ducky, shoo, don't come by me.

Ten-year-olds knew that people sat up all night with the coffin and they saw the teacup where their mothers hoarded the coins for the Bury League man. He came chatting to collect the fifty cents. This form of insurance then paid about $12.50 for a child under twelve; $15 for twelve-year-olds and up; for a wife, $25; $60 for a husband, a coffin and a stone.

When the young went on errands to the corner store after dusk, a death song might flash out like a firefly:

Now if I should die before my time should come,
I said, if I should die before my time should come,
I want you please to bury my body out on Highway 51.

Calling in homes, I discovered that illness and deaths were landmarks in the family history. They talked about them as whites talk about operations and trips to Europe. Very likely their attitude was shaped by tuberculosis. They predicted the inevitable as school children do winter cold. There were no reserves of food, clothes, blankets, fires, separate rooms. All the effort they could summon would be the doctor, the prescribed food, the living in the yard or on the porch. They never heard of any recoveries; the disease meant death. The prospects were part of what the late President of Fisk University, Charles Johnson, meant in saying, "Death is an index of cultural status."

A girl I remember as a pretty and frivolous student died of tuberculosis at twenty-two. She was a bride, entranced with her new husband and new house, but she gave up as soon as she began to cough. Her last weeks were in some apocalypse of her own where the walls were jasper, sapphire, emerald, topaz, and amethyst and where seven angels poured out of seven bowls the wrath of God.

The religious soaring of such invalids was the more important because they had the sick person's empty mind and so little to put into it: a small room, not too much light, no bright colors, books, music, or cards, and less than steady attention from the family because everyone had to be out working to meet the extra expenses of sickness and death.

The man had the harder lot. His life expectancy in 1910 was 35.6 years. The typical male was never to know wrinkles, gray hair, the slowing-down of age; probably never to know arthritis, cancer or heart trouble, never grandchildren. He was not to come into the stability of the male life pattern between thirty and thirty-five—the home, the vocational path, the life insurance, the swift motion and tall towers of the city.

The country man who was never going to be thirty-six was marked to stay in his groove. No clock, no property beyond what he could pile on a cart, no orientation in place except Downtown and the Beyond.

He could be split apart by those hostile dramas of rural life which appear from nowhere—a child of his neighborhood burned to death from crawling too near the fire; another fatally scalded from the wash kettle. A man died near him from lightning that pulled the bark off a pine from top to bottom, a second died from a scratch with a rusty nail, a third from snake bite. A woman sitting in a wagon in the churchyard had a hemorrhage over the wagon wheels; a family drowned when the river flooded the bottoms.

The white man who suffered these accidents in pioneer days had by 1910 gotten to where he could both deal with and explain the fatalities. The unfurnished mind still held them only as tenacious images. The Negro thought of death more often than he thought about slavery.

Young men often came down with a crash. A quiet and bookish former pupil came home from World War I to find that his parents, his sister, and his home were gone in a fire that happened while he was on the returning troopship. He had been a city boy, an A student, rather too trusting; he was in a strait jacket within a week. I know that the local facilities for the mentally disturbed were practically non-existent, but he died before he could be transferred to a Veterans' Hospital.

Two of my former students actually left Northern states where sanitarium care for tuberculosis should have been possible and came home to die. I went to see one of them, a white boy in looks, emaciated and sad, lying on the home porch in a deck chair. He coughed and said in his changed and husky voice, "I don't fit anywhere. Papa was at me and at me to take the porter's job in Mr. Jack's Drug Store, but I wouldn't. I told him when I cleaned floors it would be in some place where I could do something better sometime. Papa lets me alone now. He knows. I think all the time how Loreena can find somebody better."

Unless they had been very well educated, these boys would know little happiness. They had only rebuffs about jobs, therefore no prospect at all of being able to marry. After they realized they were stopped they were open to physical illness. When it came, they would not try but went down in quick collapse. I never knew until after he was dead that one of my pupils had an obsession about bullfighting. The bull took the place of man and the matador of fate; bulls were black, so he identified the Negro with the bull. Blackness had no chance.

Women took longer about dying. They had found out something about love and work and they were often happy for a little while.

When I went back to my own first school, the school beauty was already dead. They brought me two big-eyed babies to look at and the story of the long hours for the third birth and the caesarean that failed. There was no hospital; it could have been some general practitioner's first caesarean section.

The culture of the period had devised for the only unmarried daughter of a family a special vise of refinement, caste and idealism. Elizabeth Ann was the one girl in a family of boys, a fair and attractive girl, all frills and daintiness, the family treasure. She had an excellent mind, gentle manners, and a haunting contralto voice. She had to practice two hours a day and if she fell below A in a single school subject, the mother hurried to the school to find out why daughter was failing. A teacher could not argue when she said that her children had to get all A's. She was one of those women a colored man looks at and says, "Her tongue ain't got no Sunday."

As a young graduate, the girl began to teach in the country in a fury of enjoyment and devotion and did not fall in love until she was twenty-five. She applied herself to love with the impetus that delay had accumulated, but the mother began to disillusion her.

The suitor was "not balanced." No balanced man would leave college after two years to rove as a sailor. The daughter said it was because the sea called him, but the mother would not accept that. Any Negro should know he cannot work his way up on a ship, "must be lazy . . . slack moral fiber." The courtship ran swiftly from joy to pain and ended. The girl promptly came down with what a country doctor called "nervous prostration."

She was out of school lying around home for a year. When she re-entered, everything was as before until she fell in love for the second time. The new man had the prestige of the college degree and a proper job, but the mother began again, . . . "altogether too dark . . . your father and I lived in the ditch to get you children out of it . . . if you had dark children you would be there again." The man was offended and the engagement was broken.

A goitre at once developed. The girl's throat bulged. She could no longer sing, she had to visit from brother to brother in the North to get adequate medical skill. When the goitre was in abeyance she was warned never to experience excitement again. Therefore she was never able to teach, to sing or play the piano again, to love again. In the country where they were land poor, she turned to raising cotton. She liked being outdoors, she paid no attention to cautions, she worked in the field herself.

By then she must have been thirty. She was too tired to read at night and had few books and no access to a library. As she worked she brooded over the race question. Her illness and even her mother's dominance derived from problems originating deep in the past. Cotton-picking sent her imagination spinning, "I can see myself, just like the 1850 pictures in the history books." She never pinned her skirts up or tied up her curls in a bandanna; she said crossly, "That will be for later."

Soon she discovered that she had high blood pressure and had to give up the cotton. She had a high IQ, had no radio and grew tired of re-reading old text books. Very soon her pulse went up at every reminder of racial trouble. She enjoyed the character of old country neighbors but was aghast at their ignorance. When they said the Lord sent the boll weevil and that the spraying machines were of the Devil, she said nothing and went away, but her blood pressure reached 300 and she suffered from nosebleeds.

She became weary of hearing superstitions and said sharply

that if children stayed at home they would soon be no better than their parents. When she went downtown she discovered that white people irritated her with the same kind of shiftlessness. She hated the whole sharecropping business. Reading Harry Kroll's *The Cabin in the Cotton* about white tenants, she said it was also true for her people except that they were on a lower level; they would never dare to steal the owner's cotton.

Her heart beat so hard she had to keep still. Thin and stern she sat the day out on the piazza reading *Marcus Aurelius* and the *Confessions* of Saint Augustine, talking about getting really well and then getting away. Two years of this and she died of a coronary thrombosis, one of those maidens crossed in love imprisoned in Tennysonian poetry.

I knew another girl, pure African, who died of overwork and superstition. Matilda had earned a state teacher's certificate but her father made her put off using it. He set her to working the family farm and taking care of two sickly members of the family. It was a slaughtering decision. The mother died; the sister died; then, suddenly, the father. Five years had gone and she was alone in a house in the fields.

She now knew how to run the farm but did not have the strength. She was exhausted from grief, from loss of sleep, sitting up at night with the sick ones. She had no one to talk to. She went to the crops in the early morning when she could hardly stand.

She had had for a long time what they called "a touch of malaria." The calomel she took in the Little Giant Pills from the drug store left her feeling scoured and prostrated. She began to accept the belief of primitives that an individual succeeds to a dead person's place in the clan, his name and his soul.

Her dead wanted her soul. In the daytime, doors flew open and cold air swept through the rooms. At night, wraiths in vapory ovals looked in at the windows, swirled through the doors. Coming in from the field one day, Joseph's brethren were around the gate, quarreling about his coat. The disciple Peter lived under the persimmon tree, denying Him. A great figure of Christ on the cross appeared at the front door.

Callers who visited her went away saying she must have the

"yellow jaundice," the whites of her eyes were so yellow. As she progressed into mental depression, her neighbors grew afraid of her. She kept repeating and repeating that it would be better for Negroes never to hope. The illness ran into pneumonia. She died alone in the night, just after her twenty-fifth birthday.

Many of the boys who went to my school usually died of tuberculosis or of accidents. Girls had a larger range of diseases and longer periods of invalidism. They slid downhill first, innocently preparing for the actual break when illness came.

They were of good social status, but could find no way to express the uniqueness of their personality. Their work did not completely absorb them and they had no deep personal interests. They would never do anything anti-social, recoiled from "lowering the standard"; they would never take to drink, drugs, gambling, or any of the jet flights to oblivion. Violence was wrong, suicide was a sin; yet something inside them kept saying, "Nothing . . . nothing."

Such a girl was ashamed of racial exuberance and put up the bars of the intellectual life. By thirty, she was afraid to go downtown, afraid to stay in the house alone, afraid of the strange doctor and dentist, the train trip. Her delicacy avoided the automobile, the crowd, love, pain, new experience. She was vaguely interested in light men, but never in dark men; she was afraid of dark children. I sometimes thought that when she had been the eldest of six children, her biological impulses had been overcome by her long schooling in the care of children. She had already been through the washing and tending of the babies and the home pennypinching. Unless a man really cared for her, she cared nothing at all about any talk of "a home and protection."

The Southern reveries about chivalry and womanhood by now fitted her like a glove. Her parents had put her on a pedestal even more elevated than that of the white girls. For her, a whole new set of compulsions was devised: the money compulsion, the caste compulsion, and above everything, the family compulsion. A maiden of whatever age did not leave home except for school, teaching and visits to relatives. Every Sunday afternoon she stayed at home and sang:

My father's gone to glory
I want to go there too.

A good job and a summer holiday kept daughter reasonably contented under the tight rein but once something happened to her spinster's job, she declined rapidly. Insomnia began; she would lie awake until three o'clock in the morning. Eating grew finicky, nothing tasted good, she lost appetite and weight. Her stomach went on strike; sodamints, indigestion, "heartburn" and colitis. Medicine did no good; extreme fatigue. The family coaxed her into giving up the search for work for an interval.

Idleness brought brooding about the cause of her illness, worry about money. She dated events as "before" or "after" some peak of trouble, snubs that were forgotten came back to plague her. So little was left to hold onto. She began to think, "I have not succeeded; I am colored—I have to fail."

As she became too run-down to resist the first acute infection the psychic tension retreated. At the failing of the body, she relaxed in a kind of comfort. She became more religious and talked about "the promises." When the white neighbors sent custard and chicken broth, she knew what gifts of invalid food meant. In health, Negro and white rarely cross the barriers.

One lovely spring day I was sent to tell some bad news to the staff of a school on the theory that telling it face to face would be kinder than writing a letter. I succeeded only in being the messenger of a woman's death. I arrived just before dinner. The enormous spread and the air of festivity made me realize they thought the call was about something good, like a new building or more equipment. The ice cream nearly choked me and I could hardly get going when the faculty gathered around me in a circle in the living room afterwards.

I explained briefly the historic position of the Association, that its work was to proceed slowly to the point of supporting colleges only. Their school was to be turned over, plant and all, as a gift to their community and the signed agreement included a municipal guarantee that teachers continue at the same work and salary for two years. As soon as the younger teachers knew that their jobs were safe for two years and that the change was moving over the whole South, they seemed not to care. They asked me, in an objective way, about other schools being discontinued.

The principal had a different reaction; she was a childless widow, the priestess type, not really of any race or country or century. She had built up this Sahara and she regarded it as her life. In taking her school from her and giving it to the local barbarians her life had failed. Negroes always failed. Her life was gone. Only an hour away from the ice cream and the paper decorations, she was reduced to quoting from Handel's *Messiah* —"despised and rejected of men." When I left, she said, "This will be my death."

It was. She was not more than fifty years old, but the shock released some organic weakness and she died before the school opened in September.

The average Negro—even the below average—has performed a miracle of adaptation. The one who can thrive is a colossus, standing above ordinary men. I learned at great cost that the best minds were not necessarily colossal in matters of health. Many of the sick and the dead came from the highest level of scholastic ability; defeat went along with a sensitiveness that felt guilty for the race. When the dark cloud of trouble shut off a view of the horizon, they gave in. This group had fewer children; they saw their own lives ahead too clearly.

The grandparents had broken through with joy; they thought freedom was everything. The parents, making proportionate advance, were touched with skepticism. The grandchildren could not break through the vocational alienation in the dominant culture. When they felt unable to keep on transforming the meaning of their lives by shaping the future, a psychic failure opened in them comparable to suicide. I never knew anyone who committed suicide (the national total of sixteen thousand suicides a year would have seemed a sin to them), but I knew so many who went out with the tide. The lower economic group was not immune; illiterate adults slipped out of life so easily that I began to look with sympathy at bad behavior, anger, and fighting.

When a white Southerner quoted the Negro death rate as twice that of the white he went on to blame the Negroes for dying. The dying thought that death came from God and never even knew that contemptuous white talk was part of the corrosive that burned them.

My impression of the Negro's rhythm of death belongs to the dim past. It has only historical bearing now because today's patterns are so different and restrictions are much fewer. Medically, fifty years ago is like centuries. The doctor now knows more, the city knows more, and the family knows more. When a person could rarely act to correct his imbalance with the outer world, the twisting of the mind could turn into the twisting of the body and death.

The 1920 United States Census gave the Negro baby a life expectation of 45.3 years. In 1956, the forecast for a newborn white child was 70.2 years and for non-whites, 63.2 years. The Negro was still not going to collect much on his Social Security.

In periods of stress, such as during race riots, I used to think of the heart and lungs and blood vessels inside the colored body as rolling in waves of heavy colors—magenta to violet to purple to glossy black to mat black. The red and purple emanations were processional colors: harsh, obscure, creative. They meant the end of one movement and the beginning of another. Unless basic inner drives derived from a longing for life, the body could obstinately turn its great power into reverse. Death began to wash around the lungs, the liver, the stomach. The unhealthy environment favored defeat and disease took toll slowly, one organ at a time.

The Rhythm of Life 18

THE IMAGE OF WAVES rocking the heart and lungs toward illness and death went away from me all at once. Red to violet to bronze to black washed away before the sound of a trumpet. I never knew the name of the trumpeter in a Broadway theater who turned aside my melancholy about death in the race. His pure and soaring tone said that the colors of war and of mourning would move outside of the body into the arts.

The long delay in hearing the trumpet occurred because I was so absorbed in the spirituals. As a beginner among strangers I participated in the mood and belief of their musical achievement. I sang their songs with them, I collected the books of music and interpretation. Soon I traveled so much that I heard songs in the making by people who knew only the land.

The most primitive singers I heard were led by ministers at church and camp meetings. They lived in Mississippi and southeastern Georgia.

Across the South, as far as the Mississippi River, I knew the leaders engaged in the musical rediscovery, renewal and teaching. Most were in college music departments. Tougaloo College students outside of Jackson, Mississippi, had the home state in their voices. Fisk University, where the study of spirituals began, sang with marked devotion.

When I met a group of the earliest Fisk singers in Nashville, I found their pianist, Ella Shepherd, striking in the way Queen Mary was striking. She was the wife of the Reverend George W. Moore, Superintendent of Negro Congregational churches for the AMA. She was then in her sixties, tall and slender, dressed in smoky gray silk with touches of dark red velvet. She looked to be out of this world and was certainly of another century. The indefinable air of leisure and perfection and the lack of self-consciousness set her apart.

The subject matter of the songs was already familiar to Protestants, yet the music and imagery were sealed apart from whites with a sobering difference. It took a sixteenth or seventeenth century mind to think of:

Ain't no grave
That can hold my body down.

The twentieth century feels through its roots a bedazzled literary appreciation. Hearing the slave's suffering and release in "There is a balm in Gilead," the modern remembers John Donne's "Hymn to God the Father." He senses that today's versions of the spirituals as sung by gospel singers, folk singers, and night club entertainers are poor translations of the days of belief.

I never felt the blues as mine, as I had felt the spirituals. I never sang them and they did not represent my kind of blueness. I was not more than their delighted and impassioned observer. They told me much about Negro life in the music and about any life in the ideas.

Friends of my own age at once regarded my interest in the blues as a proof of alienation from their inmost feelings. To study the dregs of their race would in the end make me turn out like other white people; after seeing the racial bottomless pit, I would not care for them as persons. Girls would not have told their parents that I said the church music I had learned was almost too fragile for earth and that a student ought to hear the opposing earthy strain of the blues. They disliked the very word "earthy." To speak of "earthy" things was to confirm the opinion of the old people who said blues were devil songs, vagrant, disreputable, not-music.

I could never hear these songs adequately. Records were not made until 1920 and the John Hammond Concerts at Carnegie Hall took place even later. The night clubs where women sang were out of bounds, so what I heard first were the male voices singing in the streets.

I used to hear snatches of the blues in 1908—without knowing they were anything in particular. A young tenor voice floated in the darkness of spring evenings, singing:

Oh! that evenin' train goin' to wait for me

A lad walking by the Teachers' Home was worshipping his hero, the locomotive. He saw himself as a traveler and he had gotten as far as the names of crack trains—"The Flying Crow," "The Big 80," "The Dixie Flyer."

She whistle now,
She goin' to wait for me.

I supposed he was making it up as he went along, but such a fragment might have existed since the 1860's.

I responded to little bits of music because my father used to try to sing the sea chanteys and stevedore work songs he had heard in Europe, the Caribbean, and along the Atlantic Coast. He used to sing a child to sleep with a banjo nonsense song "Kimo-Ki-Mo":

Dar was a frog liv'd near a pool,
Sing-song Kitty, can't you ki me O!

He heard Florida stevedores load lumber to the tune and I only found out after his death that it was published before he was born in 1854.*

I was living in Memphis when I began to look forward expectantly to hearing the blues and it was before 1912, the year when James Weldon Johnson said they came to New York out of the South. A candidate for the mayoralty was running on a

* New Song Book. *George Christy and Woods: New York,* 1854.

clean-up-our-city program: E. R. Crump. He won and continued as a longtime boss of Memphis. During the campaign he employed W. C. Handy to station lively Negro bands on street corners all over town.

The prolific Handy wrote a new song—"Mr. Crump"—and his bands made people dance in the streets. The words were more or less lost in the dance steps, the street sounds and the crowds:

Mr. Crump won't 'low no easy riders here.
Mr. Crump won't 'low no easy riders here.
We don't care what Mr. Crump won't 'low
We goin' to bar'lhouse anyhow,
Mr. Crump can go catch himself some air.

It was said afterward that the song was written in 1909 and that only the guitarist sang this chorus. Publication was long delayed and when it came, "Mr. Crump" had new and unrelated verses and the title was "Memphis Blues."

The significance of blues in the beginning is that they started as black, the very blackest, and that they came from the poor. The songs join neatly with the contemporary, for they are usually songs of the self.

The confessions put on no front. No mention is made of nature, ideals, landscape, battle, children, Christmas, "Asleep in the Deep" and "The Lost Chord." Blues sigh with thought of sex, money, pork chops, and in a big way about travel.

They are short stories in music, told by one voice: "Give me back my used-to-be," a cry in the night, a plaint of homesickness, a train whistle, Mother, the memory of a woman's hair. The complaining voice of an anonymous human nightingale rises and falls. Men wandering in the open air or under the city lights were the usual composers and any stack of records is full of jealousy, women, gambling and hard luck. They sing, too, about the boss, the job, the tools, tombstones, and death.

Let the Midnight Special shine a light on me,
Oh, twenty long years in the penitentiary.

The light is the headlight of the engine which once a month brought the Midnight Special to the Parchman Penitentiary in

Mississippi. The prisoner is asking for a supernatural intercession. If the light shines on him, next day he will go free.

Country blues are about country subjects. A hunting dog is "treeing possums in the Promised Land." Scores of love songs show that "He sung this to let her go from his heart." He can let her go with repudiation. His Promised Land is Detroit:

When I start to makin' money, she don't need to come around
'Cause I don't want her now, Lord, I'm Detroit-bound.

Humor is a characteristic ending, always two-edged. Every laugh the singer turns on himself warns the listener; he, too, has got it coming—everyone is in the same fix.

The first explanation of blues I recall came from William Christopher Handy. He got his language from listening to stevedores and roustabouts, but when he composed, it was out of a formal musical education. He said that the usual song is a single verse in three four-bar lines, with the third and seventh notes flatted. The flatted sounds are the "blue" notes. Line one is the statement, line two repeats the statement with variations, and line three is the conclusion. The end is the punch line, the smasheroo.

As the songs passed from person to person, the rules changed. Blues could be of any length. The punch line is not inexorable, sometimes the story just dies away. The words alone will often not stand up to analysis. They require the voice. The singer will intercede with a guitar, or with silence, or movement in a way which compensates for difficulties in meter and rhyme.

The singing narrative sends pictures to the listener in a way hard to explain. The roughness in the voice has something to do with the intense visual images:

We gwine back
Gwine where the Southern cross the Dawg,
Cross de Yeller Dawg
Cross dat Yeller Dawg
Gwine where she . . . cross . . . dat . . . dawg.

"Yeller Dawg" is a picture of a place and a biography of a man. The place is where the Yazoo and Delta Railroad crosses the Southern Railway in Moorhead, Mississippi. Here, a little apart from the center of population—1,749 in 1950—the long shining tracks stretch out, the smokestacks stand tall above the rectangles, the pig roots, the yellow flowers grow out of the soot. If there be any humor, it is that a man is homesick for this place. The homesickness tells all about him, his looks, house, street, family, recreation, mind, and a spot which once made a child feel free.

Elements which remain fairly constant in the blues are the speech rhythms, the brevity, the liquid, succinct phrasing, the use of shock and irony, and the deliberate lack of organization. The singer likes the boy-meets-girl motive, but he goes from the situation to the solution; no conflict, no long build-up between.

If the girl longs for the man's hands around her throat, they may close there in strangulation:

High yeller, she'll kick you, that ain't all.
When you step out at night, 'nother mule in your stall.

The listener may settle down for the details in blues, but they never come. He expects a movement to stop, but it goes on. He hears a final bar coming, but the music stops short. He does not get the innuendo, the symbol, or the contradiction.

The leader of a work gang strings together a few words that have the right rhythm and his crew shouts back just one unrelated word:

Limber Jim
Shiloh!
Talk it again,
Shiloh!

The song is about as good as the singer and the best singer makes it new every time it is sung. The girls who first sang the blues did it as if they had instruments in their throats and their accompanists repeated on an instrument every tone of the voice.

The memorable voice has more than the normal overtones. It slides back and forth on either side of the gold wire of melody, shifting and undulating over a novel range. The aim is not for sweetness but rather the dark resentful notes of protest, the hoarse monologue, the guttural aside, the rasping conclusive shout.

Of living musicians who can show what the early methods were, I like best Louis Armstrong. His substantial person can almost disappear into his voice or his horn. His instrumental solos are another way of singing and he can improvise silence.

I never heard the blues discussed seriously in the South, except at Fisk University. None of the anonymous singers I heard were within miles of Huddie Ledbetter, the singer called Leadbelly, but they came out of the same life and the voices expressed this background.

Leadbelly was a lion useless in society. Alan Lomax called him "the Number One man in the Number One gang on the Number One prison farm in Texas." He was Herculean in strength, had extensive knowledge of all kinds of Negro songs, precise rhythm and the daring to make violent changes. The voice was one that comes only once in a long time. A wild rough quality of nature came out of it, the sound a rock makes as it breaks, the crackle of a tree being wrenched out of the ground. A span of man and of his history of musical development opens in his singing. The voice was all he had and I can still hear him:*

Take this hammer and carry it to the Captain,
Tell him I'm gone.

The blues are a little booklet of psalms about Negro life—full of information, delectably contemporary about Negro fancy, as reliable as any art. I already knew many of the sociological facts before I heard them. I valued blues as poetry.

They made whites think about the Negro and say, "This is he." Jazz, when it came, appealed eventually to critics and musicians who said, "This is music." The critical speculation about it in England, France and Germany has been about an art.

I did not try to play jazz, knowing in advance that I would sound white, and I disliked even the rendering of white dance bands. I had a desire to study it, as I had studied the classics.

I first heard jazz in funeral processions in the South. On the way to the graveyard, bands played slow heavy hymns in four-

* Leadbelly. *Folkways, FA2004.*

four time, perhaps, "Come, Ye Disconsolate." After the burial they marched back to town playing "Oh! Didn't He Ramble." Large city processions were spectacular and the open air and the mood of death made this music of body and nerves as easily accepted as a pastoral. It was said that Handy in his coffin was followed through Harlem by 150,000 people. At the very end of these male affairs were little boys running to keep up. When they got home they would find a pan for a drum and beat on it with chair rounds.

I could hear formal jazz only in New York. In Memphis and New Orleans, for instance, the places where it was played were considered disreputable and decadent by the Negro families I knew. I heard pianists and name bands of the early days in New York, but the first master of style I heard was Ferdinand ("Jelly Roll") Morton. Vaudeville was not the happiest place to study, because by the time a band got to be in commercial demand the director's most creative period might have passed. Or perhaps it was numbed by the volume and the clowning tricks he was urged into to hold a popular audience. The listener with the normal temperature of 98.6 thought that the jazzman's temperature must be 110, higher than the birds. The spectator was deafened and made motionless by the sound from the magnifying devices and the juggling and acrobatics thrown in. The Clef Club Concert in Carnegie Hall in 1912 had 125 in the orchestra and ten pianos. Pianists and violinists in the audience who really liked the horns and drums had to listen to them under great difficulties.

The succession of three cycles of music was entirely natural. The spirituals were exaltation, from the days that had to go beyond life. The blues were negation, refusal, turning away alone. Jazz was protest, a collective call in which the desire to affirm clashed with denial.

The performer was moored forever in some Basin Street of life, pinched at will by the closing hinges of segregation. The world was impenetrable.

When Sidney Bechet said "I play what I live," he was "playing" the hard life. The traveling players carried guns, yet might be lodged where guns were no novelty. They entered poorish hotels by the service entrance. On the street, both white and colored people insulted them, flung taunts about the immorality of jazz. Crusaders told them that it would cause insanity.

Eating and sleeping had to be at the convenience of music, travel, and their accommodations. They could not in my time sit downstairs to watch shows in the theater—not until 1927. Night club playing extended from nine in the evening to six in the morning. If they played vaudeville, it was five shows a day. If psychic wounds had shown on the skin they would have been stained as red as the seagulls dyed red in migration research along the Atlantic Coast.

The musicians left ordinary life and became birds on a flyway, night into day, train into home, riding, riding, living in sound and syncopation. Some of them died of it as soon as they stopped being young; at thirty-five, forty, forty-five they were gone.

Jazzmen adapted to their own purposes the technique the preacher used in getting responses from the congregation. They played along with different voices coming from all directions; they liked polyrhythm.

Outsiders had trouble with polyrhythm and also with the change in the accent of a beat, so that what is expected as strong comes out weak and vice versa. The syncopation which misses a beat was delightful to listeners who said they could not have invented it, but liked it when it was invented for them.

The splintering and crackling in jazz made me aware of mysteries in the musician's make-up. I liked best his inclination to improvise. Playing for fun, an orchestra would agree on a theme, a key and a tempo, then let everyone play in his own way; not so erratic as it sounds, they knew what to expect from each other. Further, the improvisation was like a dance. When it was over it was gone. The performer thus gained the upper hand over the composer; the ephemeral quality expressed the fatalism in the temperament.

They had tricks of the stripped-down style. Instead of the long drawn-out polishing before signing off, they would stop abruptly at the real end. They called this "keeping it cool," and someone called it "the pocket Hemingway." The players got it out of the same pocket in their temperament that produced the last line of the blues.

They were good at doing two things at once. They liked to play one part and sing another—playing the lead, they would sing bass; playing the alto, they would sing tenor. A player with two healthy arms was nicknamed "One-Arm" because he took a notion to cultivate all the importance in one hand.

Jazz always lay in enemy territory. The speed, the dissonance, the ear's disappointment at not hearing what it had anticipated had not yet had real criticism, only attacks. Musicians said, "It shakes but it does not flow." Negro intellectuals were reminded of Africa and "tribal accessories." Bands had not yet been invited on European tours. No one on the side of classical music would have been able to produce Leonard Bernstein's *What Is Jazz?**

This debated music explains a section of Negro life as well as X-rays. Revivals of historic jazz now are not performed in the way it was in the beginning. The early impact of savagery in the atmosphere cannot be recreated, where both the ear and the mind have grown able to accept a greater rebellion. Modern jazz has the feminine element and has grown polished and elusive.

The first I heard was hard, biting, rebellious, contemptuous, sardonic, and male only. Its expressionism was played in the spirit of a curse, the only curse I heard from Negroes except for that of voodoo. It was so smashingly male that I realized it was the first time I had heard the voice of Negro men, outside of teachers and preachers.

I had felt reassured about Negro women from the moment I met them in their homes. Men I had little hope for until I heard the young man on the trumpet. His was the voice of affirmation; he might have been the youth who jumped the fence in "Oklahoma!" singing "Oh! what a beautiful morning." He was as valid as his combative peers, a good mixture for any stage of evolution.

Religious energy had been the racial powerhouse for two generations. The blues and jazz would in time come to light in other vocations.

* *Columbia: CL919.*

Shadows Over Expression 19

AT THE TURN of the century the musician was the only artist who could more or less support himself among his own race. If he could not live on his earnings, he could drive a coal truck for self-support and let music determine his life direction.

The hardships of art were not a racial matter. Any artist had a hard time mastering the techniques and mustering the audience. White men had it hard, white women had it harder, Negro men had it hardest; colored women were hardly there at all.

Dancing, an impulse every child seemed to have in his body, was in an area of conflict as one of the church's extreme prohibitions. Cross your feet at a neighborhood party on a Saturday night and the church turned you out of membership on Sunday.

Parents bore down hard on dancing. The eighth-century Arab proverb, "If a Negro were falling from the skies he would keep time coming down," only irritated them; they said "H'm, bush-niggers!" Little boys went around whistling, clapping hands, shuffling to guitars on street corners, but a ten-year-old began to hear that no good could come of this; dancing led to liquor, fighting, razor blades. He was to stay away from temptation.

I never met a young woman who had been to dancing school or even had an interest in dancing. They laughed at the "marching" in some churches, but said their parents would be so much opposed to real dancing that it was not even worth thinking about. Mothers of my students used to tell me about country frolics when everyone brought food and drink, the fiddler played all night, and the set-caller sang out like a bugle:

If you like the way she look
Hand the lady your pocketbook.

After they were older and were church members, they did not go anymore, and in late years these parties had grown rough and were disapproved of in the very setting that bred them.

It was said in New Orleans that elements of African dances survived a long time and kept reappearing. The architect Latrobe had observed them in 1819, and George Washington Cable saw them in Congo Square as late as the 1880's. I thought fragments I saw in the backwoods might have African origin, but all that I saw in public before the 1920's were male solos or duos.

The actual status of the Negro dance up to 1919 would have looked quite different to a Negro dancer. I only knew it as an ordinary white person, having to see static repetition in vaudeville and restrained by the extreme disapproval of the Negroes I knew. They smelled brimstone around Small's Paradise and other New York night clubs. Vaudeville at the Palace or the Broadway Rialto was tap, soft shoe, acrobatic—whatever a comic and a straight man could devise. It was youthful, strong and hearty, very popular with white men. It has not changed greatly and may still be seen on television, sometimes performed by a crowd of boys and girls.

The boys I remember were giant zinnias in the bloom of their strength. The best of them had progressed to engagements at the Palace and it could be that their grit and endurance would have been equal to the Watusi ceremonial dances. I cannot remember names, but that may be because they had no publicity. They were not on the boards long enough to develop the style of Buck and Bubbles and Bill Robinson.

I never saw on the New York downtown stage any dance performed by a Negro man and woman except the cakewalk. I remember the cakewalk from very early days, probably as a part of a Broadway show.

The first version of a more romantic dance that I saw was in Gertrude Stein's *Four Saints in Three Acts*. Other Broadway producers, and perhaps the agents, thought the white audience would not identify with a waltz between a colored couple. The superlative ability of the couple might dash these commercial fears, but there was no way for a girl, and little more for a man, to achieve the accolade of "superlative."

Painting was another matter. I used to visit Harlem's five-story walk-ups—the halls lighted by 40-watt bulbs in the evening—to keep appointments with primitive painters. The strangers I met on the stairs reverentially helped me to find the apartment; they thought it was wonderful that anyone had heard that their neighbor painted. Everyone seemed to know that the painter who arrived was honored.

The first painter who leaped all the hurdles was Henry O. Tanner (1859–1937). Tanner was a painter of some distinction who went beyond the average in a risky occupation. I once listened in an adjoining room while a Negro couple bought a Picasso drawing, knowing that only a long-established museum would buy something from a Tanner exhibition on 57th Street.

Tanner's dilemma was that he was behind white taste but much ahead of the Negro pocketbook. A painter does not have to be a Negro to be faced with this dilemma. It screens him off from fame. No matter how articulate he is, when the right people do not see, it turns out like being dumb. The Negro artist knew that he had to please two races, the white first; if he did not, who would buy?

The large naturalistic canvases of religious subjects radiant with Tanner's vision are still in my mind's eye: "The Raising of Lazarus," "Christ and Nicodemus," "Two Disciples at the Tomb," "Sodom and Gomorrah," "Christ at the House of Mary and Martha." Not fully life-size, his paintings still gave the feeling of the living character. Line defined sharply. It was not like Eakins' line, but the clarity showed the early study with Eakins in Philadelphia. Later, when he studied with J. P. Laurens and Benjamin Constant in Paris, he was interested in the color blue used by the French. Colors were pale. His landscapes had an alien bloom that must have come from the space and air in Palestine. He made many trips to the Holy Land to get the right atmosphere.

Tanner's father was a bishop of the African Methodist Episcopal church in Pittsburgh. What a long time from the Sundays when a little boy learned about Nicodemus and Lazarus to the invitation to become a member of the Academy of Design when he was sixty-eight years old! It was late, but he was accepted by his guild. He is represented in the collections of the Metropolitan Museum of Art, the Pennsylvania Academy of Fine Arts, the Art Institute of Chicago, the Carnegie Institute of Pittsburgh, and he had also sold in Paris.

Tanner received from whites the recognition usual in his time. It might seem that he had no disadvantage of race. Perhaps not much, but the trend in painting made for a curious deflection. By the time he was in his prime, the people who came to look had no idea who Nicodemus was. The American fashion in painting had moved away from religion. Tanner was born in the year my mother was born. I know from what happened in her lifetime that the drift was toward other lines of exploration. Race had nothing to do with it. Any painter who chose a religious subject matter would have had slower recognition, fewer sales, fewer exhibitions.

The theater was usually on a street not far from the Negro district and when the Negro came to it he was old in acting experience. He began for the sake of his own skin, long before there could be other rewards.

The untutored made a profound study of the uses of the symbol and the mask. Indirection was healthy, so they polished it; they learned to look as if they had no concern with anything. They found symbols in sun, moon, wind, rain, trees, and water. They spoke truth from the mouth of a snake, a bird, a turtle, a fox, an opossum. The drama that is therapy and godsend was in the superstitions, wind-blown out of the depth that has invented wild religions.

The first drama library was made up of signs. The rabbit's foot was luck and the owl's hoot was death and the ground-up messes in the conjuror's packet held good and evil. All the superstitions were believed by someone and many of them are in their second century.

The Negro who threw a black cat's bones into a stream that flowed east and west, then picked out the one that flowed upstream and swore himself to the Devil upon it, was acting in a play. He could renew his fantasy, as children going to sleep make dreams, by feeling the bone in his pocket. He carried his psychoanalytic couch with him.

When he reached the commercial stage and was applauded as hilarious, his mask of happiness was his triumph. Sometimes false and sometimes true, it was a disguise. When it was true, he was just enjoying being alive. When it was false, it was one front stronger than a coat of mail. This front was to make him bushels of money later from the laughing audience which never knows that comics are first of all sad.

The names of historic actors like Ira Aldridge exist in the records of all large "theater" cities. "Hamlet" readings used to be recreation; there were always fun-makers. Dion Boucicault's "The Octoroon" was the hit of New York in 1859–60.

From the time I began to go to the New York theater I seem to remember Negroes doing slapstick. Imitators of Williams and Walker were countless, even after Walker was gone and people out of homesickness went to see Williams playing in Ziegfeld's Follies downtown. They put on blackface and white gloves and they liked to burlesque a white actor impersonating a Negro and singing "Jump Jim Crow."

These acts run together in my mind as funny, agile, penetrating, rough, no holds barred, giving bad impressions of the race. The Irishmen who alternated with them mutilated the image of the Irish and the Jews who followed left nothing to chance about Jews.

I hardly knew the names of these men unless they were on the way to becoming legends. Sam Lucas was known because he wore diamonds that could be pawned when the road show folded. He lasted on into the movies and was playing Uncle

Tom in the first screening of *Uncle Tom's Cabin.* When he jumped into the cold water to save Little Eva, he was seventy-five years old, but he refused to use a stand-in.

I went to Harlem to see "Darktown Follies" in 1913, a bit so good that Ziegfeld bought songs from it. But the first serious play with Negro actors that I saw was on Broadway and got there by means of a white playwright and producer. The program consisted of three one-act plays, so closely linked that they made a unity; the playwright was the poet Ridgely Torrence, the settings were by Robert Edmond Jones, there was a singing orchestra, the year was 1917. Considering the anguish of getting anything about a minority onto the stage, the one-act plays were a good try and still have life. Mr. Torrence was a poet of authentic vision. He once telephoned me about the AMA work with both Negroes and Indians, saying that he was trying to get at the essence of these groups.

When the curtain went up on "The Rider of Dreams" a worn mother was ironing and teaching her boy the catechism. Soon the wayward husband and father returned. He had lost the $800 to make a down payment on a home, and returned with only a guitar, having been cheated by the white man.

"Granny Maumee," the next play, moved through youthful love, the rigid old, the unwanted baby of mixed blood, and the voodoo act. In the last, "Simon the Cyrenian," the hero put on the robe that fell from the shoulders of Jesus of Nazareth and picked up both the Cross and the crown of thorns: "I will wear this, I will bear this, until He comes into His own."

Torrence represented a junction between the past and the future. The insistence on Negro actors must have been his. The actors were veterans of Small's Paradise, night clubs and vaudeville; the man who played Barabbas was from the Williams and Walker entourage.

Unless there is something in the forgotten layers of the past, these three plays were the first of the theater to receive full critical attention from the press. They brought the same sort of excitement generated by Tennessee Williams' "The Glass Menagerie" and Edward Albee's "The Zoo Story." Just as the Torrence company was settled for a long run, everything on

Broadway crashed with the United States' declaration of war upon Germany.

In only two years more, Charles Gilpin created the role of the Negro preacher in Drinkwater's "Abraham Lincoln." His acting bettered the playwright's words and stilled any anxieties about the quality of Negro actors. His acting in "Emperor Jones" a few years later marked the first time I had seen a Negro actor transcend race. While he was lost in the forest, wandering, bumping into trees, crying his aims, every soul in his white audience could feel that his life, too, had its forest, he too was a wanderer under pursuit. He too was marked for the silver bullet.

Hardly anyone I knew had seen a picture by Tanner or a Negro play, but all had contacts with books and with what writers said.

When William Dean Howells wrote the Introduction to Paul Laurence Dunbar's *Lyrics of Lowly Life*, in about 1895, he said, ". . . the first instance of an American Negro who had evinced innate distinction in literature." This was true, but Dunbar was pitiable prey to the moral impulses of some of his readers. I knew women who thought that poetry was verses on calendars, who would never have opened his books except that they had heard he was famous. They begrudged his drinking and dying at thirty-four; they hated the dialect. Told that Dunbar did not want to write dialect but was urged into it by his editor, they said he should have broken rock instead. "He haven't measure up." The woman who said this to me was a widow who had said at other times, "My work is done; I have made one girl a teacher and one a dressmaker."

I suppose Dunbar was writing for her grandchildren; my children were thirsty for him. He was the only lilting voice in their heritage. He was printed in "white" magazines; they imagined he was very rich, and he had been alive in their time, until 1906. A boy, told that he should walk with more sobriety, replied that he was hearing Dunbar's "Angelina" in his mind:

An' you couldn't hep from dancin' if you feet was boun' wif twine,
When Angelina Johnson comes a-swingin' down the line.

Within the cloisters of resentment, the upper class preferred Claude McKay in poetry:

> *If we must die let it be not like sheep . . .*
> *What though before us lies the open grave?*

They flared up every time they remembered that the first Negro poet of the contemporary wrote in dialect.

I did not for several years have access to Frederick Douglass' *Autobiography* written in 1845 or what Alexander Crummel had to say in *The Future of Africa* in 1862. When I asked for books about Negroes by Negroes, I could carry them all under one arm. Five: Booker T. Washington's *Up from Slavery* (1901), and *Life of Frederick Douglass* (1907); Dunbar's *Lyrics of Sunshine and Shadow* (1905); W. E. B. Du Bois, *The Souls of Black Folk* (1903); and Charles W. Chesnutt, *The Conjure Woman* (1899).

Many Negroes could write one book. The last three were real writers, but, as it turned out, life would not let them write. Du Bois had the most adequate academic preparation of his day; he was a graduate of Harvard and earned his Doctor of Philosophy degree there. He expressed upper-class feelings and overnight became the leader of those who could not accept Booker T. Washington as destiny.

When he and his wife were in a carriage following the hearse of their first son to an Atlanta cemetery, he heard white bystanders exclaim "Niggers!" It seemed a reason for not following the imagination in novels. He had been a sociologist; he became editor, founder, reformer, man permanently at war with the world. He died a Communist, organizing the library in Ghana, in 1963.

I felt an incensed sympathy with Chesnutt. He was a white man in appearance, brought up in North Carolina. When he published his first book of short stories he had already been a member of the Ohio Bar for twelve years. They were only tales of reminiscence, but they received attention. Not enough to impress readers of either race, but 1899 had no precedent. Perhaps he gave up fiction because he had separated himself from the South which stimulated him; he retreated to sociology, biography, and essays in the twenty-seven years left before he died.

Slowly I found a few others. James Weldon Johnson made a sensation with *The Autobiography of an Ex-Colored Man* in 1912. William Stanley Braithwaite published an annual *Anthology of Magazine Verse and Year Book of American Poetry* from about 1913. He was a Harvard graduate who must have known in advance that it would be hard to produce a whole book in hardcovers from the yearly poetry crop. It probably meant something to Robert Frost and Edgar Lee Masters when he said in 1915 that *North of Boston* and *A Spoon River Anthology* were the most important additions to American poetry of the year.

In this early stage, no Negro could begin to write seriously until he got away from the South. This was not a race problem but a writing problem. Their region had not enough February; life could go on outdoors, the vegetation provided instant aesthetic satisfaction, there were the interruptions of kinfolk and the public lack of respect for writing.

A white writer knew he had to fight reader inertia every time he did more than retell *Cinderella*, but the Negro man had to sell a black Cinderella with two stepmothers and ten sisters. No wonder he had to be above average even to get into the competition.

As soon as any young person admitted that he was trying to write a work of the imagination, his neighbors deafened him with their cries. He must get down to work—useful work for the race: journalism, protests, attacks, defense, speeches, committees, chairmanships, propaganda. They could rout him; he took their kind of job or he went away, certainly to the North, and perhaps eventually to France.

The Negro rituals showed a sensitiveness to artistic structure, but before 1919, thought would hardly have turned to architecture and sculpture. The media were too expensive and the ways to get into them were not open. I know of only one boy who became an architect; he was graduated from one of our rural high schools and earned a degree in architecture at Cornell.

I knew of just one primitive sculptor who introduced himself to Biblical figures in stone after he had learned how to carve gravestones. The art form closest to sculpture was iron work. One school had two craftsmen who were able to make the great iron campus gates. They had no real instruction in design, but I think they could have copied the New Orleans balconies.

At this distance it seems a trifle strange that I could have been so influenced by the sound of a trumpet. Probably it was because I was listening so hard. I knew perfectly well the diversified vocational balance of Negro society and that achievement in the arts was to be delayed a long time. Women were still in the home or the schoolroom. A look with half an eye would show that music, dance, and the theater attracted too many men who were not strong enough, educated enough, or talented enough to go on after thirty. The arts often led to streets marked "dead end."

And yet, I could find no other real outlets for initiative and originality, except those dependent on lengthy and expensive education or training. Arts were the tunnel under the river, the short cut to the emergence of the Negro's personality, no matter how many fell by the way. In proportion, as he emerged through the arts, his children might emerge in other occupations.

At the moment, he was edged out of trades as the whites needed jobs. Business required capital investment and so did any substantial farming. Clerical work, transportation, engineering, science, newspaper editing and reporting, sports, salesmanship, advertising, publicity, State and Federal offices—I knew white men in all such vocations, but the only Negroes were science teachers and railway porters and there were a great many more porters than scientists.

The male potential could not be judged on the evidence of a few professional men and farmers. The observer had to look at common labor. The future often lay quietly in a man's muscles. The fellow who could tear out a jail door with a few jerks or row a week on the Mississippi in flood might be the man with a message. The very violence of his life pattern was a promise that something would come.

Time makes it clear to me that my intense interest in the Negro's opportunity for expression in the arts did not come entirely from him or from me. It came out of the stirring of the New York City environment rather than that of the South.

The newish and more expansive approach to the social

sciences and the arts for which the United States was known in the 1920's was already beginning piecemeal in the New York area by 1910. It shook the young who were cloyed with the rigidity of the academy and the sweetness of popular art. I was accessible to the new, especially in visual arts and social change; I knew Lewis Mumford, Herbert Croly, and Alfred Stieglitz; as part of my graduate work I wrote about Le Corbusier.

The New York Armory Show of 1913 influenced my way of seeing. The total impression was a massive force, but I imagine that Matisse alone could have given me new eyes. It sounds unreasonable to attribute influence to a different way of painting flowers, interiors, odalisques, and sun on leaves, but the witness to Matisse's power is found in the effigy which was burned for his deviation from the norm when the Armory Show reached Chicago.

It was from the Armory visits that I began to see Negroes objectively as form, dissociated from race, history and cultures, and beautiful in the same proportion as the rest of us.

This way of seeing was uncommon in 1913. I have known Negro women who said they minded their looks more than any other burden they bore. I know white men and women who had spent a lifetime among them, who would have died for them as a matter of principle, yet called them "an ugly race."

Dr. Franz Boas thought they were beautiful; so did various artists. Our faculties did not include artists, and academic people did not possess the ability to see more than a stereotype. They always looked puzzled and began, "Well, I have known beautiful characters."

The concept of ugliness was a part of the times and the fashion, now long gone. New Englanders left home calling any opposite to their Greek ideals of beauty "ugly." Besides, their piety was always looking for the soul and for that they looked at the face alone. The body might better be inconspicuous, wooden. A fluid body like the Negro's indicated lack of self-control; it should be stiffer, nearer the norm.

It should be remembered in their favor that they were not far from the time when Sumner, Parker, and Howe risked their lives walking the streets of Boston with Frederick Douglass. They shook hands with Douglass and they walked with him but their wives were afraid of the gun at some upstairs window, the ruffian around the next corner.

People who were aliens defying a taboo must have felt it safer to approve the aesthetic of the dominant culture and think the subdominant ugly; tradition was a heavy burden.

My Negro friends understood well enough the difficulties of the Negro artist—they were near enough to artistic experience to know through their own knowledge. They were more conservative about racial beauty than whites and a long way from understanding Matisse. Their recoil was due perhaps to their dislike of every contact with Africa. They needed more time, but they did not live long enough to come to any different realization.

Man, Woman and Child

MUSIC WAS JOY and weapon but a good life was the greatest work of art. I have had three close friends among Negroes and each of them was good enough to make me trust the millions.

The first was the musician I met in my first year, a frail and delicate girl, bitter and laughing. She died young.

The other two were husband and wife transplanted from the Deep South. I met the wife there when we were both twenty-three, and the husband after their marriage. Our acquaintance lasted through the four seasons of fifty years: work, wars, race riots; the birth, schooling and marriage of children; the illness and death of parents; the grandchildren. We shared the new artistic strength of the 1920's, we were subversive together about the preachers, sociologists, and writers who made their way by publicity, the saxophone, and the lion skin. When they took the varnish off colored fakers, I supplied the names of the equivalent Great White Pretenders. We relied on each other.

My lifelong friends were remarkably objective—not for Negroes, for anybody. They never spoke of a personal racial cross and they looked at the color line in the perspective of time and economic evolution. I believe that, as much as reasonable people can, they liked their lot and believed in the eventual fulfillment of all Americans. They never acted as if they had a burden and when my friend's favorite spiritual was sung at her funeral, I assumed that it was because of the mountains of mortality that it was "We Shall Walk in the Valley of Peace."

Both died in New York City and when I came out of the church and stood watching the second coffin set out in the rain, I thought that they were angel messengers of the long future and that the part of me which had really known Negroes was gone.

I knew the first two college generations after Emancipation. The first was just going offstage and the second was in its prime. One person cannot really express a generation, but I cling to likenesses of a woman I met only twice who can stand for the striving first generation and a man who represents the successful second.

The woman comes first because the matriarch made the trail. The prominent example of the period would be Mary Church Terrell or Mary McLeod Bethune, but the average was the homemaker, loving and good, with little reach beyond teaching and maternity. She is entirely unknown except as her children have called her blessed.

The woman of the first generation, born between 1860 and 1865, was a singer. I heard her voice above the rest in a Big Meeting when I was hoping to find new music far from the railroad. It was during World War I and the congregation was singing "Stay in the Field." Voices slow, heavy, and strong, chanted over and over, "Stay in the field, stay in the field, stay in the field, until the War is ended." Suddenly a soprano raised the solo:

Green trees burning, why not the dry?
Till the War is ended.

This was a magnetic voice. The forest fire leaped from tree to tree within the meetinghouse and the old bowed in lament for the lost young.

She did not sing again until the evening ended with "Were you there when they crucified my Lord?" This spiritual as it is sung on the radio conveys a smoothed-out reverence of two verses, adapted to the ease of Sunday afternoon. The full narrative, sung by believers, never evades. The listener drops back to Golgotha. "They nailed Him to the tree . . . they pierced Him in the side . . . the sun refused to shine."

The grieving roughness of male voices brought down the darkness. A keening shriek from the sopranos tore the darkness open and lit up the three crosses. The watchers wailed. "Oh! sometimes, it causes me to tremble, tremble, tremble." The chorus let go quickly but the voice I was following held on in anguish. Slowly and terribly from *d* to high *g*, receding to e and *d* again, it foretold the irrevocable.

She was a tall woman with black curling hair in long loose waves, dusky skin, thin lips, heavy black brows, and thick lashes over gray eyes. She looked worn, but serene and eager; the revenant's look artists search for when they want joy and sorrow in one face.

She was a minister's wife and had come to the Big Meeting because her husband was giving a talk about wartime farming. Their parish was away back in the woods and if I came by there I would hear music that never reached the outside world.

The six o'clock morning train in that direction ran back into the hills until it lost itself. When it jounced to the wayside stop, I got off where the land stretched out as an approach to the sun, the sky a fierce apricot and the earth a truculent terra cotta. The old horse and buggy sidled away by roads where wayside flowers bloomed with no one to see them. Five miles and we came to the little church, the schoolhouse and parsonage in a pine grove. Children with books were milling around in the yard.

My hostess was born either in slavery or just afterward. She was brought up on a plantation and played every day with her white half-sisters. They went to college and she worked her way through a Negro institution.

When she was young, she was one of the Fisk University Jubilee Singers on the money-raising tours. She remembered bits of Europe, singing before royalty, London street scenes, Trafalgar Square, St. Martin's-in-the-Field, the British flag flying, the crowded concert halls.

During the London Concert Series, bouquets of red roses began to come to her every night. The roses followed her on the tour of the provinces and in London again she met the donor who sat in the same seat every night. He called on her, but she never went anywhere with him. He made her a written proposal of marriage. Later she said to me, "I was so excited with being in another country, that his proposal was no stranger than anything else." She told the Englishman that he did not understand the racial situation and that she already had an understanding with a schoolmate.

She came home and married her college beau and they had spent their wedded life moving from one little church and school to another, usually at the crossroads, always teaching, preaching and farming. They chose the country life because, after a fall, the husband had developed a crippling arthritis. They thought he could always preach to farmers whether able to stand or not.

They had had three little boys, named for the husband and for both their fathers; a childhood epidemic had taken them all over a weekend. The two daughters were already in college, working their way.

Dressed in their plain black, the husband and wife had already come to look alike. The little house had crepe myrtles outside the door; inside were books and easy chairs before the fireplace. The income must have been about $500 a year, plus the use of the house and land. They kept pigs and poultry and ate largely from the garden. Money was for the daughters' education, the doctor and the oculist; they could not afford the dentist and their teeth were going. Neither had ever had the conveniences of living, so they went on lifting and tugging at water and earth without knowing anything different.

The parish was scattered over the county. People drove in buggies and carts, rode muleback and walked up to eight miles to come to church. The parsonage was the first-aid station for all ills, from pneumonia to being crushed under a falling tree, from mental illness to the boll weevil.

The schoolchildren were their second family. The star was a boy who had gotten through medical school and was a doctor. Even to each other, they called him "Doctor John." They had worried over a fat rebellious girl who used to say, "Don't call me dear, call me Devil," but her stubbornness had taken her through nurses' training at Freedmen's Hospital in Washington.

The wife spent her time tutoring and patching up youngsters. It took her a year to stabilize a girl of ten who had been bribed into a raping to get a doll. It was her first doll, a store doll with real hair and afterward she had thrown it into the waterbarrel and said she wished the whole world would drown.

In the deep country I picked up from old people a few songs I had never heard before. Daddy Cudjo was said to be nearly a hundred years old; he could remember his African boyhood and his capture at the beach. He sang songs from Africa and he said, "I hates pay fi' cents for a banana." When he lifted "Poor old Laz'rus, poor as I, when he died had a home on high," all the crowd standing around would go on indefinitely, making up new verses.

The wife taught hymns and songs just by singing them. The congregation could not read much, but readily learned by heart. They liked "Religion is a blooming rose" and insinuations like:

You see that sister dressed so fine
She ain't got Jesus on her mind.

I asked her how she had found her "vocation." In college, both she and her husband had known a young man who was their ideal; he had graduated from Harvard before the Civil War. In a crisis, they asked each other, "What would Dr. X do?"

Then she had the racial heritage. She knew a girl who, as a baby, was the inspiration for "Swing Low, Sweet Chariot." Her mother, a slave of the 1850's, was about to be sold down the river, away from her baby. She wandered blindly up and down the river bank, clutching the child and thinking about jumping off the cliff. Some old Aunt Jane read her thoughts and said, "Don't you do it . . . Wait . . . Wait . . . Let the chariot of the Lord swing low and let me read the scroll . . . God's got a great work for this baby to do . . . Don't you cut her off."

After the sale, the mother kept recalling the time on the cliff when she still had her child and made a song to the rhythm of the slow walking. As it passed from voice to voice, the song became the present "Swing Low." The baby lived to be a musician who collected spirituals and when my singer closed her eyes and sang, "If you get there, before I do," images of her ancestors mingled with thoughts of salvation.

It is a comment on all red roses that this aging woman could say, "I can't say I would want to trade places with anybody. . . . My husband is my great love. He is a good man and I can be proud of him. . . . I mourn about the boys but our daughters are all we could ask for."

She showed no race consciousness and I think she had come to love the world as she knew it. When I sent this couple a box of books, including those of young Negro writers they would not have had a chance to read, Harlem was foreign to them; they read *Walden* aloud and she preferred Undset's *Kristin Lavransdatter*.

She died when she was about sixty; mature, physically defeated and hopeful. She had beauty to lose. While she was talking to me, the firelight threw shadows over what had once been a girl's beauty and was now a great face. No one need think it costs a woman nothing to look old too soon. Take away her teeth and give her only two or three black dresses and she is of the past.

I regret that poverty kept her living in the nineteenth century, though when she died the twentieth was a quarter gone. She surmounted the problems of race but was shattered by the medical problems of time and place. The sons died of diphtheria before the days of antitoxin. The husband had the kind of arthritis from which the patient does not for a long time either recover or die, but only progresses toward the wheel chair.

She had a glorious voice—not just a good voice but possibly the true potential of a singer. She was very feminine in the ancient way, and she accepted the restraints the culture put upon her and made her life the melody.

Those women who lived only for others and lasted only so long as a green tree are old-fashioned now but their descendants in the arts and professions often show that plus-quality that likes to perform more than is required.

I never accepted the stricture that Negro men were in the habit of deserting and leaving their families. This applied only to the lowest group. "He taken his foot in his hand; he gone." The men I knew personally were as stable as any Americans of their kind. They were chiefly educators and I associated them with their occupation and not with their color.

I can remember forty Negro men: twelve were principals of high schools, eleven were deans, treasurers, or professors in the college departments of economics, sociology, history, education, Latin and music; eight were Congregational ministers; three each were high-school teachers and businessmen; one each was a doctor, an executive, a Pullman porter and an office porter. Their average age would have been about forty. Eleven were so fair they could have passed for white, eleven were of full African blood. All except the two porters were college graduates, two had earned the Doctor of Philosophy degree, one the M.D.; several had the Bachelor of Divinity degree, earned after college. The executive and the musician were well-known. Considering the time, one of the businessmen had made a great deal of money. The office porter was trusted to carry large sums to the bank for forty years.

All of the thirty-six who were married had the wives they started out with, with the exception of the two individuals at the top and bottom of the earning level. The executive was divorced and remarried; the office porter had "just walked out on her" and returned to live with his sister. They averaged about three children and the children were likely to be named for grandparents. The dream of all these men was the higher education of the children. Before World War I, a man in Georgia used to write to me about his son's marks at Harvard. Dean Briggs' letters which he showed me were almost sacred to him.

One of the forty told me that he could remember his father standing at a window with a shotgun to protect their home which was in the path of a rioting mob. I asked him then if he had ever wanted to be white. He said, "No, I haven't, and I have wondered at times ever since I was a boy, why not. It must be there's something in my Negro identity I can't give up. In late years, I have realized that I am just an ordinary man. If I were white, I might have been just another high-school principal. As a Negro principal, I have had to get big enough to understand tragedy. This is something I would never want to give up."

Another, who had three thousand books around his cabin walls, told me that he was an unfaithful servant, trying to get strong enough to do right. He preached God and farming. He had the history of every farm in the area at his tongue's end; he had improved both crops and livestock. His weakness was that he had left the race problem. He had deliberately tried to exile himself in an area which had no whites.

The man most representative of the second generation professional group is an able unknown with a many-sided personality.

He was an educator and entrepreneur who would have been entirely able to build Tuskegee Institute if he had gotten there first. He was a money-raiser, but would have had the handicap of being too Northern. In Alabama, his head would have come to the point where it could not bow.

He and Mr. Washington would have been hearty enemies, but I see likenesses. Both were tall and commanding figures, practiced and mesmeric public speakers. Both were tough administrators in a semi-military way. If any complaint leaked back about the students who had to get up at four o'clock, they talked brimstone. Both were fiercely concerned with money, order, cleanliness, working habits, design, and aesthetics. I never believed that Mr. Washington selected the music the Tuskegee band played on the balcony at dinnertime, but students said so. My friend said to me directly, "We have a music teacher for singing, accompaniments, concerts, and the like, but I will not have a piano lesson on the campus yet. Once they get started the parents are worse about them than the children."

He was a man of many interests. Every day he read some *Horace* in the original. He kept bees and did all the work himself. He had a printing press and was a working printer. He studied the stars. He kept records about the lives of his alumni, year by year. He bought books steadily, works ranging from philosophy to cabbage, pigs to farm machinery. His children kept a menagerie of pets.

While he was driving me over the school acreage, we talked

about a faculty feud which he said was like an Ibsen play. He interrupted his story to show me certain tenants, a patch of transplanted Venus flytraps, and crops that were doing well.

When we stopped in dooryards I saw another side of him. He was a man cut through perpendicularly, half of him in line with my experience, half leaning toward the simplest kind of tenant. His looks and his diction did not change and he returned to Ibsen, but meanwhile, he knew how to talk with a plowman who looked like an elongated version of the turtles in his swamp.

Few well-educated people can identify so well with the lowly and this dual flexibility was not his only strength. He had to meet Southern whites. He had to have at least a third face.

A man who submits to the full grilling process of the American college and yet stands out as original is not one of the lemmings of this world. He was better balanced than most between science and the humanities, between people and principles, the world and his own race. He must have had great reserves. The culture of his time never used all of him.

The most interesting bit about the forty Negro men is that they were not very noticeable. They became enough like other professional men not to be news any more. I usually knew men only in connection with their school work, but once in a while about their children. I once arrived at a school on the day the young principal received a telegram announcing the arrival of his first child; the mother had gone North to her parents for the birth. The father was floating above the housetops. Before noon he did not know whether to keep the boy South or send him to the North for college. In all the exhilaration he spoke of his duty in teaching the child how to be colored. I have never tried deliberately to open the wounds of self-identity. This is childhood's overpowering lesson.

I knew a couple with six children at the time they were explaining the race position to their youngest. When I visited the school first she was four and came to lean against my chair. At no more than six she ran away whenever I came into the room. "She is afraid of white people, she is just beginning to understand." The father told me that the subject occupied her attention for over a year: "Can I go in there? . . . Why? . . .

Did any colored person ever go in? . . . Why? . . . What would happen if I should just go in anyway? . . . Why didn't God fix it so that I could go everywhere?"

The mother shrugged and said, "Six children are too many—I am all to pieces. We have been through this business of explaining color six times and they never let go of it."

I imagine that most parents proceed more abruptly. They give rough cautions, "You'll do it because I tell you to." In crisis, they blurted, "Keep out of it or you'll find a rope around your neck."

The child learned out of the air. He played beside the porch and the grown-ups above him laughed when they said, "If you're black, get back." When they talk about a man who has been arrested, he does not understand why they mention a hog. "A hog don't know which part of him'll season the turnip greens." There are also the double-barrelled songs:

Naught's a naught, figger's a figger,
All for the white man, none for the nigger.

The white boy threw rocks at him, the white man roared at him to get out of the way. Church made it solemn. "A thousand years it took to tame our forefathers. It has been but fifty years since Emancipation."

A woman of seventy told me that she remembered practically nothing of her father's stories of slavery. "Now, I wish I could. Daddy was always talking about it, but I learned not to hear. If I could get away, I ran out of the room. If I could not run, I learned to shut off my hearing, as we shut off commercials on the radio. He always began by telling how hard they beat him and then I felt so fierce I let the room and his voice blur."

This woman has always hated white people. She came North, worked her way through college and made herself a professional life. She never thought of doing anything against whites—she only burned to show what black people can do: "If I were white, nothing could stop me." I have known others whose hate became creative and charged them with a driving personal ambition. If they had not learned how to become creative in work, they might have gone to cutting throats.

At first I used to say casually to my children, "Save it for tomorrow." It was not long before I realized that they were not going to have a long tomorrow, they had acute need for compensation. Without pauses, they could hardly bear everything they had to bear. The red and orange and violet of a woman's Sunday dress, and the children's frilly white were breathing spells in the outside world. The nobler compensations were a hope, but I learned to sympathize with extravagance, whether it was steak or gold shoes.

At baccalaureate services I sat near graduates rustling in pink and blue silk, green taffeta and apricot satin. At Commencement, the girls on the platform billowed in white organdy, silk, lace and tulle. This bubbling up of money went against the grain of those who thought pupils of a missionary school should never splurge. Their policy was seemly, but until community education could be extended on this level, the fine feathers seemed to me an unconscious wisdom.

Children were always loved and wanted. Room always opened for one more child and one more avenue of self-denial. Parents held all children tightly. The permissive did not exist; obedience was the key word.

The importance of the mother lasted and lasted. Orphans made father and mother figures out of grandparents, aunts, uncles, or teachers they liked, and fed on stories of famous adults. When a child lost one parent, he tried to take on what he could of the duties of the family. An eighth-grade girl would manage to keep the home together for her father and brothers. A boy worked outside the home and brought the money to his mother.

The upper class added excesses to the child's education, to satisfy parental ambition. Plans for improvement stretched ahead for years. Outside reading was scheduled. Piano and violin were necessities. Manners must include deference and grace; when out of school, never one step into a dooryard outside their own caste.

Middle-class parents could not afford these embellishments, so their children had an easier time. If they got on well at school, the parents reinforced their interests and left them alone.

Lower-class children lived under such poor conditions of sanitation, sleeping, eating, playing and school that it was a wonder they lived to grow up. I think of them when I hear, "Lord, remember these children in the morning."

All children bore too heavy a load. At the very time a child was put to reading and numbers, he was also set to assimilating his inferior status. Mentality and spirit were steadily subtracted from him in early life. An experienced adult could watch the change in his manner, and the difference in his thinking showed in the brown eyes.

There Is No End 21

WHEN I LIVED in the South, for eight months of each year I became like a Negro. I swallowed my emotion and approached my goals by detour. I had the resources of work and of youth. Whenever I could not bear the life, I was white. I could get out.

After I lived in New York I forgot the precipices, and trees grew between me and the brink. Work drugged me for long intervals during World War I but in the post-war lull my long roll of observations about the Negro caused me to make some about my own life.

I had dropped by accident into a background that might remain static for my whole lifetime. I believed the winged words about an earthly Heaven but I always thought of it in terms of centuries. I knew that nations have changed by cataclysm—war, gold, gas, water, climate, invasion, discoveries—but still I never heard anyone of either race prophesy seriously about the races, except by the long road of social evolution.

From the Negro I expected prodigies of education. From the

white I expected little. During 1917, when I had my earliest thoughts about leaving my job, East St. Louis had a barbarous race riot with thirty-nine Negro and nine white deaths. In my last year, 1919, the United States had twenty-six riots, the rabid one in Chicago with twenty-three of the minority and fifteen of the majority dead.

I was thirty years old and I had the lethal deficiency of liking almost any work as soon as I was well into it. I had never had precise working aims, except that I must like my work and believe it worthwhile.

My commitment to missions had just happened. My position as supervisor was only an outgrowth of the educational trend. Supervision was not the point, but I spent over a year reflecting on whether or not I should go on in Negro education.

I had come to where I knew too much about conditions I could not affect. Anticipating the post-war difficulties, I sat like the doctor without medicine in the prison camp. I could not go beyond diagnosis.

I knew how Negroes shaped the Southerners who thought that all sculptors were white. They were also shaping me. I was letting life crush me too early. I no longer saw Negroes as aliens, or even as they saw themselves. As color became negligible to me, I forgot its barriers in opportunity and justice. As I grew Negro in feeling, I thought too much about mere endurance. I liked being the heir of black imagination but tied in with it was black fatalism. I felt an eerie growth in my understanding of transcendental values and in the faculty of translating loss into gain.

I asked no advice, because my older associates were already retired, moved away, or dead. I suffered and realized the end. I made up my mind to cut my ties, no matter how they bled, and I decided not to go to Africa—which I could have done at the time—but to let the curtain fall.

Almost at once it appeared delicious to get away from the occupational glitter of the executive. I was bored with prestige and with having to come up with instant decisions. I was getting too slick, with both the act and the mask. I actively disliked the deference heaped upon me for merely being white and representative of the abolitionist tradition. Perhaps my impulse to run was not too different from the Mississippi field hand's instinct to get to Chicago.

I went up to Dr. Warner's office and told him that I could not face the long slow drain of turning the high schools over to public instruction. I believed in the policy, but the application was too much for me. Teachers would write that the AMA had once lifted them up. Now it was casting them down. The public school authorities would not care for them as people.

Dr. Warner reminded me that in terms of service I was then the oldest person in the educational department. I should be able to establish and help supervise the order in which schools should be transferred to their towns. His generation would soon be gone and I was a bridge between the old and the new. I must not give in to being tired from the War. If I took a sabbatical year to study and travel, everything would be new again.

I had said, too, that the denominational idea about missionary salaries and life service had pinched me fatally during the War and I no longer meant to have any hand in it. He said he thought something would have to be done about missionary salaries, let me not worry, was there anything we could not get around with adequate money?

I thought that I had never fully embraced the Old Guard's devotion and sense of duty, so perhaps now none of them could understand my language of departure. I said only that I was tired of sitting on platforms. I was not willing to say that I must keep in mind the zeal of the young Negro about the old white bitch from Massachusetts. Whites in Negro education were on the way to being expendable.

My thoughts had gone too far to return. I could not brood over the matter any more. Since I meant to leave in the near future, I held to my decision.

I pulled down the rolltop on my ancient desk at one o'clock one Saturday and began over again at nine o'clock Monday morning five blocks away. I began to work on educational surveys of colleges. The questions of expansion, amalgamation and contraction were similar, but I had no personal ties and the objective soon felt like a feathery cloak to me.

My first work was so hard that all subsequent work was relatively easy. Instinct enabled me to steer away from the Lost

Cause and I never again became so emotionally involved in work.

I did not at the time realize how things go on after they end. I had begun with a national organization and it turned out that all the positions I had afterward were with national organizations.

Social and political developments were always demonstrating that history repeats itself. When I worked on the history of women, maternal mortality, industrial unemployment, and the apprenticeship of artists, the Negro past had settled into its own onyx, but I could find its traces. All these matters come to the Negro too, and sometimes come first.

My older eyes see that my stay in the South was perhaps not entirely for the Negro or for the regional meaning or even for the loved landscape. It was that journey within the self that youth makes only once.

After I left I had a heightened sense of national identity. "I looked at my hands and my hands looked new." It began through friends who did not share it. I went to college with boys and girls who wanted to get to Paris or Tahiti or anywhere far away. We knew at second hand about aesthetics at Harvard in the days of Charles Eliot Norton, Santayana, and Denman Ross. By 1919 I had already been to Tahiti.

I have tried to trace my thinking about Negroes only as far as it had reached by that year. I felt an application to them in the poem for immigrants about the Golden Door. On the way to school for two years, I passed every day the Statue of Liberty in New York harbor. Ellis Island was seething with immigrants then, coming for the prairies, the textile mills, and the garment makers' shops and Emma Lazarus said to them

I lift my torch beside the Golden Door.

The old ex-slaves I used to know had in their own way understood the secret of this light at the entrance. They would have made a song about the smallness of the national door; the Ark took in animals two by two, the Liberty Door takes us one by one.

They never saw the statue at the edge of the tossing water, they never heard the door's words in speech or in the music Irving Berlin wrote, but on their Day in the 1860's when the sky split apart, they felt they had crossed the threshold. They were inside American life.

Later I knew their children and grandchildren, charming, prosperous, inscrutable. In moments of confidence they explained that in their pilgrimage, someone on the other side was holding the door. Or when it opened it was a small false door, the kind that yawn upstairs in apartment houses the wrecker is tearing down; those doors open on empty space.

And yet, at some crisis in the life, they had had what was almost like a conversion. In spite of the denials, they had once passed through the door to the country's heritage. I have been told this by a young couple who were thrown off a Southern Pullman in North Carolina on their bridal trip. I think that tough optimism comes from some precipitate in their heritage that makes them braver than those who have not been tried.

Their ancestors that I remember could defy fact out of their profound knowledge of the invisible. The unseen sustained them and they dealt with it well. They could store apparitions and use unreality. Did a river in flood pour in to drown them? Yes; but those who got out of the water would call it Jordan. "All other ground is sinking sand."

Although living where it was hot, they had some of the outlook said to be developed in a cold climate. The ice in them lent strength to the bone.

The masses, too, had their Americanism. I have taught students who grew wildly excited about Parkman. The West of 1846 was lighted up for these teenagers by a young man sitting on wet ground beside an Indian campfire, tearing at half-cooked buffalo meat because he wanted to understand American Indians.

The masses just pulled their *Oregon Trail* message out of the air. Slow motion, but by feet and legs, eyes and ears, hands and breath, if no more, they had gotten into the continuity. The drum that others could not hear beat inside them; *on* and *on* and *on* and *on* and *on*.

The migrant hordes just beginning to travel the roads when I said goodbye had grown rich with feelings that originated here. They had in them, as much as anyone, the belief that drove the American when be blazed the wagon trails beyond the Mississippi and crossed the mountains.